Distinctive Distance Education Design:

Models for Differentiated Instruction

Richard G. Fuller
Robert Morris University, USA

Gary William Kuhne
The Pennsylvania State University, USA

Barbara A. Frey
University of Pittsburgh, USA

Information Science REFERENCE

INFORMATION SCIENCE REFERENCE
Hershey · New York

Director of Editorial Content:	Kristin Klinger
Director of Book Publications:	Julia Mosemann
Acquisitions Editor:	Lindsay Johnston
Development Editor:	Julia Mosemann
Publishing Assistant:	Travis Gundrum
Typesetter:	Deanna Jo Zombro
Production Editor:	Jamie Snavely
Cover Design:	Lisa Tosheff
Printed at:	Lightning Source

Published in the United States of America by
Information Science Reference (an imprint of IGI Global)
701 E. Chocolate Avenue
Hershey PA 17033
Tel: 717-533-8845
Fax: 717-533-8661
E-mail: cust@igi-global.com
Web site: http://www.igi-global.com

Library of Congress Cataloging-in-Publication Data

Fuller, Richard G., 1956-
Distinctive distance education design : models for differentiated instruction / by Richard G. Fuller, Gary William Kuhne, and Barbara A. Frey.
p. cm.
Includes bibliographical references and index.
Summary: "This book presents a tool to assist in the planning, conducting and evaluation of online learning, providing a way of understanding the course development and design process, drawing upon the research and theory foundations of distance education"--Provided by publisher.
ISBN 978-1-61520-865-4 (hardcover) -- ISBN 978-1-61520-866-1 (ebook)
1. Distance education--Computer-assisted instruction. 2. Instructional systems--Design. 3. Individualized instruction. I. Kuhne, Gary William, 1949- II. Frey, Barbara A. III. Title.
LC5803.C65F85 2010
371.35'8--dc22

2009050072

British Cataloguing in Publication Data
A Cataloguing in Publication record for this book is available from the British Library.

Table of Contents

Section 2
Frameworks for Designing Differentiated Instruction

Section 3
Developing Differentiated Instruction: The "Tool Box"

Foreword

The past decade has seen the rapid growth of Internet based education, commonly referred to as "distance education" or "online learning." While the technology to enable online learning evolved gradually during the previous decade, it was only in the late 1990's, with the emergence of comprehensive course management systems that faculty and college instructional development staff began to invest the time and effort to build fully online courses and, eventually, programs. Today, almost all community colleges and most four-year public colleges and universities offer some online programs; there has been significant penetration in the majority of private two and four-year institutions and a lesser amount in four-year liberal arts colleges. The current form of distance education has also spurred major growth in the for-profit sector of higher education in the U.S. Today, nearly one quarter of students in higher education do some portion of their coursework in online courses, and that percentage is continuing to grow (Allen and Seaman.[1]

Equally remarkable is that student outcomes demonstrate that students are learning as effectively online as in the classroom. The latest Department of Education meta-study, while calling for more study, goes so far as to draw the conclusion that online courses achieve marginally better outcomes than classroom courses, and that blended courses appear to achieve the best results of all.[2] The significance of these findings, which compare a form of learning that is still in its infancy with a thousand year old tradition of classroom instruction, can hardly be exaggerated. Where will online learning be in another decade, if parity with the classroom has already been achieved?

I believe that further dramatic advances will be made. These will grow out of a key difference in faculty attitudes toward distance education versus classroom-based education. That difference is the relative readiness of faculty to work collaboratively, embrace standards for course design and delivery, and commit to a process of continuous improvement in their online courses. Sadly, this is not characteristic of face-to-face higher education. While educational theory has steadily advanced in recent decades, most college faculty continue to teach their classroom courses in a manner more influenced by their own experience as students than by the research findings of those who study the learning process. A corollary of this observation is that most instructors make only minor changes in the organization and delivery of their courses over the years. They may update their course content to take account of the latest information on the subject, change discussion topics, and introduce new technology to provide visual and multimedia support, but the basic organizing principles are largely unaffected.

I make these observations, based on more than 40 years of teaching and administrative experience in higher education, in order to highlight the change in attitude that college instructors appear to undergo when they make the transition to Internet-based distance education. If we speculate about the causes of this significant change in attitude, there are a number of obvious factors:

Learning to teach in a new media, faculty cannot fall back on the models they assimilated during their own education.

The inherent community-building characteristics of the Internet appear to influence the attitude of faculty toward collaborating, sharing, and adopting best practices.

The many organizations that have sprung up to support faculty in their new roles in distance education are serving as influential communities engaging faculty on issues of technology and pedagogy in ways that have no real parallels in traditional, discipline-based, faculty organizations.

Training in course design and delivery appear to faculty as a logical step in their transition to online teaching, once they have accepted their need for training in the use of course management tools and online media.

Faculty's greater dependence on technology and instructional design staff in order to succeed in online teaching exposes them to greater staff influence on their attitudes toward course organization and pedagogy.

I am sure there are other factors as well, but it is the end result that concerns us here. That result is faculty's much greater openness to re-examining their learning objectives and teaching strategies and to re-designing their courses to be more effective. Once started down this path, many are prepared to continue the process as more research and experimentation with distance learning suggest further potential improvements.

These trends have spurred the creation of internal standards by many schools engaged in developing online courses and programs, the development of standards of best practice by accrediting bodies and national associations,[3] and the adoption of the Quality Matters Rubric[4] for the design of fully online and blended courses by schools across the country. This concern with standards is leavening the quality of distance education. Basic principles, such as the importance instructor presence, student engagement, and active learning, have been widely accepted and built into virtually all standards for online and blended course design and delivery. However, there are many avenues yet to explore and many opportunities to build on the early successes of distance education, as our understanding of the online learning environment continues to grow.

This book explores one of those opportunities. It grows out of the fundamental insight that we can categorize college courses by the type of learning they promote, and that different design and delivery strategies may be appropriate for each of these course types. Both faculty and instructional designers should benefit from the thorough exploration of the implications of this insight, and the distance learning community as a whole will benefit from subsequent efforts to build courses according to these principles and evaluate the outcomes for students. It is efforts like this that insure that distance education will continue to advance toward its potential as a no-compromise alternative to face-to-face study.

ENDNOTES

1 Allen, I. E., & Seaman, J. (2009). *Staying the Course; Online Education in the United States, 2008.* (Sloan Consortium, November, 2009). Retrieved from http://sloan-c.org/publications/survey/pdf/staying_the_course.pdf, for data on the growth of enrollment, programs, and positive attitudes toward online learning in higher education.

2 Means, B., Toyama, Y., Murphy, R., Bakia, M., & Jones, K. (2009). *Evaluation of Evidence-Based Practices in Online Learning; A Meta-Analysis and Review of Online Learning Studies.* (U.S. Depart-

ment of Education, 2009). Retrieved from www.ed.gov/about/offices/list/opepd/ppss/reports.html.

3 See, for example "Best Practices for Electronically Offered Degree and Certificate Programs," (http://www.ncahlc.org/download/Best_Pract_DEd.pdf) which has been adopted by the eight regional accrediting bodies in the U.S.

4 See www.qualitymatters.org.

Ron Legon
The University of Baltimore, USA

Ronald Legon *is Executive Director of The Quality Matters Program and Provost Emeritus of the University of Baltimore (UB), where he served as Provost from 1992 to 2003. He also served as Director of the MBNA e-Learning Center at UB, which launched the first AACSB accredited fully online MBA program in 1998, and Director of the Helen P. Denit Honors Program. Over the past 45 years, Dr. Legon has taught history and humanities at Brooklyn College, the University of Illinois at Chicago, the University of Chicago, and, most recently, at UB, where he has taught online, hybrid and face-2-face courses. He has published widely in the field of Greek History and, in recent years, on the subject of online education. Dr. Legon makes frequent presentations regarding the Quality Matters Rubric and process and the accumulating research findings regarding the impact of QM. In the past year he has presented at the Maricopa Community Colleges, the University of West Florida, DePaul University, Capella University, the Minnesota Learning Commons, the Sloan Consortium, the Instructional Technology Council, and Massachusetts Colleges Online. Dr. Legon received the 2008 award for Individual Leadership in the Field of Distance Learning from the U. S. Distance Learning Association.*

Preface

Bill designed training programs in a mid-sized industrial plant in the upper Midwest region. Since training departments are normally one of the first places targeted in any budget cuts, in the face of a tightening economy the manager of human resource development directed Bill and his fellow designers to begin a process of redesigning their training into online formats that would allow for both individual learning modules as well as group courses. Bill was further directed to design the group courses to fit either synchronous or asynchronous delivery. Such changes in training were assumed by upper management to potentially produce major savings to the training budget. Such major redesign efforts were sure to place major stress on Bill and his limited design staff. To make matters even more stressful, Bill needed to implement the changes in an accelerated schedule that would insure that at least 50% of the plant's training could move from a face-to-face format by the beginning of the following fiscal year, with a clear message that even faster transition would be appreciated.

Mary was in charge of an allied health two-year program at a community college. As both an instructor and course designer, Mary managed a program with a variety of courses, ranging from foundational theory courses, through a variety of laboratory and skill development courses, to advanced diagnostic problem-solving courses requiring analytical and synthesis skills. Recognizing that the teaching-learning process was different depending on the type of course, Mary sought to insure that each type of course was competently taught. About three months ago her dean, upon pressure from the provost and trustees, decided to move a major portion of Mary's program into a distance education format. The courses would be redesigned and offered primarily through online learning using a course management system such as Blackboard. This radical shift was justified on the grounds that the online shift held the most promise for both expansion of enrollment and reduction of facility costs for the community college. Given the nature of Mary's program, with a heavy focus on skill-based training, the question was how to best insure the development of important learner competencies outside the face-to-face environment. The broader question of how best to migrate courses into this online format, were left unanswered while the mandate for change was clear and not open to discussion. Mary began to read about distance learning and online course design, but quickly got lost in the maze of literature, feeling less certain daily that the transformed program would be successful.

Andy was a program designer for an agency that specialized in the development of continuing profession education courses and continuing professional development workshops and seminars for several large professional groups. The appeal of online designs for professionals who lost billing money whenever they were away at training was obvious. What was not so obvious was how mandated competencies could be achieved away from the face-to-face and hands on formats that characterized most of the previous decade of offerings. Andy was directed to "make it happen" and was asked for feedback on timetables for the required transitions. Of particular concern to Andy was the issue of interaction. Understanding that discussion and interaction are critical components of the development of higher critical thinking skills, the question of how to realistically foster such interaction within an online environment continued to nag at his mind.

Bill, Mary, and Andy, although not real people, represent real situations in the world of education today, particularly in higher and adult education settings (education and training beyond the K-12 world). The growth of distance education has been astounding in the past decade, particular online forms of distance education delivery. Educator and instructional designers in corporate training, higher education, professions, community agencies, and government and military settings are being charged with overseeing nothing less than a revolution in the educative process. Many charged with implementing the change feel ill-prepared for the task and uneasy (or worse) about the unique challenges of creating distance delivery of education and training. Perhaps you, the reader, are facing situations similar to Bill, Mary, and Andy. It is for people like you that this book has been written. Our goal has been to develop a practical tool to help you understand the nature of online learning and the central issues involved in effective online design. We also desire to help you recognize the distinctions in design when considering different course types, i.e., foundational courses, skill-based courses, analysis/synthesis courses, and finally, hybrid courses.

This book will present to you, the reader, a new lens to serve as a tool to assist in the planning, conducting and evaluation of online learning. While we address design considerations, we did not intend this book to replace classic instructional design model texts. We assume the reader already knows some of these classic instructional design models, or at least has some familiarity with curriculum development. We see this book as providing another way of understanding the course development and design process, drawing upon the research and theory foundations of distance education and the unique "lens" of the four course categories. We hope this approach will provide yet another tool to work alongside other models to assist course developers and instructors to better address the needs of their online students in education and training situations.

While some writers and theorists believed that the preactive (planning) and active teaching phases are unique in the online environment, we are convinced that many of the traditional principles in planning and teaching are still highly relevant. It is the intention of this book to engage the reader with those traditional principles that can best be integrated with the four course lens as a tool box of ideals that can increase the efficacy of any online program. We also provide a summary of important distance learning principles to supplement the traditional principles.

This book attempts to gather the traditional models of teaching and learning and present them in a way that is useful to both new and experienced online teachers in a manner that can assist in increasing the overall effectiveness of online courses and training sessions and provide a greater impact for both the teacher and the learner.

ORGANIZATION OF THIS BOOK

Section One: Foundations For Designing Differentiating Instruction

The book is divided into four major parts. Unit One deals with what we consider the proper foundations for a book on online distance education design. Chapter One explores the question of designing for learning outside the traditional classroom setting. We explore the nature of the distance education phenomena and how Distance Education Programs are different from traditional face-to-face learning programs. Specific design implications are suggested, as well as reflections presented on some of the forms of distance education (or online learning) and some contemporary issues within distance education. Chapter Two identifies the primary lens for the book, which is the four course model for differentiating instruction. We address the four types of courses that create the reality of differentiating instruction. After defining the four types of courses, we look in more detail at each type, including the Foundation Courses, skill based courses, analysis/synthesis courses, and hybrid courses.

Section Two: Frameworks For Designing Differentiating Instruction

In Unit Two we move from "laying foundations" to providing some important frameworks that organize the research and theory on distance education and its most contemporary expression in online learning. We intend this summary organization of information to provide an easy to use and practical tool for program designers to better understand the nature of the adult learner (most online programs focus on adults), the nature of interaction in online learning, the importance of the development of social presence within learning communities, and some important administrative concerns that impact effective online designs. Specifically, Chapter Three addresses the nature of the adult as a learner. We examine some general characteristics of adults as learners; why adults tend to participate in learning efforts, what we know from research about the relationship between age, learning, and intelligence, the possible relationship between adult development and adult learning, and finally, what we know about adult learners in distance education.

Chapter Four turns our attention to interaction in online learning. The term "interaction" refers to the broad spectrum of learning activities that engage students. In many distance education courses, online interaction promotes achievement and community beyond the expectations of both the students and instructors. We examine the forms such interaction can take, concentrating on learner-content, instructor -learner, learner - learner, and learner- interface interactions. The goal is to demonstrate the need for designing interactivity in to courses and the keys to insuring such interactivity. Recent studies show that there is a correlation between interaction levels among students and the students' levels of satisfaction, learning, and retention. Therefore, it is of paramount importance to promote active learning that requires students to engage in the coursework and collaborate with one another to increase the effectiveness of the learning experience.

In Chapter Five we turn attention to social presence in online courses. Closely related to the content, instructor, and learner interaction that occurs in distance education courses is the concept of social presence. As online students increase the amount and types of course interaction in which they engage, they also increase their social presence or the recognition that they are communicating with "real" people. Ideally, students feel that they are part of a collaborative learning community that interacts to build knowledge and meaning. Social presence is the amount to which a person feels "socially present" in their environment, the degree of feeling, perception, and reaction to being connected by technology, or the degree to which a person is perceived as 'real' in mediated communications. After carefully defining social presence, we focus on the benefits of establishing a social presence within the course. The various dimensions of social presence are identified and suggestions given for fostering meaningful social presence. Guidelines for assessing the level and nature of social presence within course and discussion of design issues linked to social presence are provided.

Chapter Six addresses a number of administrative issues impacting instructional design for online learning. We argue that, in the context of most education environments, program designers must learn to think more like administrators. Designers must clarify their own philosophy of design and understand how to integrate their philosophies with the sponsoring organization's philosophies. Designers are also alerted to a number of inescapable administrative realities for program designers, including confronting inevitable ethical issues when designing programs, improving program staffing and on-site coordination, program promotion, and learner support services.

Section Three: Developing Differentiating Instruction - The "Tool Box"

In Unit Three we get into the nuts and bolts of designing differentiated instruction through detailing the design process with foundational courses, skills-based courses, and analysis/synthesis courses. Chapter Seven begins our look at the "Preactive stage" of design by examining needs assessment. In addition to discussing the purposes and importance of needs assessment, we identify the main strategies to approach needs assessment and the primary tools and techniques employed in the needs assessment task. Finally, needs assessment is discussed within the context of each of the four course types.

Chapter Eight continues our look at the "Preactive Stage" of design by examining the need for creating measurable behavioral learning objectives, as well as the roots of lesson planning. You will discover how to align uncovered needs with specific behavioral objectives. You will also learn how to expand such objectives into cognitive, psychomotor, and affective domains. Of course we also discuss creating behavioral learning objectives within the context of each of the four course types.

Chapter Nine concludes our look at the "Preactive stage" of design by examining lesson and program evaluation. Summative and formative evaluation is explained and specific tools for each are described. Four common traps to avoid in evaluation are identified and explained, as well as some common pitfalls and ethical issues in program evaluation.

Chapter Ten begins our examination of the "Active Teaching" phase of design with a discussion of active teaching phases in foundational courses. The pedagogies employed in foundational courses are identified and the importance of instructor presence is underscored. The core cooperative learning techniques used in foundational courses are explained. The use of online direct teaching methods, as well the use of asynchronous discussion boards and synchronous virtual chat rooms, round out the practical suggestions for foundations courses.

Chapter Eleven examines the "Active Teaching Phases" of design within the setting of skills based and analysis/synthesis courses. The pedagogies used in Skill-Based courses, as well as the synchronous and asynchronous communications employed in Skills Based Courses are identified. Facilitating analysis/synthesis courses through such tools as online debates and Socratic methods of facilitation in discussion boards provides yet further practical help to any designer. Perhaps most importantly, empathetical pedagogies are discussed in light of each course type.

Section Four: Designing Differentiated Course Pedagogies

In Unit four we begin to look at specific examples of online course lessons specific to each of the four course categories. Chapter Twelve continues our look at the nuts and bolts of instructional design by examining the development of effective foundation courses in light of the previous principles. Drawing upon examples from an online anatomy and physiology course, an online economics course, and an online sexual harassment course, rationales and guidelines are shown to guide the reader in developing foundation courses within his/her professional context.

Chapter Thirteen continues this nuts and bolts approach by focusing on the issues tied to effective design of skill based courses. The chapter presents three course examples, including an online science course, an online research course, and an online hybrid course. Implications for improving skill development within the online context are underscored.

Chapter Fourteen concludes our book with a focus on the design of analysis/synthesis courses and some actual design examples. Examples from healthcare, management leadership, and education provide insights into the design issues and best practices.

It is our hope as authors that you will find this book useful as a lasting resource as you attempt to assist your agency or organization in the exciting transition to distance education and online learning as a major component of your education and training enterprise.

August 2009

Richard G. Fuller
Robert Morris University, USA

Gary William Kuhne
The Pennsylvania State University, USA

Barbara A. Frey
University of Pittsburgh, USA

Section 1
Foundations for Designing Differentiated Instruction

Chapter 1
Designing Education Outside of the Traditional Classroom

Designing effective educational courses is a critical process in much human learning. Human learning actually occurs from a combination of both planned and unplanned educational experiences. Unplanned learning, also called incidental learning, occurs when the learner is actually focused on another objective than learning and in the process gains unsought insight that increases professional competency. For example, a learner's goal might be watching a play for entertainment and in the midst of the play unexpectedly gain an insight into work relationships. While such unplanned learning experiences are definitely important to our development, our focus in this book is upon the human learning that occurs within the context of planned, organized educational experiences in which the learner's primary goal is learning. While formal course design has little or no role in the many incidental learning experiences in life, the value of planned educational experiences is very much related to the quality of the instructional design effort underlying the educational program. This is a book about the process of formal educational design outside the traditional classroom through what is known as distance education.

DOI: 10.4018/978-1-61520-865-4.ch001

Formal (as opposed to informal or incidental learning) education has been primarily offered over the past century within the setting of a face-to-face context. While these face-to-face contexts can include such settings as a classroom, seminar room, small group, or tutorial have certainly dominated the educational landscape, many learners (an increasing number in recent years) have experienced their formal educational development outside this traditional educational context. These learning experiences within a "non-traditional" context of education usually involved an educational design in which the learner and the instructor were separated by location and/or time. Such non-traditional education practice is usually described as distance education. For the purposes of this book, distance education is defined as the use of print or electronic communications media to deliver instruction when teachers and learners are separated in place and/or time. At its most basic level, distance education takes place when a teacher and student(s) who are separated by physical distance employ technology (i.e., voice, video, data, and print) to bridge the instructional gap. Millions of people around the world are choosing to learn through distance education offerings.

Those who focus on distance education as a form of formal education are primarily concerned with the theory and application of "mediated instruction" research. Distance education creates a form of "mediated instruction" because there is a separation in space and time between the teacher and learner during the majority of educational process. Distance education can also be understood as "mediated instruction" in that it uses educational media to unite teacher and learner and carry course content, providing for two-way communication between teacher and learner. Finally, distance education can be understood as "mediated instruction" because the volitional control of learning is by students rather than by the distance instructor (more about this feature later in this book).

Decades of research comparing distance education to traditional face-to-face instruction presents a solid conclusion that teaching and studying at a distance can be as effective as traditional instruction. Of course, such a conclusion comes from research studies that make some important assumptions, including:

1. The method and technologies used are appropriate to the instructional tasks
2. There is student-to-student interaction
3. There is timely teacher-to-student feedback

A good summary of such research can be explored in the following website on "no significant difference" (http://nosignificantdifference.wcet.info/index.asp).

Within this first chapter we want to explain some of the characteristics of the non-traditional classroom, including its most current expression, online learning. We will also examine some of the important issues that impact on such nontraditional learning. These characteristics and issues provide a common foundation for you, the reader, and set the stage for the primary focus on this book, which is to provide you with practical help in designing and delivering distance educational offerings for a variety of course types. As chapter two will explain, such course types will include foundational courses, skill-based courses, analysis and synthesis courses, and hybrid (or blended courses). We hope this chapter will help you to better understand the nature of Distance Education as a field of practice, recognize some of the contemporary forms of Distance Education, and investigate and synthesize the core issues and trends affecting Distance Education. But before we can turn our attention to the "outside the traditional classroom" theme, we must first look at educational design in general.

SOME GENERAL PRINCIPLES REGARDING EDUCATIONAL DESIGN

Designing educational programs or courses is normally referred to as "instructional design" in education literature, a phrase referring to the systematic procedures utilized by educators when developing educational programs. Usually these procedures form an integrated process incorporating several distinct elements or steps. While often presented in a sequential fashion, most models suggest that the steps should not be followed in a strictly linear manner. While many models of instructional design have been proposed in the literature, despite the nuances of distinction within a specific model, most include a number of similar foundational elements. These common elements of instructional course design include:

1. Assessing the learning needs in the targeted learners for the program.
2. Establishing of learning goals and objectives based upon uncovered learner needs.
3. Determining the curriculum and content to best fulfill the established objectives for the program.

4. Choosing the appropriate mix of teaching and learning methods and strategies.
5. Coordinating the support systems for delivery of the program.
6. Evaluating the various learning outcomes for the program.

These primary elements in the instructional design process will be evident whether the courses are designed for traditional, face-to-face settings, or are delivered via distance education. Each of these elements (and other related issues) will be explained within this book.

Identifying needs is the critical root of all effective instructional design because learner motivation is related to the learner's perception of whether an educational program actually addresses a perceived need. A variety of tools are used for needs assessment, including interviews, surveys, focus groups, expert opinion, and observation. Once the needs have been determined, the instructional designer develops specific learning objectives. Such objectives guide the development of content as well as create a basis for program evaluation. Learning objectives are usually organized according to the knowledge, skill, and attitudinal components of uncovered needs. Knowledge components refer to the facts, information, and thought processes essential to meeting a need. Skill components refer to the psychomotor, relational, and professional skills that must be connected to thinking to successfully address the need. Many uncovered needs will also have attitude components, which refers to the perceptions and perspectives needing developed in the learner to meet the uncovered need, such as being willing to adopt new value systems and beliefs.

Designing content for courses occurs as instructional designers take each of the identified knowledge, skill, and attitudinal components and determine the specific content to be learned to achieve each objective. Such content is often developed with the aid of content experts. After developing the specific content, instructional designers are better able to determine the appropriate pre-requisites for the course. The established content is then organized and sequenced by instructional designers, usually by starting with the familiar in order to create a link to existing schema and experiences of the learner and then building up to the new and more complex information. Instructional designers organize content using classifying strategies like taxonomies to help "chunk" information. Designers also use spatial learning strategies such as visual displays, frames or matrices, and concept mapping to organize the content, as well as bridging strategies to help learners apply prior knowledge to new information, such as advanced organizers, or creating metaphors and analogies. Finally, designers use rehearsal strategies to review material, asking questions, summarize.

Having developed and organized the content, instructional designers must then choose the proper formats for the learning, basing format decisions upon the background and experience of the participants, the expertise of the instructional staff, the available facilities and equipment, and the program content's "fit" to a particular format. Designers in distance education use a number of formats, including correspondence study, audio/video-conferencing, broadcast and cable television, satellite communication, and web-based delivery. A critical final step is to design evaluation tools to better uncover the learning outcomes in the course. Such evaluation helps to identify changes in knowledge and skills arising from the educational offering, as well as the degree to which such learning transfers to the practice setting. In additional to pre-tests and post-test, the tools for such evaluation are often the same tools used for needs assessment.

All of these steps in instructional design should be evident whether the educational programs are offered face-to-face or at a distance. Since this book is targeting distance education, we will now turn to some introductory thoughts about this form of educational delivery.

WHAT EXACTLY IS DISTANCE EDUCATION ANYWAY?

We have already explained that a central defining principle of distance education is that it is "mediated instruction". Most contemporary definitions of distance education focus on the use of print or electronic communications media to deliver instruction when teachers and learners are separated in place and/or time. Some theorists in the field emphasize distance "learning" over "education", defining distance education primarily in terms of a system and process that connects learners with distributed resources. Moore (1996) provides the most widely used definition in which he stated that distance education involved:

"... planned learning that normally occurs in a different place from teaching and as a result requires special techniques of course design, special instructional techniques, special methods of communication by electronic and other technology, as well as special organizational and administrative arrangements" (Moore & Kearsley, 1996, p. 2).

Moore (1980, 1972) built the definition above on the foundation of his "Theory of Transactional Distance". Transaction refers to the interplay among the environment, the individuals, and the patterns of behavior in a situation. Moore suggested that when we talk about distance education we are referring to a distance that is more than simply a geographic separation of learners and teachers. It is a distance of understandings and perceptions that has to be overcome by teachers, learners, and educational organizations. In any educational program there is some transactional distance. What is commonly called distance education refers to those programs in which the separation of the teacher and the learner is so significant that it affects their behaviors in major ways, and requires the use of special techniques to compensate for such effects.

Others have also sought to define the nature of the nontraditional education called distance education. Feasley (1983), in a research report for the Association for the Study of Higher Education, defined distance learning as education provided for individuals who interact with faculty physically removed from them using pre-produced course materials. Keegan (1980) defined distance learning as education having a series of characteristics including the quasi-permanent separation of teacher and learner, the influence of an educational organization, the use of technical media, the provision of two-way communication, and the quasi-permanent absence of group learning. Garrison and Shale (1987) suggest that distance education:

"...implies that the majority of educational communication between (among) teacher and students(s) occurs non-contiguously (at different times and at separate places—separating the instructor-tutor from the learner). It must involve two-way communication between (among) teacher and student (s) for the purpose of facilitating and supporting the educational process. It uses technology to mediate the necessary two-way communication" (p. 11).

Keegan (1980) proposed that distance education has six defining characteristics. The first is the separation of the acts of teaching and learning in time and/or space differentiates distance education from face-to-face education. Second, the *normal* environment for study is the student's home or workplace and *normally* the student is alone. This does not rule out the possibility of learners occasionally meeting for practical activities or accessing technology that is not available at their local settings. Third, studying alone does not qualify as a system of distance learning unless it is institutionalized, in other words, the influence of an educational organization regarding the planning, development and delivery of teaching is essential. Institutionalization enhances organizational procedures including management, and administrative aspects. Fourth, the use of communication technology for delivery of instruction and provision of administrative services is another distinct qualification of distance education. The technology brings the learning content and learning community to the learners. Fifth, the use of two-way communication (however fast or slow) in order to ensure interaction and dialogue is an obvious characteristic. Finally, the sixth component of Keegan's definition defines distance education as the application of principles of industrialization to teaching. This is a theoretical position associated with the German scholar, Otto Peters (1983). Industrialization is in many ways similar to the 'systems principles' referred to in the discussion about definitions earlier.

HOW ARE DISTANCE EDUCATION PROGRAMS DIFFERENT FROM TRADITIONAL PROGRAMS?

Whatever specific definition seems most useful to you, clearly learning at a distance is similar in many ways to learning in a classroom environment, but there are also some very significant differences. Distance educators must accomplish the same general goals as those working in face-to-face environments, but separation from the learners means some of the teacher's challenges take on special forms. The communications between learners and instructors in distance education must be provided by various technologies. There is a wide variety available, including broadcast radio and television; audio- and videotapes; interactive audio and video teleconferencing; various computer and Internet technologies, and print technologies.

Although there are many differences between distance education and traditional education, for the purpose of designing educational programs there are four differences particularly distinguish distance education (particularly the online forms of distance education) from the traditional, face-to-face education. First, there is a separation in space between the teacher and learner during the majority of educational process, a separation that removes the normal visual clues often relied upon in face-to-face settings by both instructors and learners to better understand both the teaching content and student questions. Second, there is the need to use some form of educational media to carry course content. The human voice (in the sense of lecture) can no longer be the main method of content transfer between the instructor and the learner. Third, the instructional designer must provide some form of two-way communication to facilitate interaction between the teacher and learner, as well as between learners. The most common technology tools for two-way interaction in contemporary distance education are audio/video conferencing and the use of computers to connect participants online through e-mail, bulletin boards, and chat rooms. Fourth, the volitional control of the learning process is in the hands of the learners more than the instructors since the learner makes the choice, not the instructor, about when to study, when to read assignments, when to interact with the instructor or fellow learners through the chosen media of the course, and which learning strategies to employ. Understanding these four differences between distance education and face-to-face instruction is a critical backdrop for effective instructional design.

When considering distance education as a setting for instructional design, perhaps the most important and obvious fact is that the instructor and learner (as well as the learner with other learners) are separated by space. The success of distance education instructional design is therefore dependent upon the extent to which the educational institution and instructor (aided by the instructional designer) are able to foster meaningful dialog between instructors and learners, as well as between learners and other learners. Instructional designers use varying combinations of print and electronic communications media to deliver instruction to learners. Thus the term used earlier, "mediated instruction", provides a good summation and description of distance education.

The mediation of instruction through distance education has a clear history of development. Distance education has been around for more than a hundred years. Bates (1995) suggests that three generations of distance education have taken place, generations defined primarily by the strategies employed to foster teacher-learner and learner-learner interaction. The first generation involved correspondence-based teaching where student-teacher and teacher-student feedback processes were slow, sparse, and mostly restricted to the periods when the learners submit scheduled assignments. The second generation, beginning in the 1960's, involves a much greater range of media and feedback processes similar to those of the 'first generation' systems, but expanded to include telephone counseling and some face-to-face tutorials. The third generation saw the development of systems of distance education that enable extensive communication between learners and teachers. The use of media within distance education to allow 'dynamic interaction' between learners and between learners and teachers has multiplied. One could also seek to map the history of distance education by examining technology changes. Whatever way we try to structure the historical development of distance education, the history certainly reflects an evolutionary movement, an evolution that has neither occurred overnight nor yet reached its end. The evolutionary process has taken place gradually and frequently each of the emerging educational delivery technologies has been incorporated into different distance education systems, resulting in a total multimedia-based distance educational system comprised of various generations of distance technology and media. In other words, the different technologies and media have complemented and supported each other, rather than replaced existing ones. Such trends are likely to continue in the near future.

The information and communications technology of early distance education was written and printed material distributed through the postal system which developed in every country from the end of the nineteenth century onwards. Known as correspondence courses, students generally were provided with study guides and textbooks and sometimes with supplemental reading lists. In these courses students were expected to respond to questions that distant teachers then read and assessed. Credit and non-credit Correspondence courses have been offered for more than a hundred years. For example, the Pennsylvania State University offered its first correspondence course in agriculture in the 1890s and in 1918 added credit correspondence courses for professional engineers. The University of Wisconsin and other major universities have used correspondence study courses since the 1890s to provide off-campus learning opportunities for millions of adults. Though correspondence study did not disappear, but in fact continued to grow in most countries, after the radio was invented in the 1920s and the TV in the 1950s, these "new" information and communication technologies were applied to distance education in the form of radio-based study talks and TV-led video-based courses. Sometimes print and local study groups were included. By the 1970's, various higher education institutions were experimenting with two-way communications between instructors and students through face-to-face tutorials, short residential courses, and by telephone, video and computer conferencing. As newer and more efficient technologies developed, the "media" employed gradually expanded to include audiotapes, videotapes, radios, television broadcasting, and satellite transmission. Each new form of media required instructional designers to modify their courses to reflect the strengths and weakness of each media.

Our current era of distance education has drawn upon communication technologies that are interactive, electronic, and computer based in order to facilitate communication between learners and teachers, learners and learners. Contemporary distance education course design is being shaped primarily by the use of computers and the Internet to bridge the distance between teachers and learners, as well as between learners. Online learning uses the Web as a communication media in contrast to older forms of distance education. Since most instructional designers are not communication or technology specialists, instructional designers working with distance education programs usually function as part of a larger design team. Design teams help foster a collaboration in which academic content specialists combine with instructional designers, media specialists, editors and others to create viable and effective educational programs.

Web-based distance education programs can take two different forms, asynchronous (programs in which learners and instructors are not "online" at the same time) and synchronous (programs in which the instructor and learners are "online" at the same time). Given the difficulties with distance learners being in different time zones, as well as the expense usually required for synchronous technical connections, most contemporary distance education is following an asynchronous form of course design. Some instructional designers follow an asynchronous approach in which self-study materials are posted on the web and perused by learners at their own pace, an approach that sees the Internet as primarily a distribution medium for learning materials. The majority of quality distance education programs, however, use an interactive asynchronous approach in which "classes" for learners begin on a particular day with a cohort of other learners. A cohort of learners is taught by a faculty member who interacts with individuals or the cohort through group conferencing software. Such an "interactive" model is employed because of the close parallels with quality traditional learning environments (face-to-face). In traditional settings, learners have access to learning materials, access to a professor, and access to other students. The interactive, asynchronous approach duplicates these dimensions by giving the learner, through communications media, access to learning materials, access to a professor, and access to other students. With such forms of distance education, the Internet is primarily a communications facilitator between instructor and students, as well as between students and students, and only secondarily as a medium for distribution of learning materials.

DESIGN IMPLICATIONS WHEN DEVELOPING DISTANCE EDUCATION PROGRAMS

Although similarities exist between distance education courses and traditional classroom instruction that influence the instructional design process, many important differences exist between these forms of educational programming. For example, traditional learners gather at a fixed time and place for their learning, while web-based learners are able to choose their own time and place for either totally self-directed study or asynchronous learning. Faculty and learners interact in person in face-to-face settings, while distance education forces participants to rely on electronic or print interaction. In face-to-face settings, group activities are often limited by group size and instructional time, while in distance education settings group learning activities are able to extend beyond the space and time of the classroom, particularly for those using the Web environment communication tools like e-mail, chat-rooms, and bulletin boards.

While the remainder of this book will deal in detail with the many design implication for distance education, differentiating such implication based upon program type, as an introduction it is important to understand that instructional designers must make provision for three types of interaction for in distance education programs. First, they must insure the design permits adequate interaction between the learner and the formal course content. This is done by insuring the learner has access in a timely fashion to the formal course content through textbooks, course web pages, study guides, tapes, CDs, etc., and that course assignments encourage the learner to critically reflect on the material. Second, they must insure the design permits adequate learner-to-instructor interaction. In addition to providing mechanisms for timely responses to learner questions, courses must be designed to encourage the learners to become an "active participants" in the learning episode.

The third provision instructional designers must make for distance education programs is to permit adequate learner-to-learner interaction. Constructivist learning theory suggests that people learn best when they actively construct their own understanding through interaction with fellow learners, teachers, and previous experiences with the area of knowledge. Well-designed distance education programs can actually increase this possibility by permitting learners the time to develop more reasoned responses in the course "discussions". Learner to learner interaction creates a process in which learners interpret and analyze others' writings, reflect on their own knowledge and readings, present their points of view, and provide pointers to information that support their ideas. Discussion forums enable learners to become active participants in discussing topics presented in class and in bringing to the group additional information sources. Asynchronous participation allows learners time to reflect and carefully construct their points-of-view. Learning theory also suggests that the ability to contribute to a community creates the potential for learning and discussion forums develop feelings of comradeship and community, and the sense of team sharing. Thus instructional designers need to keep "interaction" as a central consideration when designing distance education programs.

When designing instruction for distance education programs, the design process begins with a careful study of distance education research findings, becoming familiar with the strengths and weakness of mediated instruction, as well as the current debates and issues. Designers should analyze the strengths and weaknesses of possible distance delivery approaches in terms of learner needs and course requirements before selecting a mix of instructional technology. Generally distance education courses follow an integrative strategy, such as supplementing a web-based course with content narrative placed in a print-based study guide. For certain courses, the development of tapes, videos, Interactive CD-ROM's, and other learning resources could supplement the online aspects of the course. Instructional designers in distance education need to be realistic about the costs of technology – with every component added, the overall cost of the program grows and the learning curve for the students increases.

Finally, when designing instruction for distance education programs the instructional designer must be sure to provide "hands-on" training with the technology of delivery for both instructors and learners. Remember that many learners are novices in the delivery format and we must design training with limited competency in learners. Don't underestimate the time needed to develop distance education courses – the more technologically complex the course becomes, the greater the development timeline.

Distance education can take on two different forms, self-study techniques and interactive techniques. Self-study techniques include approaches to learning that require little or no human interaction, and rely primarily upon the provision of books, video tapes, interactive CD-ROMS, and computer-based instruction (CBI) as learning resources for the distant learner. Interactive techniques include those strategies that permit interaction between a teacher/facilitator and the learner(s), or as we saw above, learner-to-learner. Such collaborative or group interactions obviously require communication tools. There are two primary forms of communication utilized to deliver interactive distance education—synchronous and asynchronous. The main distinction between the two is whether or not the teachers and learners are participating at the same time. Distance programs based on asynchronous methods use technologies that permit contact between learners and educators, but not at the same time. In other words, there is some elapsed time between interactions, perhaps minutes, hours, or even days. E-mail, electronic bulletin boards, written correspondence, and other media permit asynchronous communication. Distance education programs of a synchronous nature use technologies that offer live interactive instruction. Examples of synchronous communications include audio and video conferencing and real-time computer communications, such a chats and instant messaging.

Regardless of whether the communication in an educational program is synchronous or asynchronous, a key goal of both approaches is to foster meaningful interaction. We will be looking in depth at interaction in Chapter 4. For now, interaction can be organized into three types as suggested by Moore (1996). The first is learner-to-content interaction. This is the process of intellectually interacting with the course content that results in changes in the learners' knowledge, skills, attitudes, or actions. The second is learner to instructor interaction. In this type of interaction, distance education seeks to enable the learner to receive feedback from the instructor. Such feedback is for the purpose of assessment, motivation, enhancement of learning, and facilitation. It can occur synchronously or asynchronously. Finally, the third type of interaction is learner -to-learner. This form of interaction fosters collaborative learning and allows learners to draw upon the experiences of other learners as a rich resource for learning.

SOME TYPICAL FORMS OF ONLINE DISTANCE EDUCATION

With the development of new tools for information technology and transfer, the term "distance education" is often temporarily replaced with a term linked to a specific form of mediation, such audio-conferencing, video-conferencing, computer-conferencing, or computer-based instruction. The most recent technology-based synonym, "online learning", is emerging to distinguish the use of the Web as a training and education tool in contrast to merely serving as an information source. Online learning refers to computer-based training designed around Web technologies such as Web browsers and Course Management software. Internet and the Web help overcome the barriers of time and space in teaching and learning.

Distance learning on the Internet usually takes a number of forms. Such learning can involve the sending and receiving of e-mail (for the delivery of course materials, submitting assignments, getting/giving feedback, and/or participating in an electronic discussion group such as a "listserv"). It can also involve engaging in bulletin boards/newsgroups for group discussion of special topics. Individuals can download course materials or tutorials and access interactive tutorials. Real time interaction can occur through the use of chats or some of the Web 2.0 interaction tools through such virtual environments as Second Life. Internet also permits new levels of "informatics" for the learner, i.e., the use of online databases, library catalogs, and Web sites to acquire information and pursue research related to study. Many of you are reading this book because you are either involved in internet learning and/or are charged with design responsibilities for internet-based learning programs. We hope this book will provide practical help as you carry out your professional responsibilities.

Contemporary interest in Web-based distance education is stimulated by a number of perceived advantages to delivering distance learning on the Internet. Such advantages include time and place flexibility, the potential to reach a global audience, limited concern about compatibility of computer equipment and operating systems, quick development time (compared to videos and CD-ROMs), easy updating of content, as well as archival capabilities, and usually lower development and operating costs than other forms of distance delivery. Some of the current disadvantages are limited bandwidth and slow modems that hamper the delivery of sound, video, and graphics. Another problem is that learner success depends on technical skills in computer operation and Internet navigation, and the volume of e-mail messages to read, reflect on, and respond to can be overwhelming. Finally, social isolation can be a drawback, and the lack of nonverbal cues can hinder communication.

One question extensively researched and debated within the field of distance education pertains to which technology is best for distance education purposes. The summary of the research seems to point toward an integrated approach. Few distance courses rely on one delivery technology. Even print-based courses typically use voice mail, e-mail, and facsimiles to deliver instruction. Blending technologies is beneficial by providing greater student access and appealing to multiple learning styles. The distance educator's task is to carefully select among the technological options to find the right balance to better meet the needs of the learner. For example, we know that a strong print component can provide much of the basic instructional content in the form of a course text, as well as readings, the syllabus, and a day-to-day schedule. Interactive audio or video conferencing can provide real-time, face-to-face (or voice-to-voice) interaction. This is also an excellent and cost-effective way to incorporate guest speakers and content experts. Computer conferencing or electronic mail can be used to send messages, assignment feedback, and other targeted communication to one or more class members. It can also be used to increase interaction among students. Prerecorded videos, CDs, or DVDs can be used to present class lectures and visually oriented content. Fax can be used to distribute assignments, last minute announcements, to receive student assignments, and to provide timely feedback.

SOME CONTEMPORARY ISSUES WITHIN DISTANCE EDUCATION

As distance education continues to grow as a design and delivery option within adult education, there are many issues and challenges that face students, educators, and administrators that must be addressed. Administrators must integrate distance learning into existing policy frameworks and missions. Institutions must review current policies to identify those that present barriers to distance learning and those that need to be developed to accommodate the infrastructure requirements of distance learning, including:

1. Fee assessment.
2. Out-of-state versus in-state fees.
3. Access to technology by faculty and students.
4. Incentives and disincentives to participate in distance learning.
5. Institutional structure for distance learning.
6. Class size.

Distance education also calls for a changing role for teachers. The team approach—involving faculty, instructional designers, technicians, continuing educators, and assessment experts—has replaced the autonomous teacher. Since academic preparation of teaching faculty has been in their discipline rather than educational methodology, teachers may have little understanding of instructional design, technology, or online teaching. Essential to successful distance learning is a collaborative relationship between faculty, who are the content specialists, and instructional technologists. The development and delivery of a distance course is a team effort utilizing faculty, instructional technologists, administrative support staff, and production staff. Faculty involved in distance learning share a myriad of concerns about the impact of distance learning on their roles. Some of the impacts are:

1. Control of courses.
2. Degree of institutional support for distance learning.
3. 3. Effects of distance learning on faculty rewards, incentives, tenure and promotion.

Distance education also calls for new skills in learners. Learners choosing to use distance education need to be focused, effective managers of their time, able to work both independently and in groups, self-motivated, self-disciplined, and assertive. Learners need a clear understanding of costs, policies, advising, registration, textbooks, and support personnel contact lines. Retention is a much bigger concern in distance than conventional education. It is much easier for a student to withdraw from the relatively impersonal relationship of a distance course than it is from a conventional curriculum. In response to such concerns, the distance teacher has to take various measures to ensure the course is very well structured, with clear objectives and well-considered allocation of students' time.

Student isolation is a major concern in distance education. Regardless of the delivery technology, providing student-to-student interaction seems to improve the learning and the learning experience for students. Interaction may be as simple as discussion groups and forums or as involved as collaborative writing assignments. While a certain amount of isolation is unavoidable, courses can be designed to encourage or require synchronous/asynchronous student-to-student interaction to enhance the learning experience. Such interactions will, of necessity, mean *significant time commitment by faculty in the monitoring and guiding of these interactions*. The social context for student-faculty relationships is affected by distance delivery. While both may send e-mail messages, leave voice mail, and process a variety of written assignments, there may be little or no face-to-face interaction. The lack of connection influences the learning process by making it more detached, less personal, and more formal.

A continuing issue for those considering the development of distance education courses is the perception that distance learning is second-class education. Such an attitude remains in many institutions and in the public at large despite empirical evidence to the contrary. Distance education advocates must continually reinforce commensurate performance based on research data.

Another issue is tied to the perceived cost-effectiveness of distance education. Distance learning does not necessarily save money, particularly when capital costs are considered. The success of distance education must be defined by the broader benefits of expanding access and creating responsive delivery options for students.

Finally, distance education is often affected by the tendency to "fit" technology into old patterns of teaching pedagogy rather than to assimilate technology into new teaching models. Modern technology options are expanding technological and pedagogical choices for teaching and learning. This book seeks to help you develop as designers of effective distance education for a variety of contexts. Our next chapter addressing the differentiating of instruction based upon four distinct distance education course types. Your understanding of this differentiation should be a bit easier with the preliminary considerations covered in this first chapter.

Personal Reflection Questions

1. *What forms of distance education have you participated in over the past two or three years?*
2. *What level of interaction did you discover compared with your experience in more traditional educational settings?*
3. *Were the interactions primarily synchronous or asynchronous?*
4. *What did you perceive to be the weaknesses and strengths of your distance learning experiences?*

NOTE

For a useful summary of many of the Open and Distance Learning Journals and Newsletters, examine the list compiled by the International Review of Research in Open and Distance Learning[IRRODL]: http://www.irrodl.org/journalpg.html

REFERENCES

Bates, A. W. (1995). *Technology, open learning, and distance education*. New York: Routledge.

Feasley, C. E. (1983). Serving learners at a distance: A guide to program practices. *ACSHE-ERIC Higher Education Research Report No. 5*.

Garrison, D. R., & Shale, D. (1987). Mapping the boundaries of distance education: Problems in defining the field. *American Journal of Distance Education*, *1*(1), 7–13. doi:10.1080/08923648709526567

Keegan, D. (1980). On defining distance education. *Distance Education*, *1*(1), 13–36. doi:10.1080/0158791800010102

Moore, M. G. (1972). Learner autonomy: The second dimension of independent learning. *Convergence*, *5*(2), 76–88.

Moore, M. G. (1980). Independent study . In Boyd, R., & Apps, J. (Eds.), *Redefining the discipline of adult education*. San Francisco: Jossey Bass.

Moore, M. G., & Kearsley, G. (1996). *Distance education: A systems view*. New York: Wadsworth.

Moore, M. G., & Kearsley, G. (2005). *Distance education: A systems view* (2nd ed.). Belmont, CA: Wadsworth.

Peters, O. (1983). Distance education and industrial production: A comparative interpretation in outline . In Stewart, D., Keegan, D., & Holmberg, B. (Eds.), *Distance Education: International Perspectives*. London: Croom Helm.

Chapter 2
Differentiating Instruction:
Four Types of Courses

Technology and the distance education models has no doubt changed the way that many educators view teaching and learning over the past several years. The use of online platforms or Learning Management Systems (LMS) (i.e., Blackboard, Moodle, Angel, E-College or any number of organizationally designed platforms) has brought an evolving dimension to the educational process. With the growth of online education, it is becoming clearer that modifications can enhance traditional design approaches in meeting the demands and opportunities of online learning environments (Irlbecka, Kaysa, Jones, & Sims, 2006).

As the technology grows, so do the opportunities that allow instructors to see new pedagogies and new ways to teach knowledge and skills in an online course. It is the successful educator who sees the growth potential as a great opportunity to expand teaching and learning capabilities and integrate new hi-tech pedagogies. The purpose of this chapter is to focus on four distinct categories of online courses, and the design and teaching considerations for each category.

DOI: 10.4018/978-1-61520-865-4.ch002

The concept of distance education courses has come a long way from the initial correspondence courses consisting of readings and assignments sent through the postal system. Now we have anytime anywhere, 24/7 learning with Internet connection. This immediate interactive digital arena affords a unique learning environment that many believe is a rich resource for deep learning. With these new technology changes comes the responsibility of the educator to explore new teaching opportunities and understand the possibilities that can exist, being open to the changing and growing dynamics. What was once unthinkable in the online environment, such as teaching skills, instructor lectures and real time interaction is now part of everyday online teaching. Where we could only post text, we can now function with virtual chat rooms (synchronous communications) and interactive discussion boards (asynchronous), lessons through narrated PPT lectures, videos and audio demonstrations.

The term ***differentiated instruction*** takes on many meanings and can be viewed through a variety of lenses. The concept of differentiating our instruction in the online teaching and learning environment means maximizing the learning opportunity for all students across a spectrum of curriculum and courses. This differentiated lens helps online educators to reinvent their online instructional strategies and pedagogies to provide the best possible teaching and learning opportunities. "Differentiation is not a recipe for teaching nor is it an instructional strategy" (Tomlinson, 2000b, p. 6). It is a common sense approach to address the needs of a wide variety of learners and learning situations promoting equity and excellence, focusing on best practices (Tomlinson, 2000a). The concept of differentiation is not a new concept. "The one-room schoolhouse is a prime example of teachers differentiating to meet the needs of students" (Anderson, 2007). Differentiated instruction is a philosophy based on the premise that instructors should adapt their instruction to student's differences and different instructional situations. Educators and trainers must view differentiation as a philosophy of teaching and learning that becomes tantamount as Tomlinson states to the uniqueness and possibilities of learners (2004).

Differentiating instruction is multidimensional and does not follow a step by step progression (Smith, 2005), especially in the online environment nor is it something that an instructional designer, teacher or trainer does when he or she has the time. It has to become the way we think about teaching and learning (Tomlinson, 2004). Differentiated Instruction represents a proactive approach to improving learning and learning opportunities for students (Pettig, 2000).

To attain better results and reduce variation in student achievement, Bloom (1956) reasoned that there is a need to increase variation in teaching. He proposed that instruction must be diversified and differentiated in order to address individual learning needs so all students learn well. All online courses should not be designed or taught with the same model. We need to look at each online course as a unique opportunity. Seeing that there are different types of courses offered in the online arena, can assist instructors and designers to differentiate their planning and execution of distance education pedagogies to maximize student achievement of course outcomes.

In their research, Fuller and Kuhne, (2008) identified four different types of courses that are taught in an online Learning platform. They are: *foundational courses, skills based courses, analysis/synthesis courses and hybrid courses*. Each of these four has unique properties that are approached differently in the preactive (or planning) phases of teaching and the active (or teaching) phases of the course. Each of these types of courses are approached uniquely and possess goals and objectives that require different facilitation techniques.

One of the greatest challenges in the online arena for many instructors is how best to design and facilitate interaction. This interaction focuses on the areas of student interaction with the content, the instructor, other students (Moore & Kearsley, 1996; Moore, 1989) and the technology (Hillman, Willis, & Gunawardena, 1994). Dewey's (1938) transactional conception of activity-based teaching and learning established an educational encounter as a "transaction taking place between an individual and what, at the time, constitutes his environment" (p. 43). The role of the online teacher is to decide how best to design and facilitate this learning environment with the most appropriate and interactive student activities to maximize the learning opportunity. Each of the four courses is unique and the types of facilitated interactions are designed to achieve different learning outcomes. Using the four course lens provides an opportunity to understand our courses in a unique way allowing us to assist students to master the objectives and maximize online instructional strategies.

DEFINING THE FOUR CATEGORIES OF COURSES

Foundational Courses

In any profession there is a fundamental body of knowledge that becomes the cornerstone or the basis for professional knowledge and skill that is presented in an introductory type course or format. This information provides the foundational platform of knowledge that will be used to build upon in other courses or settings. The nature or goals of the foundational course is to provide the base knowledge and skills for a particular course of study that will be utilized to develop higher thinking and application of the fundamental skills (Fuller & Kuhne, 2008). Foundational courses include courses such as anatomy and physiology, economics, fundamentals of math or science and most intro or 101 level courses. In these courses the student may not understand the application of the knowledge and information presented as the focus is on rote memorization and articulation of essential principles. The understanding of application will come in future courses where the fundamental knowledge and skills are built upon and put into function. The prioritized online pedagogies in such courses focus on helping students to make connections with and learn the core material.

In the foundational course, much of the learning is rote memorization and the student either gets it or they don't. Many of the assignments in foundational courses are emailed or posted weekly based upon module content to assure interaction with the content and understanding of key concepts. Some student-to-student interaction is fostered, primarily through the sharing of assignments on asynchronous discussion boards, something that does not routinely happen in a face-to-face classroom. The interaction and pedagogical design is to facilitate memorization and understanding of the information. Some comparing and contrasting is employed in the foundational course but the majority of the applications are left to upper level courses. Instructors need to remember that they are building a "foundation" for future learning. The course interactions are not open-ended and are designed primarily to reinforce the learning and retention of basic concepts that will be applied later in their professional studies and practice.

Where Do We Find Foundational Classes?

A foundational class can be found in any training or educational setting and are often taught using online pedagogies with relative ease for the instructor and designer. If you look at most college or university course offerings or catalogs, they are usually listed as 100 level courses. In company or governmental training and development manuals, they will be described as the entry level training courses designed to indoctrinate new employees to the fundamentals of the organization and in some cases provide foundational knowledge for job performance.

While these courses serve to establish the baseline knowledge from which the learner (employee or student) will develop and build upon with additional knowledge, many participants find them tedious as they may not initially see nor understand the value in what they are being taught. Too often we see students rotely memorize information to pass a test only to forget the information once the test is over. This is most likely due to the instructor not providing enough understanding of the value of the foundational information. Krathwohl, Bloom, and Masia, (1973) discusses the value in terms of the Affective Domain of learning. This affective or in many cases the *forgotten domain* needs to be addressed so that students can see where the information they are learning will apply in their work and in future learning.

Nursing Programs

In an initial nursing program, the foundational courses are the Anatomy and Physiology courses.

Many of these courses are taught in a traditional setting, however more and more colleges and universities are finding that these courses can and are being taught online with equal if not stronger clarity and effectiveness. These courses are foundational as they provide knowledge of the body's systems: muscles, bones, central nervous system, respiratory, cardiac etc. with the objective of having the learner memorize and discover in detail each of the areas of the body. The vast information taught in these courses becomes the foundation for all nursing courses and practice. While the student may innately understand that what they are learning will have future use as a nurse and in other courses, they may not understand how each of the concepts relate or how they are important. This deeper understanding of the use of the information will come as they progress through the program and apply this foundational knowledge of body system function to practice.

Economics

In an Economics program of study there are many higher level courses that are dealing with such concepts as econometrics that emphasizes applying statistical models such of regression analysis and estimation to economic data. This necessitates that students have the foundational understanding of statistics. Others focus on the economics of labor wage theory, unemployment and poverty, and the position of labor in alternative and comparative economic systems. Economics may include areas of price structure that explores the behavior of various market structures. These among various other high level concepts require a base line understanding of the fundamentals of economics. These fundamentals are developed in the two foundation type courses, Macro and Micro Economics. In a macro economics course, focus is on the introduction of fundamental economic institutions including the American economy, government finance and taxation, national income accounting, business cycles, the banking system, and monetary and fiscal policy. Micro economics stresses the analysis of price determination supply and demand, demand and utility, cost and supply, equilibrium of the firm, market structures, pricing of productive factors, and international trade and finance.

Both of these foundational economic courses establish the fundamental principles that allow students to grow and learn in the upper level economic concept courses. With a solid grasp of the fundamentals they can apply the foundational knowledge and skills in the more complex learning situations. Without this basic understanding, students may not be able to grasp and apply the higher level knowledge and skills.

Accounting

Intro to Accounting serves as a foundational course for many business and accounting degrees. While having knowledge and skills associated, this course introduces students to the basic accounting cycle or process of recording, summarizing, and reporting accounting information. Coverage of establishing the books and financial records for an organization through the basic accounting cycle: journalizing business transactions, posting to the ledger, developing worksheets and creating financial statements establishes the framework for understanding how managers use accounting information to make decisions. This basic understanding of the accounting process serves as the basis for all other accounting courses.

Education

In educational degree programs or teacher training degrees there are a couple of foundational courses that serve as the basis of core knowledge. A fundamentals of education course may include the History of Education and Schools and Society to provide the introductory content related to diversity and multiculturalism and the historical perspectives to understand the educational arena. Trends and issues in education, including state and national standards, are also explored. In addition, education candidates will begin their continuing exploration of the teaching profession.

Engineering

Through an Introduction or Fundamentals of Engineering course students are provided with an introductory overview of the role and functions of the practicing engineer. Many will utilize a team-based project with new students to emphasize engineering in terms of the design, fabrications, assembly, and quality functions. Cost estimation and control, inventory control, equipment specification, software and network infrastructure, and other enterprise issues are explored in a technological context. Introductory engineering courses may also include the application of engineering mechanics to problems involving equilibrium of particles and solids. Topics include resultants, equilibrium, friction, trusses, center of gravity, and moments of inertia. The foundational engineering course may also focus on strength of materials introducing the principles of mechanics necessary for the solution of engineering problems relating to strength, stiffness, and material selection and may include the initial concepts of stress, strain, torsion, beams, columns and combined stresses at certain points. While those of us who are not engineers may not understand these principles, they do provide the new engineering students with the fundamental knowledge and skills to adapt in upper level engineering learning and also provide the understanding to assist students to understand what direction in the field they wish to specialize such as Aerospace engineering, biomedical engineering, computer engineers or electrical engineer. The foundational course can assist in not only developing the fundamental knowledge of a profession but also as a conduit for personal direction and learning and career focus.

Hospitality

As with engineering, the Hospitality industry has a number of options and opportunities for students to choose and direct their careers. An Introduction to Hospitality and Tourism Management course is designed to provide students with a broad examination of the food services, lodging, and tourism industries. Many of the introductory courses will focus on the history, organization, economic and social background, and the current issues and trends of the hospitality industry as well as management's role in marketing services to the hotel, restaurant, and tourism customers is explored. This course focus not only provides the foundational knowledge of the industry, but also assists students to explore and focus on an area of career interest.

These are but a few examples of foundational courses. Each profession has a primary body of core information and or skill that serves as the basis or foundation for the rest of the professional knowledge and development. In the coming chapters of this text, we will discuss options and teaching strategies that will assist online teachers to help students see the importance of foundational course information.

Summary

The understanding of the nature of foundational courses and the pedagogies that can be used assists the online instructor to develop brain compatible ways of learning information. We know that information is hierarchical in the brain, creating certain patterns, contexts and relevance for the content being taught (Kitchel and Torres, 2006); chunking information into sizeable and understandable units (Roberts, 2007, 2002). The foundational course allows the brain to begin to organize information in a way that establishes a brain compatible platform for knowledge and application that is yet to come. Again the issue in a foundational class is "Where does this apply and how will I use this knowledge."

If students can see the future applications they become more aware of the value. Foundational courses can be difficult for students to understand as they have no reference or little understanding of the application. The elements of the affective domain or why this knowledge and skill is of value needs to be established with students in the online learning environment. They need to understand why and where this knowledge will be applied or online educators run the risk of students not retaining the information for future course applications.

In Chapter 11, we will explore further the concepts of how we can teach the online foundational course.

SKILLS BASED COURSES

Skills based courses require students to gain a particular skill(s) set that is applicable to a specific environment. These skills can range from the kinesthetic hands on skills to the mental skills required to complete a number of tasks. The kinesthetic hands on are skills similar to typing, utilization of a microscope, the physical skills associated with health care (i.e., taking blood pressure, pulse, listening for lung sounds), learning new computer software or the design skills associated with graphic design to name a few examples. The mental skills are those similar to writing and researching a paper or learning and executing the scientific process in research. These may also involve mathematical skills where real life functions are applied beyond those of completing rote textbook type problems. Harrow (1972) proposed six levels of skills: Reflex (objectives not usually written at this "low" level), Fundamental movements - applicable mostly to young children (crawl, run, jump, reach, change direction), Perceptual abilities (catch, write, balance, distinguish, manipulate), Physical abilities (stop, increase, move quickly, change, react), Skilled movements (play, hit, swim, dive, use), and Non-discursive communication (express, create, mime, design, interpret).

Teaching skills in the online distance arena takes on a different focus than the traditional face-to-face course. The prioritized interactions in such courses focus on content however expand beyond "student-to-content" connection and require instructor facilitation and presence to promote dialogue specific to the skill and the application of the skill (Fuller & Kuhne, 2008). Instructors facilitate an understanding and naturalization, the highest level of Bloom's psychomotor taxonomomy (1956), of the skill through critical thinking and understanding of the concepts with expert use of questioning to guiding the student toward skill efficiency. Instructor interaction focuses on how and where to perform the skills as well as facilitation of skill proficiency. The goal in the online arena is to have students understand the complexities and components of the skill through interaction with the instructor via email feedback and peer interaction. Assignments that facilitate student-to-content interaction in a skills-based class are weekly assignments that are emailed back to the instructor or posted in an online discussion board to assure that they are interacting with content and understanding it. Interaction with students and instructor focuses on the processes that they are going through in learning the content. With the mental skills this can be facilitated with the incorporation of group projects as well as individual practice and instructor feedback. The goal is to provide them with a set of skills that can apply in an appropriate setting.

Kinesthetic skills or activities such as those mentioned above can be facilitated through the utilization of online tutorials which may include video demonstrations or other pedagogies and assignments that facilitate practice and application. Outcomes assessment can be demonstrated through the submission of final projects that are a culmination of the skill development. This can manifest in a number of projects. If the skill were the ability to function within a software package, the instructor could create tutorials or use publisher's material that walk the student through the utilization process. The outcomes can be measured in a final project that encompasses all the skills necessary to function in the software.

More hands on types of skills that deal with manipulative outside the digital and mental skills realm can be more challenging in the distance education format. Demonstrations can be made again utilizing online videos from a publisher or instructor produced with appropriate text tutorial support. This coupled with instructor interaction through email and online synchronous and asynchronous interaction can provide sufficient instruction to develop student skill proficiency. Assessment outcomes of the skills may be more difficult and require real time interaction. Some skill assessments can be done at a distance through video demonstrations and video conferencing while others require the assessment be completed face-to-face either with the instructor or a proxy who is geographically closer and credentialed by the instructing institution.

Where Do We Find Skills Based Classes?

Let's look at some hands on and cognitive examples of skills based classes that are being taught at a distance.

Research

Research classes are an example of a mental skills class. Research classes teach the skills of quantitative and qualitative methodology development. The skills focus on the development of properly crafted research questions and the development of hypotheses, analysis of the components of the research process, the analysis and synthesis of literature reviews, design techniques and choosing the proper method to answer research questions, and applying and passing through an IRB process all culminating in the writing of a cogent research proposal and preparing for its implementation. Each of these teaches the student the research process that will assist them in developing the skills to complete independent quantitative and qualitative research projects for publication and the advancement of new knowledge both inside the university and out.

The interactive focus is on assisting students to focus their research and to develop research skills. Many students are very broad in their design of questions and methodologies. The goal of this skills based course is to assist the student in focusing their research questions and understanding what research methods they can employ that will help answer their questions and what statistics will work best. The interaction in this course is focusing skill development through contact with the instructor who can guide their ideas and through posting their assignments in asynchronous discussion boards for all to see and comment. This fosters learning from the trading of ideas and concepts among students. By seeing others student's skill development and commenting on each other's work, students can interact and learn from classmates guided by the instructor. This allows students to create their own meaning to knowledge in a self-directed manner and take more responsibility for their own learning (Knowles, 1999; 1980).

Software Courses

There are many software program courses that offer both psychomotor and cognitive skills throughout universities and in the workplace. Teaching a class in how to use PowerPoint, Word, Access or Excel are being conducted through online training in both the credit and non credit formats. Teaching a class on Web Page Design, Desktop Publishing, Computers in the Classroom or a Multimedia Design course incorporate both mental and physical skills. The physical skills of actual program manipulation and the mental skills of application development and integration into a particular setting both work together for these type courses. JAVA Programming teaches the skills to program in Java and to develop Java applications. Each of these and many others teach the physical skills of manipulating the computer and the software to maneuver and operate the software to the desired applications. This takes both the mental or perceptual skills and the physical skills to maneuver through the software and the computer hardware.

The interactive focus in teaching any of these software applications online is through initial content directions designed to illustrate the steps in procedures in each of the applications. Many instructors will use text through word processing text material or the use of a PowerPoint presentation that is automated with voice over applications illustrating the steps and procedures the student must take, posted on a learning management system (LMS) such as those mentioned above. This is easily developed as the instructor completes each step of a computer software skill taking a picture of what and how at each step using the Print Screen functions on every computer key board. This function actually takes a digital picture of what is on the screen and then can be dropped into PPT or other graphic presentation package. Using a series of arrows and descriptive text, the student can see and understand the software and hardware steps necessary to complete the skill. Not so dissimilar to how this would be taught in a face-to-face class the student sees how and then is given a task or assignment to do him/herself. Interaction with the instructor is usually to answer questions via email or discussion board for clarification or assistance with troubleshooting or with understanding the applications and where this could be utilized. Many instructors will use a synchronous format via a virtual chat room to demonstrate and work through both simple and difficult skills. The interaction with other students is in the area of how this software could be utilized through a brainstorming type function and learning from reviewing each other's work posted online for all in the course to review and comment.

Other Physical Skills Courses

The question comes, "Can I teach more traditional skills courses online?" The answer may surprise some. Traditional healthcare programs that are at least 50% clinical skills such as Registered Nurse programs can be taught online. Some of the skills are taught online using similar pedagogies of video demonstrations and other multimedia type presentations. This again is not so dissimilar from the traditional face-to-face teaching by demonstration of skills. The difference is in the practice opportunities and the formative and summative assessment. Technology has not yet brought us to the point where we can assess these skills without a face-to-face component. Clinical skills still need to be monitored in the traditional manner whether this is done with an on campus component or with a designated surrogate instructor credentialed by the degree granting institution.

ANALYSIS/SYNTHESIS BASED COURSES

To analyze something is to take the whole and break it down into its individual parts. This process allows us to understand the whole better through understanding the individual parts. By breaking it down and working with the parts, the learner is provided with an authentic perception of the whole. Once we have that deeper understanding of all the dynamics that are involved, we can synthesize our new knowledge in different settings. Synthesis is the process of taking those parts that we have broken down and applying or building them into a different whole. This becomes a higher order thinking that provides the learner significant application of the material beyond just the simple skills of rote memorization. In an analysis synthesis class, the participant is taking information that they have learned in a foundational course and are building and applying the knowledge. This provides the learner a life skill of problem solving through analyzing one thing and applying it to another.

Analysis/Synthesis Courses are used to teach students to analyze a situation and engage in problem solving (Fuller & Kuhne, 2008). These are courses where core info is presented but there may not necessarily be a right or wrong view.

Examples are those classes in any discipline that may be titled as issues classes or policy type classes. These classes will generate a number of issues and potentially polarizing ideals. The focus is on exploring all sides of the issues to assure that students understand the facts from all angles. The key is to flesh out all aspects of the subject and have the students explore and support the differing viewpoints with the facts. While there are many opinions, there may not be one single correct view of a subject. The instructor's role is to facilitate the knowledge and the understanding of all the facts. The interaction can be facilitated in a number of pedagogies that explore all views and facts and culminate in a synchronous or asynchronous discussion board. For the instructor in this type of class the key is not to intervene too much in the discussion but serve as a facilitator of understanding and direction. Instructors may wish to avoid authoritative postings as they may tend to shut down dialogue. If the instructor posts their particular opinions about a topic it can change the discussion in that students stop posting or just restate instructor opinions. Students will simply parrot instructor ideas or postings (as most students do not want to challenge the instructor and risk receiving a lower grade) or quit posting and exploring new angles and ideas as they view the instructor as the final authority. The instructor should post more personal experience than personal thoughts and beliefs.

Dialogue among participants provides regular opportunities for reflection and inquiry and requires the least intervention in the discussion boards of all course types. Simulated contact in this manner through subject matter presentation can subsume part of the interaction by causing students to consider different views, approaches and solutions and generally to interact with a course.

In the analysis/synthesis course there is a need to establish the culture of independent collaborative learning with the overarching goal of student development of independent critical thinking. Instructors do not respond to the majority of postings but facilitate all students to discuss and interact. Instructors will read all postings in this type of course and respond to key ideas and elements to guide the learning process through guiding questions. The instructors must facilitate the discussion board to assure that students are focused in their discussion and aren't allowed to go off on tangents. Instructors can pose questions that will stimulate or lead the discussion in a direction as well as "perturb the system" (Beaubin, 2002) to assure that all concepts are being explored. This takes careful facilitation and monitoring by the instructor. If the discussion is getting one-sided or negative, the instructor can, through a posted thought, direct the dialogue to view another side. "That is true but what would 'so and so' say regarding this and why?" Or the instructor can pose additional thought provoking ideas and questions to guide the analysis and synthesis of concepts. One technique in this type of course is to create an online debate where students don't get to pick but defend an assigned point of view which forces them to see all sides. Another technique is for students to choose a topic, interview someone then write a paper discussing their issue and what they have found by leading a discussion board thread.

Where Do We Find Analysis/ Synthesis Classes?

Analysis/synthesis courses are found in most programs of study and serve to allow participants to delve deep into critical and controversial issues in their field. Many of the courses are titled with Trends and Issues in their title and provide an overview of history and philosophies for application of information, employment, current issues, political concerns, fiscal and budgetary concerns or issues that are unique to the profession.

In a class such as *Issues in Health Care*, the course may focus on the current health care delivery system and spotlight the major trends, issues and problems challenging policy makers and health care professionals. The structures and processes attributed to the delivery of health care services are stressed and analyses of management problems that are of importance may be explored. This is a course where a module or lesson might focus on "Comparing the Canadian versus the USA health systems. This would obviously prompt many opinions and views that would fall along political and personal views. The goal is to have students analyze all aspects of the issue and understand the facts from all educational and applicable vantage points. Another course such as *American Foreign Policy* from the Political Science realm may serve as an analysis of the development and objectives of United States foreign policy with attention on Eastern, Middle Eastern, and Latin American policies, the involvement in world wars, the end of the policy of isolation, and the expansion of the American role in foreign affairs. This is a course that would focus on the historical aspects of world politics and decisions and how they shaped U.S. policies. This course would provide many political views which may polarize students to view one side as the student enters the class with one political view. The goal for the online instructor is to assure that all students flesh out the relevant facts from all sides of the political issues allowing students to breakdown the concepts and analyze all elements. This can be a daunting task as students may enter the class with a preconceived political view. There are several techniques and online instructional strategies to assist students to analyze information and to synthesize it in new ways allowing them to develop their own understanding.

Other courses may not be as controversial, but still provide the analysis synthesis opportunity for learning and applying. This type of course is of significance as it innately deals with the affective domain through illustrating the value and application of information. An information technology course such as *The Information Age Organization* may focus on the dramatic changes within organizations in the late 20th century as affected by information technology and such elements of change as restructuring, entrepreneurship, and managing the complex organization. Through a series of case analyses, students explore the design of the information age organization and the information infrastructure required to support it. The course will look at organizational designs and includes consideration of problem analysis strategies. While not providing controversial issues for online discussions, it does present case based information to analyze with the ideals that students will be able to understand and synthesize or apply in other venues.

Additional analysis/synthesis courses may be found as *Issues and Controversies in Adult Education, Problem solving in Organizations, Special Topics in Political Communications* to mention but a few. We will explore the pedagogical opportunities in Chapter 13.

HYBRID COURSES

A hybrid by definition is the combining of two or more items of different natures targeted at achieving a certain outcome. A hybrid course can work toward the same end by combining two or more educational methods to achieve a set of educational goals and objectives.

We've discussed three of the four course types in the previous pages: foundational courses, skill based courses and analysis/synthesis type courses. A hybrid course includes a combination of the foundational, skills and/or analysis/synthesis courses and requires a mixing of techniques to facilitate online instruction, interaction and assessment. A course such as a basic *Statistics* course is foundational as it provides the baseline understanding of how and where statistics can be applied. The course uses general examples to provide a baseline understanding of the theories and applications of the different statistical calculations. In most university or college graduate and undergraduate programs students are required to take an Intro to Statistics course. This is a foundational course for a variety of programs of study but also serves as a skill based class as students will leave with a skill set to calculate and use calculating software to apply the numeric values. The skills are both mental and physical to a degree as they provide an ability and understanding of the mathematical equations for descriptive and inferential calculations that help prove or describe situations in numerical values and demonstrate methods for solving equations through computer programs such as Excel or SPSS. Some courses may incorporate the use of graphing calculators which further adds to the skills. This is foundational as it provides the basic knowledge to complete the computations and have a general understanding of what the values represent. Most research courses require a statistics course as a prerequisite to understanding quantitative research design and analysis and many business and math related courses use as both the foundation and the skills basis for higher level concept courses. Students apply the statistics they have learned in this hybrid course by coupling it with the new research content.

The term hybrid course has also taken on the meaning of blending face-to-face instruction with online approaches to learning where a portion of the course learning is conducted online resulting in reduced face-to-face seat time. Blended Learning is the planned integration of online and face-to-face instructional approaches in a way that maximizes the positive features of each delivery mode." The goal is to create an innovative and effective learning experience for students (Regan, 2007). Such courses, are sometimes called "hybrid", "mixed-mode", and "flexible learning", appear to be gaining in popularity (Picciano & Dzuiban, 2007).

Table 1. Summary of four types of courses

	Foundation	**Skills**	**Analysis/ Synthesis**	**Hybrid**
Objectives Or Outcomes	Objectives from low levels of thinking according to cognitive domain but serve as the basis for higher thinking	Objectives involving physical movement and coordination in the psychomotor domain	Objectives from high levels of thinking according to cognitive domain	Objectives from course (e.g., Foundation + Skills or Skills + Analysis)
Instructor	Teacher	Coach	Facilitator	Ranges from directive to supportive
Interaction	Interaction with content and instructor	Interaction with content and instructor	Interaction with peers and content	Interaction includes content, instructor, and peers
Activities	Lecture Flash cards Word games Jeopardy Matching Annotated bibliographies	Demonstration Simulations Role play Field trip	Debate Case study Problem based learning Discussion Guest speaker	Activities from two types of courses
Assessments	Quiz Exam Low stakes writing Homework	Rubric Checklist Demonstration Presentation	Participation Synthesis papers Essay Presentation Project	Assessments from two types of courses
Instructional Resources	Textbook PowerPoint	Video Images PowerPoint	Journal articles Websites Charts/Tables	Resources from two types of courses

This blended learning opportunity is provided for a variety of reasons that include scheduling availability, resource allocation, instructor and student time, and student recruitment and retention. The blended learning approach integrates the best of the traditional face-to-face with the advantages and resources of the online learning opportunities. Utilizing the innate capabilities and the more self-directed approach, the online component can add to the student learning with asynchronous discussions of information resources coupled with the clarity of traditional classroom pedagogies. This can facilitate a deeper learning experience as it differentiates instruction to a high degree allowing students greater flexibility and control of their education. Hybrid or blended learning courses can be up to 80% online with 20% face-to-face (other courses may include levels of a 50/50 blend). Other hybrid courses are 100% face-to-face but utilize the online platform to augment the presentation of information and interaction by including additional resources and weekly asynchronous discussions.

In the coming chapters we will look at these four courses: *foundational courses, skill based courses, analysis/synthesis and hybrid courses* to understand how best to design each and to teach each. If we as educators understand the different intent of each of these four courses, then we can better design and teach in the online to meet the student's needs and the goals and objectives of the education. By viewing course design and online instruction through the lens of these four types of courses, we provide ourselves as educators with yet another tool to differentiate our instruction and maximize the learning opportunity for online participants and ourselves as educators and trainers. Table 1 illustrates the potential opportunities through summarizing and comparing the four course models of online courses. Online courses have a wide variety of goals and purposes which determine the course design strategies. Each of these will be discussed throughout this book.

Personal Reflection Suggestion

Think of all the courses that you teach in either the traditional face to face and online. Which do you believe fit into each of the four course categories of foundational courses, skill based courses, analysis/synthesis and hybrid courses. List them out and describe what makes them fit that particular category.

REFERENCES

Anderson, K. M. (2007). Differentiating instruction to include all students. *Preventing School Failure, 51*(3), 49–54. doi:10.3200/PSFL.51.3.49-54

Beaubien, J. (2002). Harnessing the power of complexity in an online learning environment . In Rudestam, K. E., & Schoenholtz-Read, J. (Eds.), *Handbook of Online Learning: Innovations in Higher Education and Corporate Training* (pp. 221–236). Thousand Oaks, CA: Sage Publications.

Bloom, B. (1956). *Taxonomy of educational objectives*. New York: Longman.

Dewey, J. (1938). *Experience and education*. New York: Collier Macmillan.

Fuller, R. G., & Kuhne, G. W. (2008, January). Fostering Meaningful Interaction in Health Education Online Courses: Matching Pedagogy To Course Types. *International Journal of Information and Communication Technology Education, 4*(1).

Harrow, A. (1972). *A Taxonomy of the Psychomotor Domain. A guide for Developing Behavioral Objectives*. New York: McKay.

Hillman, D., Willis, D. J., & Gunawardena, C. (1994). Learner-Interface Interaction in Distance Education: An Extension of Contemporary Models and Strategies for Practitioners. *American Journal of Distance Education, 8*(2), 30–42. doi:10.1080/08923649409526853

(2007). Introduction . InPicciano, A. G., & Dziuban, C. D. (Eds.), *Blended Learning Research and Perspectives*. Needham, MA: The Sloan Consortium.

Irlbecka, S., Kaysa, E., Jones, D., & Sims, R. (2006). The phoenix rising: emergent models of instructional design. *Distance Education*, *27*(2), 171–185. doi:10.1080/01587910600789514

Kitchel, T., & Torres, R. M. (2006). Meaning as a factor of increasing retention. In *Proceedings of the 2005 American Association for Agricultural Education National Research Conference*, San Antonio, Texas.

Krathwohl, D. R., Bloom, B. S., & Masia, B. B. (1973). *Taxonomy of Educational Objectives, the Classification of Educational Goals. Handbook II: Affective Domain*. New York: David McKay Co., Inc.

Moore, M. G. (1989). Three types of interaction. *American Journal of Distance Education*, *3*(2), 1–6. doi:10.1080/08923648909526659

Moore, M. G., & Kearsley, G. (1996). *Distance Education: A systems view*. San Francisco: Wadsworth Publishing Company.

Pettig, K. L. (2000, September). On the road to differentiated practice. *Educational Leadership*, 14–16.

Ragan, L. (2007 November). Best Practices in Online Teaching – Pulling It All Together – Teaching Blended Learning Courses. *Connexions Program of Rice University*. Retrieved November 26, 2007, from http://cnx.org/content/m15048/latest/

Roberts, J. W. (2002). Beyond learning by doing: The brain compatible approach. *Journal of Experiential Education*, *2*(2), 281–285.

Roberts, J. W. (2007). *A handbook: Teaching at the University of Maitoba*. Winnipeg, Canada: University of Teaching Services.

Tomlinson, C. A. (2000a). Differentiated instruction: Can it work? *Education Digest*, *66*, 25–31.

Tomlinson, C. A. (2000b). Reconcilable differences? Standards-based teaching and differentiation. *Educational Leadership*, *58*, 6–11.

Tomlinson, C. A. (2004). Sharing responsibility for differentiating instruction. *Roeper Review*, *26*(4), 188–189. doi:10.1080/02783190409554268

Section 2
Frameworks for Designing Differentiated Instruction

Chapter 3
Learners and Learning

One factor that must be considered by all course designers and is independent of the type of the course being designed is the characteristic of the targeted learners. For many reading this book, one major learner consideration is that adults, not traditional age learners, are usually the focus of corporation or community training efforts. Certainly many in the higher education arena also are targeting adult learners since more than half of those attending college in the United States are now over the age of 21. This chapter focuses upon what research has demonstrated about adults as learners, their special characteristics and needs that distinguish them from traditional age learners. Such characteristics must be understood and indrawn upon if effective distance education programs are to be developed.

In this chapter we will examine together some of what is known about adults as learners and the possible interplay between adult development and the learning process. Despite the fact that adult learners come in all shapes and sizes and are encountered in nearly every conceivable setting, it is still possible to draw some generalizations about their characteristics as learners--characteristics that set them apart from youth and call for different approaches to the teaching and learning process. In addition to examine some of the major characteristics of adult learners, this chapter will also consider what we know about adult participation in learning efforts, as well as take a brief look at how adulthood and intelligence are related.

DOI: 10.4018/978-1-61520-865-4.ch003

SOME GENERAL CHARACTERISTICS OF ADULTS AS LEARNERS

An accumulating body of both experience and research has enabled adult educators to draw some important conclusions about what adults are like as learners. Such conclusions, or principles, can provide a solid foundation for designing educational programs for adults. They can also provide insights into teaching that can greatly increase the effectiveness of educational efforts. The ten characteristics summarized below are of particular importance for program designers.

Conclusion #1: Adults Generally Desire To Take More Control over Their Learning than Youth

Adults tend to be self-directed in their lives, although responsibilities with jobs, families, and other organizations can remove a degree of their freedom to act. Adulthood brings an increasing sense of the need to take responsibility for our lives and adults strongly resent it when others take away their rights to choose. This fact is clearly seen in educational efforts among adults. When not given some control over their learning, most adults will resist learning and some will even attempt to sabotage education efforts. They do not like being relegated to a "passive" position. Certainly this implies that program designers should always seek for ways to include the adult in the planning of educational efforts. Certainly we should seek ways to foster self-assessment and evaluation. The very fact that the learners are adults underscores the reality that adult learners generally desire a peer relationship with instructors, rather than a hierarchical one. Most adult also expect greater availability of instructors.

Conclusion #2: Adults Tend To Draw Upon Their Experiences as a Resource in Their Learning Efforts More Than Youth

The adult's life and professional experiences are a key resource in any learning effort. Adults have a greater reservoir of life experiences simply because they have lived longer and seen and done more. This is a critical distinction between adults and traditional learners. Consciously or unconsciously, adults tend to link any new learning to their prior learning, a body of knowledge that is rooted in their life experiences. They evaluate the validity of new ideas and concepts in light of how the idea or concept "fits" their experience. Certainly this suggests that the designer and instructor schedule the time to get to know more about the experiences of our learners and seek to help them link new ideas to prior learning. The professional experience can also be a resource for learning when discussion is encouraged regarding how new ideas fit the experience of learners.

Conclusion #3: Adult Tend To Be More Motivated In Learning Situations than Youth

This distinctive of higher motivation is probably closely linked to the fact that most adult learning is voluntary. Adults are making personal choices to acquire education, even when such schooling is tied to professional development or job skills. Whenever individual are able to choose to learn, they are much more motivated to learn. One design implication is that instructors can spend less effort trying to motivate adult learners and concentrate time on facilitating the learning they are already motivated to pursue.

Conclusion #4: Adults Are Normally More Pragmatic In Learning Situations than Youth

Adults are particularly motivated to learn information that seems immediately applicable to their situation and needs. They tend to be frustrated with learning abstract "theory" that has no immediate application. Many also tend to resist "learning for the sake of learning" forms of education or training. Certainly there are exceptions to this principle, but the majority of adult learners seem to reflect this pragmatism. This pragmatic orientation can be drawn upon in course designs by being sure to tie the content of programs to the application needs of the learners. Certainly the use of effective needs assessment strategies (covered elsewhere within this book) is supported by the importance of applicability to practice needs that is demanded by adult learners. Another implication is to be sure to lean the content of a course toward the utilitarian more than the theoretical.

Conclusion #5: In Contrast To Youth, the Learner Role Is Usually Secondary For Adults

For most adults, the "student" role is a relatively minor and secondary role. This is in sharp contrast to traditional age learners for whom the learner role is both their primary social role and the main basis for their self-identity. Adults fulfill multiple roles in their lives and these multiple roles inevitably create conflicting and competing demands on the adult learner. Multiple roles result in most adults having far less time and energy to read, study, or learn. Such a reality has many implications for program designers. First, more flexibility is generally required in adult education programs than in traditional education. Make allowance for competing roles by giving assignments far ahead of time. Accept that jobs and families can create obstacles for the learner, and be willing to extend deadlines for assignments. Also accept that the learners will not see their educational efforts as necessarily the highest priority in their lives. Finally, understand that your targeted adult learners may be preoccupied at times with other roles and responsibilities.

Conclusion #6: Adults Are Forced To Fit Their Learning into Life's "Margins"

The many adult roles identified above take energy and time to fulfill. Everyone faces the reality that there are limits on their energy and time. An important principle to understand is that learning takes time and energy. If an adult is going to undertake a learning activity, s/he must realistically evaluate his/her life and see that there is actually room for the added demands of the learning. Adult learners must learn to carve out some margin in their lives to allow learning to occur, in other words, a learner must go through a process of priority setting. If the existing demands on an adult require all the energy they possess, then the learning will be compromised. One practical implication of this reality is that designers and instructors of adults must prioritize student advising to provide guidance to help learners to be realistic about the demands of learning and provide time management and study suggestions. Certainly institutions must be cautioned that merely providing training without also providing a realistic amount of time to actually learn the material is to risk minimal benefits from all training efforts.

Conclusion #7: Many Adults Lack Confidence in Their Learning

Many adults have had somewhat negative learning experiences during their traditional schooling years and carry into their adult life some of the baggage of such experiences. As a result, many adult learners tend to feel inadequate when learning through formal educational programs. Even in cases where earlier learning experiences were positive, many adults lack confidence for further schooling efforts due to what they perceive as rusty study skills, poor reading skills, test anxiety, or other such learning barriers. Effective designers and instructors will take this confidence concern into consideration in the program they design and or teach. One strategy is to employ specific learning strategies that build higher confidence in adult learners. Certainly taking the time to teach better study skills and ways of improving reading comprehension will bear rich dividends in terms of learning outcomes. Studies have shown another practical step is to use collaborative learning approaches in the classroom to alleviate educational anxiety, i.e., turn the classroom from a competitive environment to a collaborative one.

Conclusion #8: Adults Tend To Be More Resistant To Change than Youth

Learning often involves changes in our attitudes or actions. Adults tend to be somewhat resistant to such changes because life itself teaches that change is not always for the better and that many of the outcomes of change are unpredictable. Youth tend to be more idealistic and are often open to change just for the sake of change. A clear implication of this reality is to provide more explanation of the "why" of changes, not just the "how" for adult learners. Make an effort to link new concepts to older, understood, and accepted concepts for adult learners. Change theory also underscores that building incremental changes in an education program tends to be more useful than global changes because it allows the "proof" gained from the positive experience stemming from an incremental change to encourage the adult learner to explore yet more change.

Conclusion #9: Adults Are More Diverse Than Youth

Adults vary from each other as learners in terms of age and experience much more than traditional age learners. Such differences can be used as a powerful resource for adult learning. Through collaboration in small groups, adults can benefit from their variety of experiences. Dialogue with other adults enables adult learners to perceive more nuances of application, and possible problems with new concepts, than could ever be gained from private reflection. Certainly this implies the need to allow more time for adult learners to network together and share perspectives and experiences. Designers should also seek to present material in a variety of ways to accommodate different learning styles.

Conclusion #10: Adults Must Compensate For Aging in Learning

Finally, aging brings with it a number of physical complications that can impact on adult learning efforts. The percentage of such complications increases with age. As we will see later, such complications are not really due to intelligence. Although the speed of learning tends to decrease with age, the depth of learning tends to increase. In other words, adults tend to learn less rapidly with age, but what they learn is learned at a deeper and more integrative level. As adults age, vision and hearing can also create barriers in educational programs. As adult educators, we must pay much more attention to issues such as font size in our online offerings when dealing with adult learners.

Personal Reflection Suggestion

Spend some time reflecting on your experiences as a learner in light of the conclusions above. Think about what you were like as a learner at the age of 16 and what you are like today. How have you changed in your approach to learning since becoming an adult?

UNDERSTANDING WHY ADULTS PARTICIPATE IN LEARNING EFFORTS

Another important body of information regarding adult learners that designers should consider when designing and promoting their programs involves understanding why adults choose to participate in educational efforts. Research into adult education participation was one of the major research interests in adult education from the 1960s through the 1990s. Part of the interest in this subject was driven by market considerations (i.e., the need to understand why people attend educational programs so better recruit plans could be developed to attract new people for programs). More importantly, research into adult education participation was easily quantifiable (i.e., such research lends itself to numbers and statistics). Two major types of participation research were carried out in adult education: descriptive and explanatory. The descriptive research sought to answer the questions of "who" participates and in "what kinds" of learning opportunities. Indirectly, descriptive research pointed out underrepresented groups. Explanatory studies sought to answer the question of "why" or "why not." They focused on the motivations of learners and uncovered barriers to participation. One confusing factor in participation research is that not all the research is examining the same phenomenon. Some researchers were defining adult learning efforts as anything that was organized, while others limited their analysis to formal schooling or organizational offerings.

The question of "who" participates in adult learning activities has been fairly well answered in the literature, although such studies must be done on a continuing basis to uncover changes and trends. Actually, most adults (approximately 9 out of 10) participate in adult learning efforts if we define such efforts broadly enough to include self-directed learning efforts. The groundbreaking research done by Allan Tough confirmed this surprising fact (Tough, 1978). Even using such broad definitions, certain groups still end up underrepresented, including the poor, the minorities, the rural, and the elderly. Studies on participation in more formal educational efforts have shown that the higher the level of prior formal education, the higher the level of participation in continuing educational efforts. Age and accessibility to educational programs have also been revealed as important considerations. In the more formal educational efforts, minorities, poor, and elderly are still clearly underrepresented.

The question of "what" adults study in their learning efforts has also been extensively researched. The evidence shows that adults tend to study the practical more than the academic, the applied more than the theoretical, and skills more than knowledge. The question of "why" adults participate has been also been partially answered in the literature, at least in terms of formal educational efforts. The vast majority of formal adult learning efforts are pursued for job-related reasons. Less than a third of such learning is done for personal, non-job related reasons. A small percentage of adult learners seek out new learning opportunities in order to meet new people, or to pursue personal development unrelated to job needs. The situation shifts when informal learning is examined. Since such learning includes self-directed projects and community learning opportunities, the importance of problem-solving on a personal or community level begins to become a major motive in learning efforts.

Research into "why not" has been particularly useful and has uncovered important barriers to formal adult learning efforts. Such barriers can be situational, as when cost, job conflicts, or time become the reason for non-participation. Such barriers can also be institutional, as when school policies, course scheduling, or support services become the reasons for non-participation. Such barriers can also be dispositional, as when fear, energy, or family opposition become the reasons for non-participation. More recent research on formal adult learning efforts has focused upon the sociological barriers to participation, or those linked to issues of socioeconomic status and the structure of society in general. Such research has underscored the reality of societal barriers that tend to prevent participation on the part of marginalized groups in the society.

Personal Reflection Question

1. *In light of the preceding summary research on participation by adults in learning projects, reflect on your own experiences as an adult learner over the past two or three years. Include in your considerations both formal and informal learning efforts.*
2. *How closely do your answers to the following questions align with the research conclusions?*
    a. *What reasons did you have for pursuing your learning efforts?*
    b. *Where did you go to pursue the learning efforts?*
    c. *If you quit a learning effort before completion, what were the reasons?*

d. *Were there any learning efforts you desired to pursue but were prevented from pursuing?*
e. *What barriers stood in the way of such learning efforts?*

3. *Finally, how should such facts influence your design and promotional efforts with the educational programs you are designing?*

THE RELATIONSHIP BETWEEN AGE, LEARNING, AND INTELLIGENCE

One important question linked to adults as learners is what happens to intelligence as we age. Does our level of intelligence increase or decrease as we grow into adulthood and eventually older age? This question has been a focus of argument for a long time. For many years the common wisdom was that after the mid- to late teen years, we began to lose our "peak" of intellectual functioning. This view was so widely accepted that the only real question that seemed worth investigating was how much and how quickly we deteriorated. With the advent of more formal research studies in the twentieth century, notably by Thorndike, it became clear that adults' learning ability does not drop significantly after the teen years, and measurable declines are primarily a fact of old age, not adulthood in general (Thorndike, Bregman, Tilton, & Woodyard, 1928).

Although research could confirm that adults were able to maintain high levels of learning ability, the question of what actually happens to intelligence in the adult years was not so easily answered. The best answer to this question of the effects of aging on intelligence is "it all depends on what we mean by intelligence." Over the past eighty years the meaning of the word "intelligence" has been the focus of much debate by researchers and theorists. Some have defined intelligence to be the ability to learn or reason. Those who adopt this definition try to measure such an ability by linking it to a formal measurement or score, such as an "IQ" (Intelligence Quotient). Most tests to measure such ability tend to focus on verbal meanings, speed of reasoning, and spatial organizing skills. On the basis of measurements (tests) believed to identify such abilities, adults' "intelligence" was found to start to decline with age, but not dramatically until rather late in life.

But many researchers, theorists, and practitioners were dissatisfied with the identification of intelligence with a single factor such as "learning ability". As a result, some researchers and theorists begin to postulate other conceptions of intelligence. Theorists began to view intelligence as a combination of biological and environmental factors as expressed not only in learning ability, but in such things as wisdom and creativity. In the 1960s, Cattell and Horn broke new ground in these new lines of inquiry into intelligence and suggested that instead of looking for a single factor called "intelligence," there are actually two factors in human intelligence: Fluid Intelligence and Crystallized Intelligence. (Cattell, R., 1963). Fluid Intelligence referred to the ability to perceive complex relationships and engage in short-term memory, concept formation, reasoning, and abstractions. This factor in intelligence showed up with tests of memory and speed of processing information. This factor in intelligence decreased over age, starting in the late teen years. Crystallized Intelligence had to do with acculturated information--those skills linked to vocabulary, verbal comprehension, judgment, wisdom, and ability to evaluate experience. This factor in intelligence showed up as a form of practical and social intelligence. Crystallized Intelligence was found to increase slowly over the adult life span, dropping only in very old age. Cattell and Horn suggested that Crystallized Intelligence tended to compensate for reductions in Fluid Intelligence in most adults. As a result, adults could continue to learn effectively throughout their lives. Adult education needed to focus more on judgment and analysis and less on short-term memory and speed of processing.

Once Cattell and Horn successfully called into question the whole concept of a single factor called "intelligence," other theorists began to look at intelligence as a multiple-factored reality. For example, Sternberg (1985) suggested that human intelligence actually had three aspects or components, including Componential Intelligence (synonymous with analytic thinking or common academic ability), Experiential Intelligence (synonymous with creative thinking or the ability to apply academics in practice), and Contextual Intelligence--synonymous with practical thinking or wisdom and "street smarts". Sternberg suggested that a person's true level of intelligence was a combination of these three elements. As far as adult education is concerned, Sternberg suggested that experiential and componential intelligence seemed unaffected by age. He also suggested that important aspects of intelligence cannot be measured by existing tests of mental abilities, a fact that seems to be born out by the superior performance of many adult learners in schooling despite lower traditional measures of intelligence. Finally, Sternberg also suggested that experiential and contextual intelligence can be taught--that well-designed educational programs can actually increase the intelligence, not just the knowledge, of learners. Adult educators seeking to foster transformative learning find a strong ally in such theoretical possibilities.

There is simply not enough space in this chapter to explore other intelligence theories such as Gardner's view of multiple intelligence (Gardner, H.,1983) and Goleman's emphasis on the idea that intelligence has both rational and emotional aspects (Goleman, D.,1995). The point for our consideration of all of these theories is to argue that adults are certainly not compromised in their learning due to "diminishing intelligence" as a result of entering adulthood, or even growing older. If a measurable decline in certain aspects of intelligence occurs during adulthood, effective educational programs can help adults to more than compensate for such declines by reliance on other intelligence factors. Our exciting task as adult educators is to design our courses with an eye on these intelligence implications. Although we may need to rely less on speed of processing and cover our material more slowly, the material we choose to cover can be learned in more depth and with greater opportunities for reflection. Such learning holds the promise of actually increasing the intelligence (or certain aspects of intelligence) in our adult learners.

Personal Relection Question

1. *Reflect upon the various views of intelligence above and their relationship to adult education and aging. Which seem to be the most useful for understanding the adult learners you have taught?*
2. *What implications do you see for programs you are designing?*

THE RELATIONSHIP BETWEEN ADULT DEVELOPMENT AND ADULT LEARNING

There are important relationships between various developmental changes in adulthood and the teaching-learning process in adults. Research into adult learning reveals the importance of "teachable moments" or "trigger events" in motivating both learning and application. Often these moments or events are directly related to various problems, issues, or tasks encountered in the midst of developmental changes. Research into adult learning also shows that important changes in psycho-social, moral, spiritual, and cognitive areas occurring during adulthood have a major impact on a number of issues directly and indirectly linked to learning, including motivation, ways of organizing information, levels of independence and self-directedness, ways of conceptualizing the world, the nature of relationships with instructors, and reasoning ability. While space will not permit an in depth look at all research into the relationship between adult development and learning, we will briefly examine some representative theories of different aspects of adult development and suggest implications for teaching and learning with adults.

Psychoanalytic views of development concentrate upon discovering how adults make sense of their worlds and how they decide to relate to their world. Representatives of this view generally trace their roots to Freud or Jung, focusing upon unconscious dynamics within adults that impact on their learning and educational experiences (Merriam, S. & Clark, M.C., 1991). Perhaps the most useful of these psychoanalytic views for adult educators has been Erikson's Theory of the Psycho-social Stages of Development (Ericson, 1980). Erikson proposed that adult personality development follows a predictable course. As adults age, their egos alter to meet changing social demands and expectations. (NOTE: Ego, the Latin word for "I," usually refers to the self-consciousness of an individual, the controlling aspect of one's personality.) The need to adjust, or alter, creates an emotional crisis within each adult. This "crisis" can be resolved positivity or negatively, i.e., in ways that help to develop the personality or in ways that debilitate the personality. The goal is for an adult to develop a healthy, integrated personality. The educational implications of the psycho-social theorists like Erikson are obvious. Adults at various stages in their ego development construe their lives and experiences in different ways. Depending on the stage of development and the positive or negative resolution, adults differ greatly in the relationships they create with fellow learners and teachers, in the role they expect knowledge and education to play in their lives, and how they cope with stresses of the educational process. At higher levels of positive ego development, education is seen as leading to a deeper understanding of oneself and others, leading to deeper values, creativity, and self-fulfillment. Adult educators understand the counseling and advising function inherent in their role and seek to use educational experiences to foster positive resolutions of ego crises if for no other reason then such assistance impacts on the learning of the adult.

Perhaps the most intuitively obvious link between adult development and learning is seen within the theories on cognitive development. The most important early research and theory on cognitive development was done by Jean Piaget during the 20s and 30s. Piaget (1966) was intrigued by the question of how people went about making sense out of their worlds. He concluded that people are active processors of information, not simply "conditioned" organisms as the behaviorists were suggesting. He believed that the knowledge structures in the mind--the mental schema--changed with changes in stages of human development. In other words, meaningful cognitive development occurred as the brain interacted with the social and physical environment. This interaction had two parts, assimilation and accommodation. When a person assimilated new information, they simply interpreted it in a way consistent with their existing schema. When a person accommodated information, they modified the existing schema in their brains to account for new concepts and facts. When the existing schema couldn't be modified enough to account for the new information or perspectives, the person went through a process of equilibration, in which a totally new cognitive structure replaces the old. This is when major shifts in paradigms occur within the human being, or to put it in Piaget's words, when a new stage of cognitive development is achieved. Piaget concentrated his work on youth and identified four major stages of cognitive development.

1. The sensory-motor stage (lasting from birth through approximately two years of age) is when the child makes sense out of their world primarily through the senses.
2. The pre-operational stage (lasting from two years old through around seven years old) is when the child makes sense out of their world through pre-logical thought and language.

3. The concrete operations stage (lasting from seven through about eleven years of age) is when the child makes sense out of their world through logical thought without abstractions.
4. The formal operations stage (entered in the early teen years) is when the child makes sense out of their world through abstract thought processes and hypothetical thought.

Obviously, the educational implications are that educational programs should be fit to the cognitive development stage of the child. To spend time teaching abstract concepts prior to the formal operations stage of development would yield limited benefits for the learner.

Within adult education literature, the research and theory has focused on whether Piaget's stages went far enough. Many believed that new stage(s) of cognitive development were likely in adulthood, stages marked by just as radical a paradigm shift as in the movement between early stages of cognitive development. If such further stages of cognitive development were possible, the implications for teaching adults and educational design would be just as significant. Patricia Arlin (1975) has suggested that a fifth stage of cognitive development can occur in adults, a stage she labels Problem-Finding. She sees the ability to find problems as requiring a different cognitive processing than the ability to solve problems. Such a problem-finding level would involve the ability to contextualize information, to look beyond the setting to the underlying implications. Klaus Riegel (1973) has proposed another level of cognitive development that he labeled Dialectic Operation. Such a level involves the ability to synthesize information, discovering new concepts through the resolution of thesis/antithesis analysis. The point of these examples is to suggest that one of the important differences when working with adult learners is to understand that they may be capable of a qualitatively different form of cognitive processing than youth. This difference might be just as real as the difference between the concrete operations stage and the formal operations stage in terms of the ability to think with abstractions and hypothetical thought.

A very different approach to adult development issues is taken by the theorists focusing on psycho-social tasks (Merriam & Clark, 1991). They are concerned with aspects of development that are unrelated to stage changes in either cognitive, moral, or personality development. Instead, this body of research examines issues linked to the changing psycho-social tasks at different phases of life--developmental tasks requiring adjustments, adaptation, or new competencies rather than the comprehensive changes normally seen with the stage theories previously identified.

Psycho-social theorists and researchers focus upon the changing social roles in adulthood and how changes in such roles impact adjustment in life. The underlying assumption of these theories is that individuals go through socially regulated role cycles throughout life (particularly in adulthood) in which predictable changes in social roles force adults to accept new duties and obligations to reflect their changed roles. The developmental changes in focus are social and context changes, not internal developmental changes. The timing of such "role cycles" can vary from person to person, but the issues encountered tend to be similar for similar groups. Recent research has tended to focus on differences in such issues between different cultural, ethnic, age, or gender groups. The focus of adult development within this stream shifts from a study of inner development to a study of life events and tasks. Adult educators have long argued that learning in adulthood is strongly related to role demands in the learner. Many have advocated that adult education programs be designed with the demands of social role requirements in the learners as the primary content issue. Learning programs thus designed would address the competencies required for adult roles, a concept linking motivation for learning to current role demands.

Widely-used phase theories of adult development drawn upon by adult educators include Havighurst (1972), Levinson (1986), Gould (1978), Neugarten (1979), and Sheehy (1976). Havighurst (1972), for example, suggested adulthood contains three phases of development tasks within its natural cycle:

1. Early adulthood tasks (ages 18-30) - Early adulthood tasks can include such things as selecting a mate, starting a family, and starting an occupation.
2. Middle adulthood tasks (ages 30-60) - Middle adulthood tasks can include such things as relating to spouse as a person, adjusting to aging parents, and moving from active parenting.
3. Later maturity task (age 60 to end of life) - Later maturity tasks can include such things as adjusting to aging, adjusting to retirement, and adapting to changing social roles.

Each of these tasks creates teachable moments in the adult learner, which, in turn, create a proper timing for educational efforts.

Personal Reflection Questions

1. *Reflect upon possible explanations for differing responses to adult education efforts in your experience that might be related to Erikson's views of ego development.*
2. *What do you think about the idea of further stages of cognitive development beyond Piaget's formal operations stage?*
3. *What do you think about the appropriateness of psycho-social task views of adult development when considering designing adult education programs?*

A CONCLUDING NOTE ABOUT ADULT LEARNERS IN DISTANCE EDUCATION

Research has shown some important characteristics of learners who are successful in a distance education program (Moore & Kearsley, 2005, 1996). Designers of distance education programs must always take into account that students vary in their ability to practice self-directed learning, depending on their personality characteristics and previous learning experiences. Those who participate in education can be grouped in any number of ways: by gender, age, ability, ethnicity, profession, etc. Moore (1980) presents a helpful list of eleven traits of successful distance education learners (true of learners in a variety of distance education settings, including online learning environments):

- They like to plan ahead – a day, a week, a month – and longer.
- They usually stick to a plan, modifying it as they go along, but never abandoning a plan without improving it to serve their convenience and to help them "keep at it."
- They organize their lives to make the best possible use of time, the most critical ingredient of successful independent study.
- They realize they can't start a new activity (learning) without giving up something else that formerly took the time now set aside for study.
- They enjoy reading, writing, listening, and discussing.
- They have open minds to learning new things.
- They enjoy questioning, testing, and analyzing.
- They are not afraid of being different.
- They like to form generalizations, look for principles, and find the basic structural ideas in any subject.

- They have developed skills in note taking, remembering, and relating.
- They work cooperatively with others, but enjoy being "on their own" in learning.

A important consideration for distance education offerings is that young adult learners, between the ages of 18 and 24, make up the majority of the student population in the traditional classroom, while adult learners, between the ages of 25 and 50+, are the majority in online learning. As we saw from earlier in this chapter, this age group of adult learners take online education to learn something practical today and apply the new knowledge at work or in life tomorrow. Moore (1980) agrees that for adult learners, learning is desired or an essential extra; for them formal learning is not the main task of their day. These adult learners need to be considered vessels of information as many of them have professional, leisurely, and daily experience; many are seeking to learn more in fields that they already know a great deal; and to a point, they all have an understanding about themselves and their interpersonal relationships. The motivation of students is one of the key factors that will determine the success of an online learning experience.

REFERENCES

Arlin, P. (1975). Cognitive Development In Adulthood: A Fifth Stage? *Developmental Psychology*, *11*, 602–606. doi:10.1037/0012-1649.11.5.602

Cattell, R. (1963). Theory of Fluid and Crystallized Intelligence: A critical approach . *Journal of Educational Psychology*, *54*(1), 1–22. doi:10.1037/h0046743

Erickson, E. (1980). *Identity and the Life Cycle*. New York: Norton.

Gardner, H. (1983). *Frames of Mind*. New York: Basic Books.

Goleman, D. (1995). *Emotional Intelligence: Why It Can Matter More Than I.Q*. New York: Bantam Books.

Gould, R. (1978). Transformations: Growth and Change . In *Adult Life*. New York: Simon & Schuster.

Havinghurst, R. J. (1972). *Developmental Tasks and Education* (3rd ed.). New York: McKay.

Levinson, D. J. (1986). A Conception of Adult Development. *The American Psychologist*, *41*(1), 3–13. doi:10.1037/0003-066X.41.1.3

Merriam, S., & Clark, M. C. (1991). *Lifelines: Patterns of Work, Love, and Learning in Adulthood*. San Francisco: Jossey-Bass.

Moore, M. G. (1980). Independent study . In Boyd, R., & Apps, J. (Eds.), *Redefining the discipline of adult education*. San Francisco: Jossey Bass.

Moore, M. G., & Kearsley, G. (1996). *Distance education: A systems view*. New York: Wadsworth.

Moore, M. G., & Kearsley, G. (2005). *Distance education: A systems view* (2nd ed.). Belmont, CA: Wadsworth.

Neugarten, B. (1979). Time, Age, And The Life Cycle. *The American Journal of Psychiatry*, *136*, 887–893.

Piaget, J. (1966). *Psychology of Intelligence*. Totowa, NJ: Littlefield, Adams.

Riegel, K. F. (1973). Dialectic Operations: The Final Period of Cognitive Development. *Human Development*, *16*, 346–370. doi:10.1159/000271287

Sheehy, G. (1976). *Passages: Predictable Crises Of Adult Life*. New York: Dutton.

Sternberg, R. (1985). *Beyond I.Q.: A Triarchic Theory of Human Intelligence*. Cambridge, UK: Cambridge University Press.

Thorndike, E. L., Bregman, E. O., Tilton, J. W., & Woodyard, E. (1928). *Adult Learning*. New York: Macmillan.

Tough, A. (1978). Major Learning Efforts: Recent Research and Future Directions. *Adult Education*, *28*(4), 250–263. doi:10.1177/074171367802800403

Chapter 4
Designing for Interaction in Online Courses

The most valuable advancements in online learning have been in the area of interaction. The passive and unwieldy communication once accepted in online learning has been replaced with dynamic and engaging interaction enhanced with a wide spectrum of strategies and technologies. Interaction is not limited to text-based dialogue and Web sites, as online simulations, tutorials, games, and virtual worlds have introduced a new level of interaction. This high level of interaction enhances student learning, satisfaction, and persistence (Berge, 1999; Mabrito, 2004). In many distance education courses, online interaction promotes achievement and community beyond the expectations of both the students and instructors.

The purpose of this chapter is to summarize four different types of interaction in online courses–learner-content, instructor-learner, learner-learner, and learner-interface–and the primary considerations for planning and facilitating these instructional interactions. The four types of interaction are not rigid, mutually exclusive styles of engagement. Swan (2001) suggests that the types of interaction are intertwined: interaction that takes place between students is created by the teacher who enables and supports this interaction, based upon the content. For example, online problem solving discussions involve learner-to-learner communication but also require synthesis of course content, or course content presented through an audio conference involves instructor-learner interaction as well as learner-content interaction.

DOI: 10.4018/978-1-61520-865-4.ch004

FORMS OF INTERACTION IN ONLINE COURSES

A key component in designing distinctive online courses is the instructional interaction with all of its forms and purposes. The term "interaction" refers to the broad spectrum of learning activities that engage students. Thurmond (2003) wrote, "Ultimately, the goal of interaction is to increase understanding of the course content or mastery of the defined goals" (p. 4). In this chapter, interaction refers to the learner's engagement with course-related content and stakeholders, which may be in the forms of reading, writing, researching, discussing, practicing, collaborating, or reflecting on a body of knowledge. Wagner (1994, 1997) highlights the difference between interactivity and interaction by pointing out that interactivity is best thought of as a property that is afforded by a medium, while interaction is a behavior where individuals and groups directly influence one another. We make this distinction to highlight the importance of interaction within distance education and the need not to confuse it with the affordances of interactivity.

Mason (1994) emphasizes the educational importance of interaction, but appears to use interactivity and interaction as synonymous terms. Mason points to the range of uses for the term interactivity, and then states that "It would be useful if the word 'interactivity' were reserved for educational situations in which human responses–either vocal or written–referred to previous human responses." (p. 25). The rationale for interaction is clear: "Interaction has been shown to benefit learners at the affective level. It increases motivation and interest in the subject….Opportunities for learners to express their own points of view, explain the issues in their own words and to formulate opposing or different arguments, have always been related to deep-level learning and the development of critical thinking" (p. 26).

Focus on various forms of interaction began in 1989, when Moore noted three types of interaction in a distance education editorial–learner-content interaction, learner-instructor interaction, and learner-learner interaction. In 1994, Hillman, Willis, and Gunawardena argued that these three types of interaction could not take place unless the learner interacted with the medium. Consequently, they introduced learner-interface interaction as a fourth type of interaction that is especially pertinent in the Web-based learning environment. While the types of interaction may overlap, each type fulfills a unique and critically important purpose in online learning.

- Learner-Content Interaction refers to the student's engagement with the course subject matter, such as reading or outlining a textbook chapter, writing a research paper, studying a chart, self-testing with a practice quiz, or interviewing a subject matter expert. The learner is influenced by the learning content.
- Instructor-Learner Interaction may be in the form of private one-to-one communication between the instructor and student or one-to-many communication between the instructor and a group or class of students. One-to-one communication may be in the form of emails or feedback on an assignment. Online course examples of one-to-many interaction include the instructors' welcome announcements and discussion forum postings.
- Learner-Learner Interaction involves communication among two or more students. Examples may be in the form of asynchronous discussion forums, real-time team review sessions in chat, collaborative wiki Websites, or an audio conference call to review an assignment. Much of the learner-learner interaction is based on the constructivist philosophy in which learners collaborate to construct knowledge based on their experiences.
- Learner-Interface Interaction involves technology tools that engage learners, such as online practice quizzes, blogs used for journal entries, statistical software packages, or business simulations. In Web-based courses, learner-content, instructor, learner, and learner-learner interaction all occur within the learner-interface context.

LEARNER-CONTENT INTERACTION

In resident on-campus courses, subject matter content is generally presented in the form of textbook chapters, readings, lecture notes, classroom discussions, and an occasional guest speaker or video. The Web-based learning environment provides opportunities for additional teaching formats such as computer software, Web sites, audio and video recordings, tutorials, and simulations. Northrup (2002) describes learner-content interaction as "any type of interaction directed at achieving instructional success" (p. 220). Ideally, content is presented as intellectually challenging information "which elicits deeper thinking on the part of the students, and which presents, for better or worse, more equality between instructor and student" (Smith, Ferguson & Caris, 2002, p. 67). In online courses, "faculty are no longer the keepers of the knowledge" (Smith, 2008, p. 15) as self-directed students have access to a large body of information from a variety of primary and secondary sources. Van Dusen (2002) describes learner-content interaction as the "hallmark of education" (p. 243) as students dissect material in a way that allows them to develop new knowledge and skills.

In another study, Mayes (2002) recognizes three stages of interaction – two of which deal with learner-content interaction. *Conceptualisation*, or interaction with concepts, forces the learner to analyze and compare his or her framework of understanding against a new exposition. For example, corporate trainers might examine three models of course development, and determine which model is closest to the model used at their organizations. *Constructions*, or interacting with tasks, is applying and testing new conceptualisations in the performance of meaningful tasks. This stage involves the building of the learner's own framework of understanding, such as developing a research paper or designing a patient's treatment plan. The third stage of interaction involves *dialogue* or interacting with people. Learners create and test their new conceptualizations during conversations with the instructor and fellow learners in discussion forums, chat rooms, or audio conferences.

When course content and interaction are structured and planned Murphy and Cifuentes (2001) believe that the learner is involved in a much deeper level of understanding. Structured learning designed with a strong foundation that leads to higher levels of processing, critical thinking, and problem solving helps students to retain knowledge and transfer its application to new settings. Daugherty and Funke (1998) found that Web-based learning can promote satisfying and effective communication between instructors and students; however, the topics of discussion require careful consideration and active facilitation. Swan (2001) agrees that a learner's interaction with course content has been proven to be "an important course design feature" (p. 315).

Planning Content Interaction

The learner-content component of online courses is generally the most time-consuming for faculty to develop. The challenge is often not what to include in a course, but what to leave out. Smith (2008) advises faculty or course developers to "think learning, not teaching" (p. 11) in identifying critical course content. Consider the course outcomes or course objectives and what material students need to learn in order to achieve those desired outcomes. What knowledge and skills will students need beyond the end of the course? The following examples of learning outcomes include observable, measureable behaviors which point to a specific body of content:

- Identify the characteristics of depression in a population of senior citizens.
- Develop a proposal for grant funding from the National Institute of Health.
- Assess guidelines for quality control in the production of computer software in a small manufacturing company.
- Compare and contrast the economic and environmental effects of energy conversion processes.

Online programs must be organized in clear, specific modules, units, or lessons. Learners juggling multiple life roles will complete the course in fragmented time segments; therefore, they need to easily and quickly find their place in the many pages of Web content. Consistent names, colors, and fonts for headings and subheadings will help students manage their learning progress. The following course layout (see Figure 1) represents an organizational overview for an online 15-week course. Each weekly lesson consistently presents an introduction, objectives, lecture notes, handouts, exercises, sample tests, and readings.

In a face-to-face course, the instructor naturally breaks course content into manageable learning chunks during the class session. In the online environment, the naturally related segments of information are not as obvious. Chunking, or presenting small pieces of related content, is a strategy that will organize material and direct students' attention to the most important concepts. Garrison, Anderson, and Archer (2001) found that "chunking the content into absorbable pieces helped keep students from feeling overwhelmed and provided them with the essential information for completing the exercises and grasping the concepts without exhausting them with too much written content" (p. 7). Faculty can logically organize course content in many formats including from broad to specific, simple to complex, problem to solution, known to unknown, or chronologically. As Oliver (1999) notes, "content is presented as a means to an end rather than an end in itself" (p. 251).

The non-profit organization Quality Matters (www.qualitymatters.org), developed from a 2003 Fund for the Improvement of Postsecondary Education (FIPSE) grant, introduces a research-based process to certify the quality of online courses in higher education. Their model focuses on the alignment of the following five critical course components: (1) learning objectives, (2) learner interaction, (3) assessment and measurement, (4) resources and materials, and (5) course technology (see Figure 2). These five course components must all logically relate to one another. If a course objective states that "students will be able to compare and contrast the ethical issues of genetic engineering", the learning resources, learner interactions, assessment strategies, and technology tools should all support mastery of this objective. One example for aligning key course components with this objective could be teams of students using the discussion board to present a class debate. In addition to online journal articles about genetic engineering, course materials might include Web resources on how to conduct a debate and a grading rubric to assess student performance.

Figure 1. A consistent course structure enhances the organization and navigation of the course

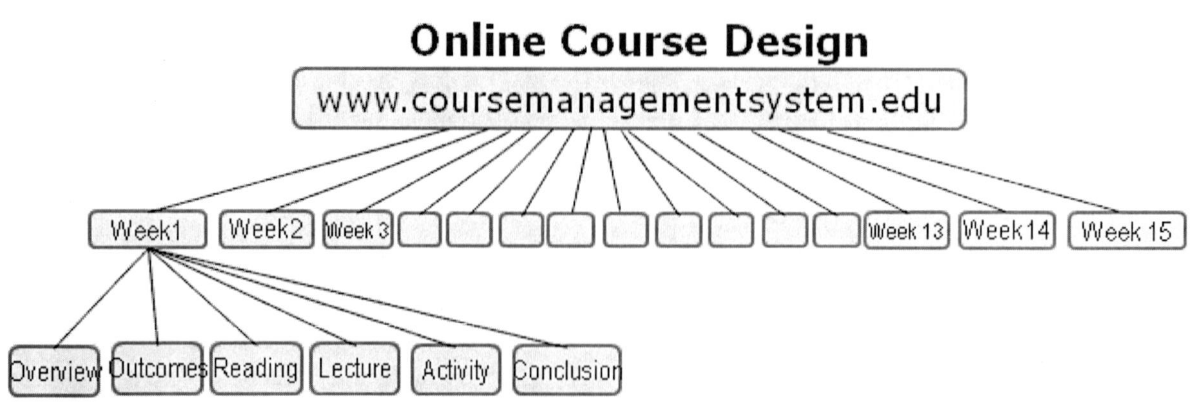

Figure 2. Quality Matters promotes alignment between learning objectives, assessments, resources and materials, interaction, and technology. © 2009 MarylandOnline. Used with permission of Maryland-Online and the Quality Matters Program.

Facilitating Content Interaction

A key challenge in developing course content is to incorporate active learning strategies into what can easily become a passive pursuit of reading page after page of content. The style of writing can engage students with reflective questions, examples, and authentic experiences. Many faculty deliver content with media such as audio or video to motivate and gain learners' attention. In a well designed course, there is a balance between the amount of content and the depth of interaction with the content. Just as Chickering and Gamson (1987) noted the importance of *time on task* in their Seven Principles of Good Practice in Undergraduate Education, research conducted by Swan (2001) points to *contact with content* as a valuable instructional component in online learning.

Robert Gagne's (1985)*Nine Events of Instruction* offers a systematic approach to help faculty facilitate interaction with course content. This seminal theory of instruction has been applied to all ages of learners and all modes of course delivery. As noted above, chunking course content into manageable bites of information will assist learners in digesting large amounts of content. After presenting a chunk of content, Gagne's theory asks teachers to consider how learners can practice or apply the learning content to improve their retention and retrieval of the information. For example, learners may respond to study questions at the end of a chapter, solve math problems, create a scientific poster, or enter data into a new software program.

These events of instruction are presented as interactive guidelines to facilitate the transfer of knowledge rather than a rigid, linear prescription

Table 1. Gagne's nine events of instruction applied to online courses

Steps of Instruction	Strategies for Online Courses
1. Gain attention	Present an interesting and relevant problem, idea, event, or situation to peak learner interest.
2. Describe the goal	Describe the goal or objective of the lesson; State what students will be able to accomplish and how they will be able to use the knowledge; Make learners aware of expectations.
3. Stimulate recall of prior knowledge	Remind the student of prior knowledge relevant to the current lesson (facts, rules, procedures or skills); Show how knowledge is connected; Provide the student with a framework that helps retention and retrieval of information.
4. Present the material to be learned	Use appropriate media for content such as text, graphics, simulations, figures, images, sound, or video; Follow a consistent presentation style; Chunk information into logical segments.
5. Provide guidance for learning	Help learners perform task; Provide instructional aids, resources, or step-by-step instructions to support learning; Present information in a different medium or communication channel.
6. Elicit performance	Practice using new knowledge or skill; Produce a product; Repeat task or process; Respond to study questions;
7. Provide informative feedback	Provide specific instructor or peer feedback to analyze learner's behavior; Provide a check-list.
8. Assess performance	Administer a formal or informal assessment plan to determine mastery of knowledge or skill.
9. Enhance retention and transfer	Inform the learner about similar problem situations; Provide additional practice in real life situations; Put the learner in a situation to transfer knowledge; Review the lesson.

for success in online teaching. Some of Gagne's guidelines can be implemented as metacognitive strategies. For example, Northrup (2002) recommends advanced organizers, graphical representation of concepts, a calendar of structured due dates for assignments, and note-taking guides. Ultimately, the content is only as good as it is accurate and up-to-date. In addition to being well-organized and relevant, it must be periodically analyzed (McAlister, Rivera and Hallam, 2001) and reviewed by qualified support staff.

Personal Reflection Suggestion

How much content is too much? Reflect on how much content is a reasonable amount for learner-content interaction. Learning takes time. Consider the balance between quality of learning and quantify of reading material. How can you prioritize the concepts that require deep interaction?

INSTRUCTOR-LEARNER INTERACTION

Modern distance education theory acknowledges the importance of interaction and places a heavy emphasis on the interaction between student and teacher (Swan, 2001). Interestingly, Lenhart, Lytle, and Cross (2001) found that students reported the quality of online instructor-student interaction to be equal or better than interactions in resident courses. Garrison (1989) agrees that "Distance education must involve two-way communication between (among) teacher and students(s) for the purpose of facilitating and supporting the educational process" (p. 6). Such communication, or interaction, is necessary for the negotiation of meaning between the teacher and student. This interaction may be in the form of informal emails, virtual chats, or class announcements, or in a more formal style of recorded video or audio conferences. Regardless of whether its formal and informal communication, students value instructor feedback to validate their opinions, perspectives, and course work. Moore and Kearsley (1996) explain, "For a program to be educational there must be a relationship between learners and teachers" (p. 34). Even when distance education students are adult learners, Porter (2004) acknowledges "they will require guidance, coaching, and approval from their teachers" (p. 149).

Moore's work often provides the conceptual basis for distance education research. One prominent theory, the theory of transactional distance, asserts that the geographical separation of the instructor and students is not a significant factor in distance education. Moore (1980, 1989) describes transactional distance as "...a function of two crucial variables in the learner-teacher transaction, which we have chosen to call dialogue and structure" (p. 21). In Moore's theory, the success of distance education is dependent on the extent to which an institution and instructor can "provide the appropriate structure of learning materials, and the appropriate quantity and quality of dialog between teacher and learner, taking into account the extent of the learner's autonomy" (Moore & Kearsley, 1996, pp. 205 – 206). Dialogue and structure are dynamic course components and it is the instructor's role to determine the ideal balance of dialogue and structure to maximize learning while reducing the students' feelings of isolation.

Additional study conducted by Simonson, Smaldino, Abright, and Zvacek (2009) notes that when learners are geographically separated, dialogue is described as two-way communication and structure is "the extent to which a program is responsive to the needs of the individual learner" (p. 43). Evans and Nation (1989) agree that dialogue is central to distance education and note "dialogue involves the idea that humans in communication are engaged actively in the making and exchange of meanings, it is not merely about the transmission of messages" (p. 37). They urge distance educators to reconsider the value of interaction in education and suggest "connecting distance education theory to theoretical endeavours in education and social sciences more generally" (p. 38).

Planning Instructor-Learner Interaction

Well designed communication from an instructor can help students manage their time and workload, plus enrich learning through elaboration and clarification of course material. Furthermore, interaction with the instructor humanizes the learning experience for students. Email, the most commonly used form of instructor-student communication, is timely, personal, and flexible. To reduce the deluge of email messages from students, many faculty create a class question and answer discussion forum so all learners can post questions and share information that is of interest to the whole class. Another form of communication is the announcements page. Here, the instructor can share one-way, timely information with the entire class such as updates, previews, or corrections. Synchronous and asynchronous discussions are generally planned for learner interaction with instructors participating in the discussions at a level that is appropriate for their courses. Providing both public and private synchronous and asynchronous interaction has been correlated with student satisfaction, motivation, and learning (Shea et al., 2001; Northrup, 2002; Sherry, 1996).

In both resident and online courses, lecturing is one-way interaction strategy that faculty use when communicating with their class. In distance education courses, instructor lectures may take the form of audio or video presentations usually enhanced with slides such as Microsoft PowerPoint™. Effective lectures have the advantage of providing a large amount of information in an organized format. Frequently, the challenge is to deliver an engaging lecture that promotes higher-order thinking. Moore and Kearsley (1996) caution against designing lectures as the primary pedagogy of instructor-learner interaction:

From existing research it is already clear that teaching by correspondence or electronic tech-

nologies is an art that is different from the art of broadcasting or even of conducting a teleconference meeting of business persons, or conducting interaction in a classroom. The key to being effective is that the teacher takes full advantage of the interactive nature of the media and resists the temptation to lecture (Moore & Kearsley, 1996, p. 71).

Listening to long lectures can be challenging, but some students prefer listening to content from an instructor rather than reading it from the Internet (Faux and Black-Hughes, 2000; Northrup, Lee and Burgess, 2002). Muirhead (2004) recommends that faculty personalize the online learning environment by using a conversational style that reflects their personality. Additionally, instructors can integrate personal and professional experiences and discussion questions into their lectures. Text-based lectures should be easy to read without being simplistic in content.

Facilitating Instructor-Learner Interaction

The role of the instructor is somewhat different in online course as compared to resident courses. Online instructors are not the center of attention because students are empowered to control many aspects of their learning such as what, when, and where they complete the course requirements. Learner control is exercised within the parameters established by the course instructor, but students have access to numerous resources and great flexibility in how they learn the course material. Generally, the instructor provides a friendly introduction and sets the tone for online learning by modeling the desired communication behavior. Additionally, the instructor may write in an informal style, provide support, ask follow-up questions, and interject appropriate humor to create a positive learning environment.

Timely instructor feedback regarding a comment, process, concept, or event has demonstrated a positive effect on student learning (Young and Norgard, 2005; Berge, 1999; Northrup, 2002; Chickering and Ehrmann, 1996). Due to the geographic separation and lack of visual cues, responsive and encouraging feedback is believed to have a significant impact on students' satisfaction with Web-based courses (Stevenson, Sander, & Naylor, 1996). Thurmond and Wambach (2004) emphasize that instructors need to provide students with timely feedback to keep them engaged in the learning and to help them maintain a structured learning pace. Young and Norgard (2005) recommend consistent and frequent interaction between the instructor and students. In Northrup's (2002) study, graduate students indicate that instructor feedback is a highly valued attribute and they recommend that faculty provide feedback to students at least twice per week.

Personal Reflection Suggestion

Take some time to reflect on your role as a student and how you identified and developed relationships with key faculty members. Consider how the relationships between faculty and students develop in distance education environments. What are some of the challenges and barriers to developing meaningful relationships? How can the design of a course reduce these barriers?

LEARNER-LEARNER INTERACTION

Most online instructors recognize that learner-learner interaction can lead to deep learning as participants building community, share ideas, analyze course concepts, and develop critical thinking skills. In traditional on-campus courses, McMillan and Chavis (1986) recognized the importance of building a community of learners and define this sense of community as "a feeling that members have of belonging, a feeling that members matter to one another and to the group, and shared faith that members' needs will be met through their commitment to be together" (p. 9).

While learning communities were not likely to develop in early forms of distance education, Palloff and Pratt (2005) recognize their value in today's Web-based distance education by writing "that a learning community is the vehicle through which learning occurs in the online course" (p.7). Building community in an online course involves "moving from issues of instructor control to the empowerment of online learners and recognizing that learning is a socially constructed project requiring reciprocal relationships" (Falvo & Solloway, 2004, p. 57).

For most faculty, an online sense of community is imperative because learning is a social experience that "is no longer viewed as a transmission of knowledge from a teacher to a student, but a process of knowledge construction in which each participant contributes to and benefits from the ideas by others" (Han & Hill, 2007, p. 91). Three common concepts associated with social theories are learning occurs within a community, knowledge emerges through interaction, and intelligence is distributed among learners. Harasim (2002) proposed a discussion framework in which learners generate ideas, elaborate on each other's ideas, and actively co-construct a knowledge base. Also built on the constructivist view, Gunawardena, Loew, and Anderson (1997) suggest a Interaction Analysis Model for Examining Social Construction of Knowledge in Computer Conferencing with the following five phases of knowledge co-creation: (1) sharing/comparing of information, (2) discovery and exploration of dissonance of inconsistency among participants, (3) negotiation of meaning or knowledge co-construction, (4) testing and modification, and (5) phrasing of agreement and application of newly constructed meaning.

In most online courses, learner-learner interaction in online courses is a pervasive factor occurring throughout each day and week of a course (Harasim, Hiltz, Teles, & Turoff, 1995; Hiltz, 1995). Learners socialize with one another, support one another, grow with one another, and may even learn to challenge one another. Since the late 1980s, there has been a large-scale implementation of online courses involving interaction among students through a wide variety of computer tools for both synchronous and asynchronous communication. Today, there are also numerous social networking tools such as Facebook, My Space, LinkedIn, and Instant Messanger that promote a "back channel communication" network outside of the structure of a course (Frey & Kearns, 2009). In his case study research, Poole (2000) noted that most messages were posted from home on Thursday, Saturday, and Sunday. The most popular times to post a message were 4-8 pm or 8 pm to midnight. From a review of postings in his course, Fung (2004) reported that 87% of all postings were academic, 10% were nonacademic, and 3% were technical.

Adult learners bring a wealth of life experience to a course including cognitive, linguistic, generational, and cultural styles that enrich the learning environment. Small group or team learning experiences have the potential to utilize students' strengths in addition to building of strong relationships and a sense of community. Ko and Rossen (2001) suggest that faculty take the lead in dividing students into small groups rather than having students self-select their group members. If the group is to collaborate on an assignment, they recommend four as the optimal number. Small groups often lead students to engage in more in-depth discussion without a large number of discussion board postings (Han and Hill, 2007). Palloff and Pratt caution that students may be resistant to online teams and group assignments. Structured assignments with clear expectations will help to counter their resistance. Computer mediated communication tools create an archive of team interaction and allow instructors to oversee individual student participation in group assignments. Instructors may "need to intervene in cases on over- or under- participation" (Palloff and Pratt, 2005, p. 40) of individual team members.

Planning Learner Interaction

The ability to plan in-depth intellectual discussion is one of the most valuable aspects of online learning. In asynchronous discussions (e.g., threaded discussion and list-servs), all students have an opportunity to participate and time to reflect prior to posting their contributions. Synchronous or real-time discussions (e.g., audio or video conferencing, virtual chat) are effective for timely or less complex discussions. Hrastinski (2008) found synchronous communication to for planning tasks and providing social support. She wrote, "other things being equal, synchronous e-learning better supports personal participation and asynchronous e-learning betters supports cognitive participation" (p.55).

Instructors can enrich online dialogue by posing a "diverse range of questions that cause individuals to examine their assumptions, beliefs, ideas and rational" (Muirhead, 2004, p.3 of printout). Muilenburg and Berge (2002) suggest questions that focus on the central topic of the lesson, require students to evaluate ideas, relate to current events, consider contrasting views, present scenarios, analyze case studies, address controversial issues, or require students to complete online activities and summarize their experience for the class. Smith and Winking-Diaz (2004) suggest metacognitive questions that encourage students to construct their own meaning through self-questioning; follow-up questions that further explore assumptions, perspectives, or experiences; student-created questions that tend to be impromptu questions which clarify and extend the discussion; and evaluation and reflection questions that bring closure to discussions with lingering questions and final thoughts. These types of discussion topics are effective because there is not one correct answer or response.

Faculty can set the stage for learner-learner interaction by explaining the purpose of each learning activity and providing clear guidelines for students to complete the assignment. "If students are clear about the nature of the activity and how they are to complete it, they are more likely to pick up the gauntlet and move forward with minimal instructor intervention" (Palloff and Pratt, 2005, p. 20). However, Berge (1999) and Northrup (2002) found there may be a limit to the number of online discussions which can effectively enhance learning in an online course. "Too many" weekly online discussions may lead to frustration and overload for course participants. Small discussion groups may be more effective for balancing the work load and promoting in-depth exploration of specific topics.

Facilitating Learner Interaction

The course instructor is an integral part of the learning community and needs to take an active role in modeling and facilitating online interaction. Faculty engagement and verbal immediacy lessen the psychological distance among learners and increase the sense of social presence (Richardson and Swan, 2001). Besides responding quickly, Baker and Rynearson (2006) identify verbal immediacy behaviors as asking questions, using appropriate self-disclosure, addressing students by name, and using inclusive pronouns. Faculty can build trust by encouraging students to support one another and share experiences. Impromptu, optional discussions rarely develop into engaging forums of divergent thinking, problem solving, and critical thinking; therefore, graded participation that considers both qualitative and quantitative aspects of students' postings are recommended by many online educators (Mabrito, 2004; Ko and Rossen, 2001; Jiang and Ting, 1999). Vonderwell and Zachariah (2005) found students who were assigned discussion roles (e.g., facilitator or summarizer) participated more frequently in online discussions. In particular, students assigned to the role of facilitator commented "they learned more about the topics in the discussions while that were facilitating" (p. 221).

When designing asynchronous discussions, Mishra and Juwah (2006) recommend that instructors make student expectation specific and clear, use open ended questions, create a separate discussion for social dialogue, invite participation from all learners, and periodically summarize the discussions. For asynchronous discussions, many facilitators empower students to take the lead in reading and responding to their classmates. Ko and Rossen (2001) advice faculty not to respond to every posting, but to reply to several postings in one message. Give students a chance to build the discussion prior to jumping in with answers or comments. Generally, facilitators contribute by moving the discussion forward with probing questions, additional resources, and thoughtful comments. In synchronous chat rooms, Mishra and Juwah (2006) suggest that the instructor identify a specific goal and outcome, provide learner training for using chat, prepare 30 to 40 open ended questions, develop a protocol for student participation, and limit the session to less than one hour, Class size is an important consideration for synchronous discussion. Hofmann (2004) recommends "no more than 75 percent of the number you would invite to the same program taught in a traditional manner" (p. 65).

Personal Reflection Suggestion

Reflect on strategies that will encourage independent adult learners at various locations around the world to work together to become a community of learners. This is a huge challenge in a one-term course. How can you help learners build trust, share ideas, take risks, and, ultimately, build knowledge?

LEARNER-INTERFACE INTERACTION

The first three types of interaction—learner-content, instructor-learner, and learner-learner interaction—have been common types of interaction throughout the history of classroom education. The fourth type of interaction, learner-interface interaction, is unique to online courses and is recognized as having a strong effect on student learning (Hillman et al., 1994). The terms interface, graphic user interface, or human-computer interface all focus on interaction between the learner and specific technologies, platforms, and applications. The computer interface is responsible for "visualizing concepts, conveying order, clarifying meaning, directing focus, stimulating interest, facilitating interactions, confirming choices, supporting recall, directing navigation, creating ambience, and otherwise engaging the learner" (Hedberg and Metros, 2006, 200-201). To further recognize the value of a clear user interface, just consider the frustration and confusion created by a poorly designed Web site and how this can have a negative effect on finding relevant information, reading Website content, and spending time on task. Ideally, technology should be transparent and learners should be challenged by the course content and not the technology.

Today, most faculty and course developers work within the framework of a course management system (CMS). CMSs have been through several iterations and have incorporated many improvements in interface design through the past decade. Even so, Metros and Hedberg (2002) caution that many CMSs "perpetuate the use of teacher-directed methods by lock-stepping the author into a set of constrained templates" (p. 192) that do not necessarily promote social or content interaction valued in constructivist learning theories. They recommend an integrative and holistic design process in which the "interface elements should visually communicate the educational objectives and goals" (p. 193).

Swan believes (2004) that the course interface can significantly affect the quality and quantity of course interaction. Specifically, Vonderwell and Zachariah (2005) note the discussion board interface effects participation and learning. Students who feel disoriented and confused are often experiencing information or cognitive overload (capacity of working memory) and are less likely to participate in online discussions. Visually organized discussions and clear subject lines enable the learners to participate in a more coherent manner. Vonderwell and Zachariah suggest that multiple-thread discussions rather than single-thread linear discussions should be considered to enhance the organization of topics and student postings.

Faculty and designers must also consider how to combine text, audio, video, images, and animations for effective interface interaction. Van Dusen (2002) writes, "The technology itself, such as multimedia or hypertext, does not teach; it is, however, the vehicle for instruction" (p. 242). Mayer (2001) studies the design of multimedia components to reduce cognitive load and support learning. For example, Mayer recommends presenting narration and animation simultaneously, delivering dialogue in a conversational style, allowing learners to control the pace of learning, removing irrelevant elements from the computer screen.

Planning Interface Interaction

Prior to taking online courses, educators and trainers should ensure that participants have the prerequisite equipment and technology skills to successfully complete the learning experience. Online learners report feeling fear, anxiety, apprehension, eagerness, and even excitement when asked to describe how they feel about starting a new course (Conrad, 2002). "This response held true among the program's novice learners who were beginning their first online course; among the program's experienced online learners who had completed one or more courses; and among nonprogram learners who were taking courses as electives" (Conrad, 2002, p. 208). Vonderwell and Zachariah (2005) report that students' technology skills influence their participation in the course with less prepared students participating less in online discussions. Ross (1996) notes that learners with low technology communication skills are more aware of the technology than of the content of their communication. Another important attribute needed by today's online learner is typing skills (Zafeiriou, Nunes and Ford, 2001).

Ideally, the institution will provide student training prior to the beginning of online courses; however, if the institution does not provide student training, it becomes the responsibility of the instructor. Online orientation guides or getting started tutorials may be necessary to introduce students to the Web-based learning interface. Palloff and Pratt (2003) recommend the orientation topics of how to use the internet, how to study, how to manage time, how to communicate, how to use the online library resources, and how to get technology help. Orientation programs may be presented in welcome letters sent through the postal service or email, face-to-face workshops conducted in campus computer labs, or online tutorials with examples and screen captures.

"Research in the area of user interface design for computer-based learning environments found that screen and interface design should be considered at the same time during the design and development process" (Jones and Okey, 1995, para. 1). In other words, it is more time efficient to incorporate effective interface interaction during the development process than to fix a course that is already developed. Faculty and course developers should be familiar with basic Web design and accessibility issues. Designing text is a primary consideration because

reading information from a computer screen is different than reading from a paper hard copy. Reading from a screen is often slower than reading printed text on paper (Gregory, 2004), but is ultimately affected by many interface variables such as font, screen resolution, and background color.

Facilitating Interface Interaction

Having addressed some of the larger planning issues to improve the interface interaction, it is also important to consider the practical application of interface design. For online text, Hansen and Haas (1988) found shorter lines of text were more effective for learning. Some authors recommend instructional text presented on a computer screen should be 50 percent less than text presented in hard copy (Nielsen, 1999; Holtz, 2001) because users tend to scan keywords, headings, and points of interest on computer screens (Garrand, 2001) . When using hyperlinks, be certain that they are labeled and serve a clear purpose in the course (Schneiderman and Kearsley, 1989) and provide learners with guidance on where to go and what to read at the linking Website.

In online courses, Mabrito (2004) recommends that every course should have a central home page, a navigation structure that is apparent to students, and a search option. He also recommends that learners be able to navigate to any course page with three or fewer clicks. Fong and Kwan (2003) emphasize consistency in concepts, terminology, graphics, and visual style which allow users "to learn something once, and then apply that knowledge again and again as they use the computer" (p. 296).

CONCLUSION

Online education is a fast growing segment of higher education and can produce learning results equivalent to traditional face-to-face teaching methods. Given that global access to the Internet continues to spread, online learning will continue to grow as a valued and rewarding educational medium for learners. Its flexibility of allowing students to learn anytime and any place is unmatched by resident instruction methods. Furthermore, the technology used to deliver online courses has improved the speed, efficiency, and connection between students, instructors, and course content. Online learners no longer have to feel the isolation and geographic separation from the institution, professor, and their fellow classmates.

The distance education literature reveals four dominant interactive relationships in online learning: learner-content, instructor-learner, learner-learner, and learner-interface. Learner-content interaction in the intellectual thinking and learning that occurs as students engage with a variety of course materials. Instructor-learner interaction validates the students' learning progress through feedback, support, and dialogue. While all types of interaction are important, learner-learner interaction tends to be a major focus of research due to its vital contributions to a course's educational outcomes. Especially with adult learners, the knowledge and skills they bring to a course serve as a powerful body of enrichment and resources. A strong sense of communities strengthens both the social and academic interactions which enhance the learning experience. Recent studies show that there is a correlation between interaction levels among students and the students' levels of satisfaction, learning, and retention. Therefore, it is of paramount importance to promote active learning that requires students to engage in the coursework and collaborate with one another to increase the effectiveness of the learning experience.

REFERENCES

Baker, C., & Rynearson, K. (2006 October). *Verbal immediacy: Effective online interactions*. Paper presented at the 2006 EDUCAUSE Conference, Dallas, Texas.

Berge, Z. (1999). Interaction in post-secondary Web-based learning. *Educational Technology, 39*(1), 5–11.

Chickering, A., & Gamson, Z. (Eds.). (1987). *Seven Principles for Good Practice in Undergraduate Education*. The American Association for Higher Education Bulletin.

Chickering, A. W., & Ehrmann, S. C. (1996). *Implementing the seven principles: Technology as lever*. Retrieved January 30, 2009, from http://www.tltgroup.org/programs/seven.html

Conrad, D. L. (2002). Engagement, excitement, anxiety, and fear: Learner's construction in computer bulletin board discussions. *Computers & Education*, *42*, 243–265.

Daugherty, M., & Funke, B. L. (1998). University faculty and student perceptions of Web-based instruction. *Journal of Distance Education, 13*(1), 21-39. Retrieved January 20, 2009, from http://www.jofde.ca/index.php/jde/article/view/134/411

Evans, T., & Nation, D. (1989). Dialogue in practice, research and theory in distance education. *Open Learning*, *14*(2), 37–42. doi:10.1080/0268051890040207

Falvo, D. A., & Solloway, S. (2004). Constructing community in an online course. *Tech Trends: Journal of the Association for Educational Communications and Technology*, *48*(5), 56–64.

Faux, T. L., & Black-Hughes, C. (2000). A comparison of using the Internet versus lectures to teach social work history. *Research on Social Work Practice*, *10*, 454–466.

Fong, J., & Kwan, I. (2003). Effective e-learning by using HCI and interactivity on data modeling. *International Journal of Computer Processing of Oriental Languages*, *16*(4), 293–310. doi:10.1142/S0219427903000917

Frey, B. A., & Kearns, L. R. (2009 January). Back-Channel communication: Web 2.0 technologies for social learning. In *Educause Learning Initiative*, Orlando, FL.

Fung, Y. Y. H. (2004). Collaborative online learning: interaction patterns and limiting factors. *Open Learning*, *19*(2), 135–149. doi:10.1080/0268051042000224743

Gagne, R. (1985). *The Conditions of Learning* (4th ed.). New York: Holt, Rinehart & Winston.

Garrand, S. (2001). *Writing for multimedia and the Web* (2nd ed.). Woburn, MA: Focal Press.

Garrison, D. R. (1989). *Understanding distance education: A framework for the future*. London: Routledge.

Garrison, D. R., Anderson, T., & Archer, W. (2001). Critical thinking, cognitive presence and computer conferencing in distance education. *American Journal of Distance Education*, *15*(1), 7–23. doi:10.1080/08923640109527071

Gregory, J. (2004). Writing for the Web versus writing for print: Are they really so different? *Applied Theory*, *51*(2), 276–285.

Gunawardena, C. N., Lowe, C. A., & Anderson, T. (1997). Analysis of a global online debate and the development of an interaction analysis model for examining social construction of knowledge in computer conferencing. *Journal of Educational Computing Research*, *17*(4), 397–431.

Han, S. Y., & Hill, S. R. (2007). Collaborate to learn, learn to collaborate: Examining the roles of context, community, and cognition in asynchronous discussion. *Journal of Educational Computing Research*, *36*(1), 89–123. doi:10.2190/A138-6K63-7432-HL10

Hansen, W. J., & Haas, C. (1988). Reading and writing with computers: A framework for explaining differences in performance. *Communications of the ACM*, *31*, 1080–1089. doi:10.1145/48529.48532

Harasim, L. (2002). What makes online learning communities successful? The role of collaborative learning in social and intellectual development . In Vrasidas, C., & Glass, G. V. (Eds.), *Distance education and distributed learning* (pp. 181–200). Greenwich, CO: Information Age.

Harasim, L., Hiltz, S. R., Teles, L., & Turoff, M. (1995). *Learning networks: A field guide to teaching and learning online*. London: MIT Press.

Hedberg, J. G., & Metros, S. (2006). Engaging learners through intuitive interfaces . In Hung, D., & Khine, M. S. (Eds.), *Engaged Learning with Emerging Technologies* (pp. 107–125). Dordrecht, The Netherlands: Springer. doi:10.1007/1-4020-3669-8_6

Hillman, D. C., Willis, D. J., & Gunawawrdena, C. N. (1994). Learner-interface interaction in distance education: An extension of contemporary models and strategies for practitioners. *American Journal of Distance Education, 8*(2), 30–42. doi:10.1080/08923649409526853

Hiltz, S. R. (1995). *The virtual classroom: Learning without limits via computer networks*. Norwood, NJ: Ablex.

Hofmann, J. (2004). *The synchronous trainer's survival guide: Facilitating successful live and online courses, meetings, and events*. San Francisco, CA: Pfeiffer.

Holtz, S. (2001 October). *Writing for the wired world*. Sydney, Australia: International Association of Business Communication.

Hrastinski, S. (2008). Asynchronous and Synchronous E-Learning. *Educause Quarterly, 31*(4), 51-55. Retrieved January 24, 2009, from http://connect.educause.edu/Library/EDUCAUSE+Quarterly/AsynchronousandSynchronou/47683

Jiang, M., & Ting, E. (1999). *A study of students' perceived learning in a Web-based online environment*. Paper presented at the WebNet 99 World Conference on the WWW and Internet, Honolulu, Hawaii. (ERIC Document Reproduction Service No. ED 448721).

Jones, M. G., & Okey, J. R. (1995). *Interface design for computer-based learning environments*. Retrieved December 22, 2008 from http://www2.gsu.edu/~wwwitr/docs/idguide/index.html

Ko, S., & Rossen, S. (2001). *Teaching Online: A Practical Guide*. New York: Houghton Mifflin.

Lenhart, K. A., Lytle, J. S., & Cross, C. (2001). Analysis of large Web-based courses at the University of Central Florida. *Society for Information Technology and Teacher Education International Conference, 2001*(1), 1117-1119.

Mabrito, M. (2004). Guidelines for establishing interactivity in online course. *Innovate, 1*(2). Retrieved December 31, 2008, from http://www.innovateonline.info/index.php?view=article&id=12&action=article

Mason, R. (1994). *Using communications media in open and flexible learning*. London: Kogan Page.

Mayer, R. (2001). *Multimedia learning*. Cambridge, UK: Cambridge University Press.

Mayer, R. E. (2001). *Multimedia learning*. New York: Cambridge University Press.

Mayes, J. T. (2002). The technology of learning in a social world. In R. Harrison, F. Reeve, A. Hanson, & J. Clarke (Eds.), *Supporting Lifelong Learning Volume 1: Perspectives on Learning*. London: Routledge.

McAlister, M. K., Rivera, J. C., & Hallam, S. F. (2001). Twelve important questions to answer before you offer a Web-based curriculum. *Online Journal of Distance Learning Administration, 5*(2). Retrieved January 31, 2009, from http://www.westga.edu/~distance/ojdla/summer42/mcalister42.html

McMillan, D. W., & Chavis, D. M. (1986). Sense of community: A definition and theory. *American Journal of Community Psychology, 14*(1), 6–23. doi:10.1002/1520-6629(198601)14:1<6::AID-JCOP2290140103>3.0.CO;2-I

Metros, S. E., & Hedberg, J. G. (2002). More than just a pretty (inter) face: The role of graphical user interface in engaging eLearners. *The Quarterly Review of Distance Education*, *3*(2), 191–205.

Mishra, S., & Juwah, C. (2006). Interaction in online discussion and chat sessions . In Juwah, C. (Ed.), *Interactions in online education: Implications for theory and practice* (pp. 156–170). London: Routledge.

Moore, M. G. (1980). Independent study . In Boyd, R., & Apps, J. (Eds.), *Redefining the discipline of adult education* (pp. 16–31). San Francisco: Jossey-Bass.

Moore, M. G. (1989). Editorial. Three types of interaction. *American Journal of Distance Education*, *44*(9), 1–6. doi:10.1080/08923648909526659

Moore, M. G. (1993). Theory of transactional distance . In Keegan, D. (Ed.), *Theoretical Principles of Distance Education* (pp. 22–38). London: Routledge.

Moore, M. G. (Ed.). (2007). *Handbook of distance education* (2nd ed.). Mahwah, NJ: Lawrence Erlbaum Associates.

Moore, M. G., & Kearsley, G. (1996). *Distance education: A systems view*. Belmont, CA: Wadsworth.

Muilenburg, L., & Berge, Z. (2002). *A framework for designing questions for online learning*. Retrieved January 24, 2009 from http://www.emoderators.com/moderators/muilenburg.html

Muirhead, B. (2004). Encouraging interaction in online classes. *International Journal of Instructional Technology & Distance Education, 1*(6). Retrieved December 8, 2008, from http://www.itdl.org/Journal/Jun_04/article07.htm

Munro, J. S. (1998). *Presence at a distance: The educator-learner relationship in distance education (ACSDE Research Monograph No. 16)*. University Park, PA: The American Center for the Study of Distance Education.

Murphy, K. L., & Cifuentes, L. (2001). Using Web tools, collaborating and learning online. *Distance Education*, *22*(2), 285–305. doi:10.1080/0158791010220207

Nielsen, J. (1999). *Designing Web usability: The practice of simplicity*. Indianapolis, IN: New Riders.

Northrup, P. T. (2002). Online learner's preferences for interaction. *The Quarterly Review of Distance Education*, *3*(2), 219–226.

Northrup, P. T., Lee, R., & Burgess, V. (2002). Learner perceptions of online interaction. *Educational Resources Information Center*. (ERIC Document Reproduction Service No. ED 477 075)

Oliver, R. (1999). Exploring strategies for on-line teaching and learning. *Distance Education*, *20*(2), 240–254. doi:10.1080/0158791990200205

Palloff, R. M., & Pratt, K. (2003). *The virtual student: A profile and guide to working with online learners*. San Francisco: Jossey-Bass.

Palloff, R. M., & Pratt, K. (2005). *Collaborating online: Learning Together in Community*. San Francisco: Jossey-Bass.

Poole, D. M. (2000). Student participation in a discussion-oriented online course, A questionnaire for predicting online learning achievement. *Distance Education*, *24*(1), 31–47.

Porter, L. (2004). *Developing an online curriculum: Technologies and techniques*. Hershey, PA: Information Science Reference.

Richardson, J., & Swan, K. (2001). *An examination of social presence in online learning: Students perceived learning and satisfaction*.

Ross, A. R. (1996). The influence of computer communication skills on participation in a computer conferencing course. *Journal of Educational Computing Research, 15*(1), 37–52. doi:10.2190/6TYW-ADV1-W0LC-N9H0

Schneiderman, B., & Kearsley, G. (1989). *Hypertext hands on!*Reading, MA: Addison-Wesley.

Shea, P., Fredericksen, E., Pickett, A., Pelz, W., & Swan, K. (2001). *Measures of learning effectiveness in the SUNY Learning Network*. Retrieved January 6, 2009, from https://urresearch.rochester.edu/retrieve/6491/MeasuresofLearningEffectiveness2001.pdf

Sherry, L. (1996). Issues in distance learning. [from http://carbon.cudenver.edu/~lsherry/pubs/issues.html]. *International Journal of Educational Telecommunications, 1*, 337–365. Retrieved January 30, 2009.

Simonson, M., Smaldino, S., Albright, M., & Zvacek, S. (2009). *Teaching and learning at a distance: Foundations of distance education*. New York: Allyn & Bacon.

Smith, G. G., Ferguson, D., & Caris, M. (2002). Teaching over the web versus in the classroom: Differences in the instructor experience. *International Journal of Instructional Media, 29*(1), 61–67.

Smith, M. C., & Winking-Diaz, A. (2004). Increasing students' interactivity in an online course. *Journal of Interactive Online Learning, 2*(3). Retrieved January 25, 2009, from http://www.ncolr.org/jiol/issues/PDF/2.3.3.pdf

Smith, R. M. (2008). *Conquering the content: A step-by-step guide to online course design*. San Francisco: Jossey Bass.

Stevenson, K., Sander, P., & Naylor, P. (1996). Student perceptions of the tutors role in distance learning. *Open Learning, 11*(1), 22–30. doi:10.1080/0268051960110103

Swan, K. (2001). Virtual interactivity: Design factors affecting student satisfaction and perceived learning in asynchronous online courses. *Distance Education, 22*(2), 306–331. doi:10.1080/0158791010220208

Swan, K. (2003). Learning effectiveness: what the research tells us . In Bourne, J., & Moore, J. C. (Eds.), *Elements of Quality Online Education, Practice and Direction* (pp. 13–45). Needham, MA: Sloan Center for Online Education.

Swan, K. (2004). Issues of interface. *European Journal of Open and Distance Learning*. Retrieved January 13, 2009 from http://www.eurodl.org/materials/contrib/2004/Karen_Swan.html

Thurmond, V. A. (2003). *Examination of interaction variables as predictors of students' satisfaction and willingness to enroll in future Web-based courses while controlling for student characteristics*. Retrieved January 30, 2009, from http://www.bookpump.com/dps/pdf-b/1121814b.pdf

Thurmond, V. A., & Wambach, K. (2004). Understanding Interactions in Distance Education: A Review of the Literature. *International Journal of Instructional Technology and Distance Education, 1*(1), Retrieved January 19, 2009, at http://www.itdl.org/journal/Jan_04/article02.htm

Van Dusen, G. C. (2002). Classroom learning: Interaction and interface . In Foster, L., Bower, B. L., & Watson, L. W. (Eds.), *ASHE Reader Distance education: Teaching and learning in higher education* (pp. 242–248). Boston, MA: Pearson Custom Publishing.

Vonderwell, S., & Zachariah, S. (2005). Factors that influence participation in online learning. *Journal of Research on Technology in Education, 38*(2), 213–230.

Vrasidas, C., & McIssac, M. S. (1999). Factors influending interaction in an online course. *American Journal of Distance Education, 13*(3), 22–36. doi:10.1080/08923649909527033

Wagner, E. D. (1994). In support of a functional definition of interaction. *American Journal of Distance Education*, *8*(2), 6–29. doi:10.1080/08923649409526852

Wagner, E. D. (1997). Interactivity: From agents to outcomes . In Cyrs, T. E. (Ed.), *Teaching and Learning at a distance: What it takes to effectively design, deliver, and evaluate programs* (pp. 19–26). San Francisco: Jossey Bass.

Young, A., & Norgard, C. (2005). Assessing the quality of online courses from the students' perspective. *The Internet and Higher Education*, *9*, 107–115. doi:10.1016/j.iheduc.2006.03.001

Zafeiriou, G., Nunes, J., & Ford, N. (2001). Using students' perceptions of participation in collaborative learning activities in the design of online learning. *Education for Information*, *19*(2), 83–105.

Chapter 5
Social Presence

Closely related to the content, instructor, and learner interaction that occurs in distance education courses is the concept of social presence. As online students increase the amount and types of course interaction in which they engage, they also increase their social presence or the recognition that they are communicating with "real" people. Ideally, students feel that they are part of a collaborative learning community that interacts to build knowledge and meaning. However, interaction and social presence are different concepts, and it is possible that students can interact with their instructor and their co-learners without feeling socially connected.

The purpose of this chapter is to define social presence, identify the qualities that foster social presence, and review instructional strategies that build social presence in online courses. The social presence that naturally occurs in traditional campus courses cannot be assumed in distance education Web-based courses. Students are challenged by the geographic separation and the lack of visual cues in computer medicated communication (CMC). Classes of online students are social networks with their words, actions, responsiveness, communication styles, intelligence, humor, and supportiveness all contributing to their online presence. Even at a distance, learning is a social experience.

DOI: 10.4018/978-1-61520-865-4.ch005

DEFINING SOCIAL PRESENCE

Social presence theory, a sub-field of communication theory (Richardson & Swan, 2003), includes several definitions of social presence that relate to a variety of communication mediums. As the number of social networking technologies has increased and their effectiveness has improved, the amount of interest and research in the area of social presence has also increased. Early in the social presence literature, Short, Williams, and Christie (1976) suggest social presence is the level at which people involved in a transaction via that media feel socially aware of each other. Tu (2002) writes that a higher level of social presence "confers the attributes of being more sociable, more personal, more sensitive, and warmer" (p. 3) than lower levels of social presence.

Social presence has also been defined as the amount to which a person feels "socially present" in their environment (McIsaac & Gunawardena, 1996, p. 408). Tu and McIsaac (2002) offer that "social presence is the degree of feeling, perception, and reaction to being connected by CMC" (p. 140) to another person through text. In yet another definition, Gunawardena and Zittle (1997) define social presence as the "degree to which a person is perceived as 'real' in mediated communications" (p. 8). Their research recognizes that social presence is a combination of the medium and the communicators. Similarly, Carabajal, LaPoint, and Gunawardena (2003) note that social presence is a factor that is influenced by the technology as well as the students. They define social presence as "the degree of salience of the other person in the interaction and the consequent salience of the interpersonal relationship" (p. 224).

BENEFITS OF SOCIAL PRESENCE

Biocca and Harms (2002) emphasize the importance of social presence because interaction through technology increasingly substitutes for face-to-face communication. In online courses, teachers and researchers find that social presence is necessary for students to advance to cognitive presence or the ability to construct meaning (Stacey, 2002). Richardson and Swan (2003) note students with high overall perceptions of social presence also score high in their perceived learning and perceived satisfaction with the instructor. Picciano (2002) reports a significant relationship among learner perceptions of interaction, social presence, and learning. Also related to learning, social presence positively impacts the depth and critical thinking demonstrated in online discussions (Maurino, 2007; Polhemus, Shih, & Swan, 2001). Whereas most studies connect social presence to learning, Wise, Chang, Duffy, and del Valle (2004) contradict most studies and find students do not feel they learn more when social presence is high. However, their study appears to be the exception rather than the rule in social learning benefits.

The support provided to students in an online course contributes to their success (Stacey, 2002), and Nunez (2005) points to social presence as contributing to student satisfaction, motivation, and retention in online programs. Without human touch, students feel as though it is just them and the computer (Weiss, 2000). Social presence literature makes "it clear that a student's degree of presence, engagement and interaction with others in an online educational setting had a significant influence on the attrition rate and the overall outcomes of the course" (Jolivette, 2006, p. 536).

Richardson and Swan (2003) add that social presence may also increase the instructor's satisfaction with online learning. Faculty are part of the learning community and value the opportunity to know their students as more than just a name of the screen (Wang & Newlin, 2001). Online classrooms offer faculty a way to shift from the high pressure "sage on the stage" to the social constructivist "guide on the side." Mentoring students as they engage in meaningful dialogue and actively build a community of knowledge provides faculty with a sense of fulfillment in a job well done (King, 2002).

Social presence is a critical factor in developing an online learning community where students learn together through group activities (Garrison & Anderson, 2003; Tu & Corry, 2003; Kazmer, 2000). Reid (1995) proposes the following steps leading from social presence to community: (1) social presence, (2) social interaction, (3) common communication, (4) common culture, and (5) community. Community and social presence both depend on a sense of relating and caring among participants (Wise et al., 2004). When social presence is low, group dynamics suffers (Short et al., 1976) and messages become more impersonal (Whiteman, 2002). Palloff and Pratt (2005) also recognize the relationship between social presence and community and write "that social presence is a critical element of the online community and one that is critical to collaborative work" (p. 9).

Personal Reflection Suggestion

Most faculty find personal fulfillment in sharing knowledge and developing relationships with learners. As an instructor or trainer, how important is social presence in your course(s)? Do you make an conscious effort to develop a sense of social presence between yourself and students?

DIMENSIONS OF SOCIAL PRESENCE

Social presence involves complex personal dimensions that vary among students and instructors such as intimacy, immediacy, community, interaction, trust, transactional distance and off-topic exchanges. Many of these dimensions have been studied in face-to-face courses, and only recently examined in the online learning environment.

In early research on social presence, Argyle and Dean (1965) identified *intimacy* as an important dimension of face-to-face social presence, and Wiener and Mehrabian (1968) identified *immediacy* as an important dimension related to social presence. Intimacy is the closeness defined as a function of eye contact, physical proximity, smiling, and the topic of conversation. Immediacy is the psychological distance between communicators and includes eye contact, smiling, vocal expressiveness, physical proximity, appropriate touching, leaning forward, gesturing, being relaxed and spending time (Short et al., 1976). Even though these visual indicators are absent from online courses, the concepts are nonetheless critically important to establishing a positive learning environment. In Web-based courses, participants communicate the intimacy and immediacy that they value through sharing, agreeing, or affirming the postings of their co-learners. It is easier to form relationships with people in which we have common goals, interests, and values.

Two additional key dimensions of social presence are *community* and *interaction*. Community, the convergence of interaction and connection between students and between the students and the teacher, relates "to interactivity, sense of well-being, quality of the learning experience, and effective learning" (Rovai, 2002, p. 45). Interaction comes in the forms of learner-content, learner-instructor, leaner-learner, and learner-interface. While all forms of interaction are critical, the success of the online learning classroom is often tied to the nature of interaction via the discussion board, email, or chat tools (Picciano, 2002).

Part of a strong community is the dimension of *trust,* which develops between participants when they sense that the community is safe. They believe that feedback will be offered with some immediacy and that members of the community can rely on one another. Trust works hand-in-hand with intimacy and engagement; greater trust leads to increased and more honest communication (Rovai, 2002). Trust also leads to a willingness to engage with people they cannot see (Wise et al., 2004). In order to develop social presence, trust must be gained by students and among students (Tu & McIsaac, 2002).

Developed by Moore (1990), *transactional distance* is a dimension of social presence assessed in terms of how much dialogue takes place between teacher and learner and how much structure the class provides. Moore (1993) defines transactional distance as the "psychological and communications space to be crossed" (p. 22) by instructors and students who are geographically separated. A highly distant online classroom would feature very little dialogue between teacher and student and very little structure; the opposite, much dialogue and high structure would offer the least distant (Moore, 1990; Garrison, 2000; Stein & Wanstreet, 2003).

Closely related to the dialogue of a socially present online learning classroom is the more *off-topic exchanges* within the community (Rovai, 2002). These comments consist of personal information, supportive comments, humorous asides, or emoticons. Emoticons express emotions and mimic facial expressions through text (Aragon, 2003) such as ☺ for smiling and ;) for winking. Focusing classroom discussions solely on-topic, on-context leads to the gradual evaporation of feelings of social presence (Tu & McIsaac, 2002). Sidebar, off-topic conversations often allow social presence to develop more rapidly than a focus solely on course content.

FOSTERING SOCIAL PRESENCE

Tu and Corry (2002) identify three aspects of an online course that contribute to social presence: (1) *social context* or the "user's characteristics and perceptions of the CMC environment" (Tu, 2002, p. 2); (2) *online communication* which is the user's online language and attributes of the CMC; and (3) *interaction* is defined as "people being engaged together in activities" (Tu, 2002, p. 16). From the student perspective, qualities that enhance social context include being familiar with other learners and finding the right balance between too much and too little participation. Assertive students who participate frequently are sometimes intimating to other participants who struggle to keep up with the dialogue. Behaviors that build online communication are strong computer keyboarding skills, use of spell check, expression of emotions, and control of the number of discussion board postings. Qualities that develop interaction are quick response times and appropriate length of messages.

The social presence of the course instructor may be more important than the presence of students in determining student satisfaction. Instructor social presence has also been positively correlated to student motivation, satisfaction, and learning (Swan and Shih, 2005). To build social presence, Wheeler (2005) recommends that faculty respond to students with comprehensive, encouraging messages sent in a timely manner. Many faculty and instructional developers begin a course with student introductions and model the behaviors that they want students to emulate. Nunez (2005) identifies expressions of emotion (e.g., capitalization and emoticons), humor, and self-disclosure as affective indicators of social presence. Scollins-Mantha (2008) also emphasizes the importance of adding *tone* to informal messages with words or symbols that communicate emphasis, surprise, or confusion. By adding a statement such as "I'm joking!" or "Wow – can you give me an example?" teachers can foster relationships that develop social presence (Aragon, 2003). Strategies to build cohesiveness include inclusive pronouns and social communication.

An instructor can also build social presence by interacting with all learners and showing respect for them and their contributions. Students value instructor presence in online courses, and, if particular, value timely feedback from instructors (Scollin-Mantha, 2008). Furthermore, the instructor may foster social presence by modeling appropriate communication behaviors, demonstrating care, addressing students by name, and engaging is casual conversations. Students will follow the lead offered by their teachers (Savery, 2005)

Research on teacher immediacy behaviors takes into account many of the same factors as social presence, but without considering the effect that media has on the communication.

Bozkaya (2008) notes that "teachers displaying verbal and nonverbal immediacy behaviors may enhance social presence of learners" (p. 190) in both face-to-face and videoconferencing environments. In online discussions, both the quality and quantity of student participation can improve with greater teacher immediacy (Lobry de Bruyn, 2004). When compared to high teacher immediacy behaviors, Rifkind (1992) relates a lack of immediacy to lower levels of social presence, lower levels of affective student learning, higher levels of student frustration, and a more critical attitude demonstrated by the instructor.

Also related to social presence is media richness or the ability of a medium to carry information (Newberry, 2001). Short and colleagues (1976) contend that "different communication media convey varying degrees of social presence based of their ability to transmit nonverbal and vocal information" (p. 116). For example, McIsaac and Gunawardena (1996) report video conferencing can create high levels of social presence because it is similar to face-to-face interaction. In CMC, real time chat messages tend to be the shortest and discussion board postings tend to be the longest forms of communication. In a comparison of email, real time chat, and the asynchronous bulletin or discussion board, Tu (2002) "finds email is perceived to possess the highest level of social presence, followed by real-time discussion and bulletin board" (p. 1). Newberry (2001) proposes the following hierarchy of media richness: (1) face-to-face, (2) video conferencing, (3) synchronous audio, (4) text-based chat, (5) email and asynchronous audio, and (6) threaded text discussions.

The more limited the verbal and visual cues of communication, the more challenging the development of social presence. In addition to the mode of communication, the unconstrained interaction time within many online courses may also contribute to social presence. Stacey (2002) finds the length of the learning experience affects participants' feeling of connection with longer sessions enhancing interpersonal impressions and the gathering of social information. While interpersonal impressions formed more slowly in CMC than in traditional classroom settings, strong persistent personal connections can and do form among students and faculty.

Wheeler (2005) believes that it is important for online students to recognize that they are communicating with people—not machines. The leanness of text-based communication often limits the sociability of CMC. Kehrwald (2007) concludes that the conditions that limit text-based communication include a lack of contextual information, a significant social and psychological distance among learners, and an imbalance in the sender-receiver relationship. Gunawardena (1995) found that communicative failures are more likely to occur at the social level than at the technological level in text-based. Even though CMC is perceived as being low in social cues, students often perceive their online courses as being interactive, interesting, and stimulating (Whiteman, 2002).

Communication anxiety, the feeling of speaking in a vacuum, can result when a student does not receive a timely response to online posts. The student takes this lack of response as rejection, which hinders the cohesiveness of the class (Carbajal, LaPoint, and Gunawardena, 2003). Students also become "quiet" when etiquette is breached or tension occurs among learners. In these cases, it is the role of the instructor to address the issue (Conrad, 2002). Instructors must also manage the socio-emotional side of the classroom by quenching any flames, drawing out lurkers, and toning down the "loud" participants (Rovai, 2001).

Biocca and Harms (2002) emphasize that research exploring the technological influences of social presence is still in its infancy. Although there are few studies on text messaging, it may be yet another method of communication which improves social presence. The Technology Advancement Center at East Carolina University found that 94 percent of their students had cell phones and most use text messaging on a regular basis. DuVall, Powell, Hodge, and Ellis (2007) conclude that "if text messaging is integrated effectively into an online class and used for well-defined objectives, it provides a useful tool for enhancing social presence and communication among learners" (p. 28). One of the beneficial features of text messaging is the immediacy it offers because it is delivered through a small portable device such as a cell phone. If using text messaging, faculty should be aware that some cell phone providers charge an extra fee for the service.

As another mode of communication, instructors may wish to consider audio files attached to emails. Free and easy to use software, Audacity (http://audacity.sourceforge.net), enables teachers to record .mp3 files to share with students as an additional social cue to connect with students. Microsoft Word® 2007 allows 60-second audio files to be embedded in files through the insert Objects feature. Podcasting or broadcasting of audio files such as lectures is yet another way that instructors can bring their voice into the student's learning environment. Spoken information appears to be received more accurately by students than written information (Card, Polin, Parra, Rhoads, & Sartori, 2006). In addition, the audio files foster social presence; less confused learners feel greater levels of comfort and engage more freely.

Blogging is another technology that may be linked to social presence, but more research is needed to clarify the relationship. Blogs are often hosted on commercial websites outside of the course management system, which removes a layer of formality and control. By extending the course beyond the course management website, students can increase their social and content connections with each other (Beldarrian, 2007).

And blogs give students the opportunity to share unique creative expressions personalized with photographs, images, audio recordings, and video files (Scollins-Mantha, 2008).

Personal Reflection Suggestion

Consider each medium used in your course (e.g., text, audio, video). How do you communicate social presence in each type of media?

ASSESSING SOCIAL PRESENCE

There are several studies and methodologies for assessing online social presence. In one prominent study, Tu (2001) studied social presence in CMC (e-mail, bulletin board and real-time chat) from the perspective of Chinese students who often collect information and cues from non-verbal channels. Because they cannot collect information in their traditional methods, the level of social presence in their online learning environments can be extremely low. Tu employed observation and a dramaturgical approach involving script analysis and interpretation. Dramaturgy is an intentional motive behind communication that seeks to portray the speaker in the best possible light (Goffman, 1959). Tu concluded that engaging Chinese students with a more interactive online learning environment will increase the level of social presence.

Rourke, Anderson, Garrison, and Archer (2001) created a content analysis template to assess the interactive, affective, and cohesive components of social presence communicated by learners. Content analysis is an assessment strategy which assigns numeric value to code transcripts in order to infer meaning from text-based communication . The interactive component refers to the threaded interchanges combined with messages of a socially appreciative nature. In the affective component of content analysis, researchers focus on emotions, feelings, and mood indicators such as expressions of emotion, capitalization, humor, irony, sarcasm, warmth, and self disclosure. The cohesive indicators included the use of phatics (communication that serves a social function such as "you're welcome"), vocatives (name or noun used to address a person), and salutations that build a sense of group commitment.

In a another social presence study that uses content analysis methodology, Ubon and Kimble (2004) found emotion expressed through affective responses was used most frequently in the first module when students were in the early phases of community building. Group cohesive responses were highest in the second or third module as students build community and create knowledge. To express interactive communication, online students extend the dialogue by frequently asking for clarification or advice from other participants.

Picciano (2002) studies student perceptions of interaction, presence, and performance in online graduate students. He collected data through a student satisfaction survey based on the Inventory of Presence Questionnaire developed by the Technische Universiteit Eindhoven, Netherlands and on a questionnaire developed by Tu (2001). Picciano's survey incorporated the following Likert Scale survey items to measure social presence:

1. I enjoyed the online course.
2. Even though we were not physically together in a traditional classroom, I still felt like I was part of a group in the online course.
3. The online course stimulated my desire to learn.
4. An online course provides a personal experience similar to the classroom.
5. An online course allows for social interaction.
6. An online course allows me to express my feelings, and to learn the feelings of others.
7. An online course provides a reliable means of communication.
8. An online course is an efficient means of communicating with others.
9. I did not find the online course threatening to me.
10. I felt I got to learn a great deal about the instructor in the online course.
11. I felt I got to learn a great deal about the other students in the online course.

Lin (2004) revised the questionnaire of Picciano (2002) and added additional items based on a review of the social presence literature. The final questionnaire consisted of 20-Likert Scale items. After validity and reliability analyses conducted with a small response group (n=15), 12 of the 20 items items reflected social presence. In addition to items similar to the eleven items listed above, Picciano found students valued humor, group activities, and group support.

Personal Reflection Suggestion

In most online learning initiatives, there are cues that indicate the course is progressing smoothly such as the students are engaging in timely discussions, completing assignments, and submitting appropriate questions or comments. What are the indicators of social presence in your course?

INSTRUCTIONAL DESIGN ISSUES LINKED TO SOCIAL PRESENCE

Developing social presence in an online course corresponds with the constructivist philosophy of creating knowledge through student-centered interaction with content, peers, and faculty (Palloff & Pratt, 2005; Piaget, 1969; Vygotsky, 1962). It is the instructor and course developer's responsibility to "create a sense of online community and make a space for social interaction to take place" (Maurino, 2007, p. 245). Many learners who are new to online learning, and even students who have previously taken Web-bases courses may be anxious in a new course with a new instructor. They do not have the traditional visual cues to judge the instructor and the environment. Many instructors begin their online courses using friendly welcome messages and student introductions to set the stage for collaborative learning. Some instructors require their students to create web pages that include appropriate personal and professional information and perhaps their photographs. "Typically, inclusion of pictures in a web page is a low-cost and easily accomplished option for raising social presence" (Newberry, 2001, p. 5-6).

McInnerney and Roberts (2004) find a forming (initial stage of group development) or warm-up period assists in the development of an online learning community. The Penn State World Campus provides an orientation course which introduces students to the online learning environment. The University of Colorado – Global Campus offers a synchronous open house prior to the first day of class which allows students to communicate with advisors, administrators, faculty, and other learners. Additionally, many instructional designers recommend an asynchronous discussion forum for social interaction within courses, such as a "water cooler" or "cyber cafe" forum. Here, students can informally discuss movies, books, sports, or other social topics. As learners identify interests they have in common, they also increase their comfort level and an online sense of self.

Social presence can be further developed with clear netiquette guidelines. Students under time pressure often quickly type their replies to fulfill the course requirements, and dash on to the next challenge of their day. With the frantic pace of life, students may lose site of their classmates on the receiving end of their interaction. Providing netiquette guidelines provides students with a strong foundation for establishing a socially present classroom and a community of learners (Weiss, 2000). In addition, practitioners may want to use a variety of communication mediums and instructional strategies to develop learner feelings of social presence. Synchronous and asynchronous tools, plus audio and video mediums each introduce a different level of social presence in an online course environment. To build community, McInnerney and Roberts (2004) recommend synchronous communication in addition to asynchronous communication. Synchronous chat rooms increase immediacy, connections between students and the teacher, and a sense of community. Chat rooms require faculty to step back from their traditional leader role to a less controlled, informal facilitator role. Asynchronous discussion boards tend to the more structured, formal communication that is required and graded. Because asynchronous discussion boards can be overwhelming, Scollins-Mantha (2008) recommends requiring a small number of required postings, clearly labeling forums, and changing the subject line headings for replies within a discussion thread.

Stein and Wanstreet (2003) suggest "that it is worthwhile to offer different methods of collaborative learning" (p. 197) to develop different dimensions of social presence. Small group activities are effective because students have an opportunity to share common goals and information in a student-led and less formal environment (Tu & McIsaac, 2002). Additionally, students benefit from the personal support network that forms in team assignments. Each small group activity will have to be analyzed for the ideal balance between instructor and student control. Students with little experience in online learning may best be served with pre-determined groups, schedules, communication tools, and roles (e.g., coordinator, recorder, summarizers). Experienced non-traditional learners may prefer selecting group members and the roles of each member within the group. Whether the group activity is a case study, simulation, role play, problem solving, or another instructional exercise, Palloff and Pratt (2005) suggest that both the individual and group effort be graded.

Students in cohort groups and students who have the opportunity to meet face-to-face demonstrate increased levels of communication and etiquette (Conrad, 2002). Students in the University of Pittsburgh FastTrack program earn a Master's of Library and Information Science degree in a two-year, cohort-based program that meets one weekend per semester in an on-campus learning experience. Because social presence takes longer to develop in online courses than traditional campus courses, there seem to be benefits to the cohort-based design in which a group of students stays together throughout their online program. There may also be some connection between social presence and class size. Most online classes seem to be within the range of 15 to 25 students, but the number of students depends on the type of course. A foundational course with less interaction may be larger than the higher interactive analysis/synthesis course. These are all aspects of social presence that require more research.

CONCLUSION

The evolution of online learning has presented practitioners with both barriers and opportunities as they strive to keep the human connection in the learning experience. The isolation barriers of time and place can be partially addressed with advancements in technology, but the social networks that are taken for granted in traditional campus courses must be carefully planned and orchestrated in online courses. The social presence that develops among learners is critical to their motivation, satisfaction, learning, and cognitive development. Modes of communication as email, discussion board, chat, videoconferencing, and other social networking tools each contribute to different dimensions and levels of social presence. Trainer, faculty, and course developers will want to integrate a variety of asynchronous and synchronous tools and media to efficiently develop social presence. In addition, practitioners can use a variety of instructional strategies including orientation programs, virtual office hours, small group activities, and collaborative wikis to foster learning communities or social networks. Just as social technologies are evolving, so is the concept of social presence.

REFERENCES

Aragon, S. R. (2003). Creating social presence in online environments. *New Directions for Adult and Continuing Education*, (100): 57–68. doi:10.1002/ace.119

Argyle, M., & Dean, J. (1965). Eye-contact, distance and affiliation. *Sociometry*, *28*, 289–304. doi:10.2307/2786027

Beldarrian, Y. (2007, August). Distance education trends: Integrating new technologies to foster student interaction and collaboration. *Distance Education*, *27*(2).

Biocca, F., & Harms, C. (2002). What is social presence? In Gouveia, F., & Biocca, F. (Eds.), *Presence 2002 Proceedings*. Porto, Portugal: University of Fernando Pessoa Press.

Bozkaya, M. (2008). The relationship between teacher immediacy behaviors and distance learners social presence perspectives in videoconfering applications. *Turkish Online Journal*, *9*(1), 180–192.

Carabajal, K., LaPointe, D., & Gunawardena, C. N. (2003). Group development in online learning communities . In Moore, M. G., & Anderson, W. G. (Eds.), *Handbook of distance education* (pp. 217–234). Mahwah, NJ: Lawrence Erlbaum Associates.

Card, D., Polin, L., Parra, J., Rhoads, J., & Sartori, T. (2006 January). *Can you hear me now? The return of voice to distance learning*. Paper presented at the Proceedings of the 5th IASTED International Conference on Web Based Education, Puerto Vallharta, Mexico.

Conrad, D. (2002). Inhibition, integrity, and etiquette among online learners: The art of niceness. *Distance Education*, *23*(2), 197–212. doi:10.1080/0158791022000009204

DuVall, J. B., Powell, M. R., Hodge, E., & Ellis, M. (2007). Text messaging to improve social presence in online learning. *EDUCAUSE Quarterly*, *3*, 24–28.

Garrison, D. R., & Anderson, T. (2003). [*st century*. London: Routledge Falmer.]. *E-learning*, 21.

Garrison, R. (2000). Theoretical challenges for distance educationin the 21st century: A shift from structural to transactional issues. *International Review of Research in Open and Distance Learning*, *1*(1). Retrieved March 15, 2009, from http://www.irrodl.org/index.php/irrodl/article/viewFile/2/22

Goffman, E. (1959). *The presentation of self in everyday life*. Garden City, NY: Doubleday.

Gunawardena, C. N. (1995). Social presence theory and implications for interaction and collaborative learning in computer conferences. *International Journal of Educational Telecommunications*, *1*(2/3), 147–166.

Gunawardena, C. N., & Zittle, F. J. (1997). Social presence as a predictor of satisfaction within a computer-mediated conferencing environment. *American Journal of Distance Education*, *11*(3), 8–26. doi:10.1080/08923649709526970

Jolivette, B. J. (2006). *Social presence and its relevancy to cognitive and affective learning in an asynchronous distance learning environment: A preliminary literature review*. Retrieved March 12, 2009, from http://eric.ed.gov/ERICDocs/data/ericdocs2sql/content_storage_01/0000019b/80/1b/df/60.pdf

Kazmer, M. M. (2000). Coping in a distance environment: Sitcoms, chocolate cake, and dinner with a friend. *First Monday, 5*(9). Retrieved March 15, 2009, from http://www.firstmonday.org/issues/issue5_9/kazmer/index.html

Kehrwald, B. (2007) The ties that bind: social presence, relations and productive collaboration in online learning environments. In *ASCILITE Conference Proceedings*, Singapore. Retrieved February 27, 2009, from http://www.ascilite.org.au/conferences/singapore07/procs/kehrwald.pdf

King, K. (2002). Technology catalyzing change in how faculty teach and learn. *Journal of Continuing Higher Education*, *50*, 26–37.

Kregins, K., Kirschner, P., & Jochems, W. (2002). The sociability of computer-supported collaborative learning environments. *Educational Technology & Society, 5*(1). Retrieved on March 7, 2009, from http://ifets.ieee.org/periodical/vol_1_2002/kreijns.html

Lin, G. Y. (2004). *Social presence questionnaire of online collaborative learning: Development and validity*. Paper presented at the annual meeting of the Association for Educational Communications and Technology, Chicago, IL.

Lobry de Bruyn, L. (2004). Monitoring online communication: Can the development of convergence and social presence indicate an interactive learning environment? *Distance Education*, *25*, 67–81. doi:10.1080/0158791042000212468

Maurino, P. S. M. (2007). Looking for critical thinking in online threaded discussions. *Journal of Educational Technology Systems*, *35*(3), 241–260. doi:10.2190/P4W3-8117-K32G-R34M

McInnerney, J., & Roberts, T. S. (2004). Online learning: Social interaction and the creation of a sense of community. *Journal of Educational Technology & Society*, *7*(3), 73–81.

McIsaac, M. S., & Gunawardena, C. N. (1996). Distance Education . In Jonassen, D. (Ed.), *Handbook for research on educational communications and technology* (pp. 403–437). New York: Scholastic Press.

Moore, M. G. (1990). Recent contributions to the theory of distance education. *Open Learning*, *5*(3), 10–15. doi:10.1080/0268051900050303

Moore, M. G. (1993). Theory of transactional distance . In Keegan, D. (Ed.), *Theoretical principles of distance education* (pp. 22–38). New York: Routledge.

Newberry, B. (2001). *The name assigned to the document by the author. This field may also contain sub-titles, series names, and report numbers. Raising Student Social Presence in Online Classes.* (ERIC Document Reproduction Service No. ED 466 611).

Nunez, Y. S. (2005). Assessing faculty's social presence indicators in online courses. *Focus (San Francisco, Calif.)*, *4*(1), 47–49.

Palloff, R. M., & Pratt, K. (2005). *Collaborating online: Learning together in community*. San Francisco, CA: Jossey Bass.

Piaget, J. (1969). *The mechanisms of perception*. London: Routledge & Kegan Paul.

Picciano, A. G. (2002). Beyond student perceptions: Issues of interaction, presence, and performance in an online course. *Journal of Asynchronous Learning Networks*, *6*(1), 21–40.

Polhemus, L. Shih, L.F., & Swan, K. (2001, April). *Virtual interactivity: The representation of social presence in an online discussion*. Paper presented at the annual meeting of the American Educational Research Association, Seattle, WA.

Reid, E. (1995). Virtual worlds: Culture and imagination . In Jones, S. G. (Ed.), *Cybersociety: Computer-mediated communication and community* (pp. 164–183). Thousand Oaks, CA: Sage.

Richardson, J. C., & Swan, K. (2003). Examining social presence in online courses in relation to student perceived learning and satisfaction. *Journal of Asynchronous Learning Networks*, *7*(1), 66–88.

Rifkind, L. J. (1992). Immediacy is a predictor of teacher effectiveness in the instructional television classroom. *Journal of Interactive Television*, *1*(1), 31–38.

Rourke, L., Anderson, T., Garrison, R., & Archer, W. (2001). Assessing social presence in asynchronous text-based computer conferencing . *Journal of Distance Education*, *16*(2), 1–14.

Rovai, A. (2002). Building sense of community at a distance. *International Review of Research in Open and Distance Learning, 3*(1). Retrieved March 7, 2009, from http://www.irrodl.org/content/v3.1/rovai.html

Rovai, A. P. (2002). A preliminary look at the structural differences of higher education classroom communities in traditional and ALN courses. *Journal of Asynchronous Learning Networks, 6*(1), 41-56. Retrieved March 7, 2009, from http://www.sloan-c.org/publications/jaln/v6n1/v6n1_rovai.asp

Savery, J. R. (2005). BE VOCAL: Characteristics of successful online instructors. *Journal of Interactive Online Learning, 4*(2), 141-152. Retrieved on March 21, 2009, from http://www.ncolr.org/jiol/issues/PDF/4.2.6.pdf

Scollins-Mantha, B. (2008). Cultivating social presence in the online learning classroom: A literature review with recommendations for practice. *International Journal of Instructional Technology and Distance Education*, *5*(3), 23–38.

Short, J., Williams, E., & Christie, B. (1976). *The social psychology of telecommunications*. London: John Wiley and Sons.

Stacey, E. (2002). Social presence online: Networking learners at a distance. *Education and Information Technologies*, *7*(4), 287–294. doi:10.1023/A:1020901202588

Stein, D., & Wanstreet, C. (2003). *Role of social presence, choice of online or face-to-face group format, and satisfaction with perceived knowledge gained in a distance learning environment*. Paper presented at the 2003 Midwest Research to Practice Conference in Adult Continuing and Community Education.

Swan, K., & Shih, L. F. (2005). On the Nature and Development of Social Presence in Online course Discussions. *Journal of Asynchronous Learning Networks*, *9*(3), 115–136.

Tu, C. H. (2000). *Strategies to increase interaction in online social learning environments*. A unique accession number assigned to each record in the database; also referred to as ERIC Document Number (ED Number) and ERIC Journal Number (EJ Number). (ERIC Document Reproduction Service No. ED 444550).

Tu, C. H. (2001). How Chinese perceive social presence: An examination of interaction in an online learning environment. *Educational Media International*, *38*(1), 45–60. doi:10.1080/09523980010021235

Tu, C. H. (2002). The impact of text-based CMC on online social presence. *The Journal of Interactive Online Learning*, *1*(2), 1–24.

Tu, C. H., & Corry, M. (2002). Research in online learning community. *Journal of Instructional Science and Technology*, *5*(1). Retrieved July 18, 2009, from http://www.ascilite.org.au/ajet/e-jist/docs/Vol5_No1/chtu_frame.html

Tu, C. H., & Corry, M. (2003). Building active online interaction via collaborative learning community . In Tu, C. H., & Corry, M. (Eds.), *Distance Education: What works well* (pp. 51–59). New York: Haworth Press.

Tu, C. H., & McIsaac, M. S. (2002). An examination of social presence to increase interaction in online classes. *American Journal of Distance Education*, *16*(3), 131–150. doi:10.1207/S15389286AJDE1603_2

Ubon, A. N., & Kimble, C. (2004). Exploring social presence in asynchronous text-based online learning communities. In *The 5th International Conference on Information Communication Technologies in Education* (pp. 292-297).

Vygotsky, L. S. (1962). *Thought and language*. Cambridge, MA: The MIT Press. doi:10.1037/11193-000

Wang, A. Y., & Newlin, M. H. (2001). Online lectures: Benefits for the virtual classroom. *T.H.E. Journal*, *29*(1), 17–24.

Weiss, R. E. (2000). Humanizing the online classroom . In Weiss, R. E., Knowlton, D. S., & Speck, B. W. (Eds.), *Principles of effective teaching in the online classroom* (pp. 47–51). San Francisco: Jossey-Bass.

Wheeler, S. (2005). *Creating social presence in digital learning environments: A presence of mind*. Featured Paper for the TAFE Conference, Queensland, Australia. Retrieved on February 27, 2009 from http://videolinq.tafe.net/learning2005/papers/wheeler.pdf

Whiteman, J. M. (2002). *Interpersonal communication in computer mediated learning*. Orlando, FL: University of Central Florida. (ERIC Document Reproduction Service No. ED 465 997).

Wiener, M., & Mehrabian, A. (1968). *Language Within Language: Immediacy, a Channel in Verbal Communication*. New York: Appleton-Century-Crofts.

Wise, A., Chang, J., Duffy, T., & del Valle, R. (2004). The effects of teacher social presence on student satisfaction, engagement, and learning. *Journal of Educational Computing Research*, *31*(3), 247–271. doi:10.2190/V0LB-1M37-RNR8-Y2U1

Chapter 6
Administrative Issues Impacting Instructional Design for Online Learning

Instructional designers must never forget that designing online programs and courses is not done in isolation from the institutional context in which the programs are to be offered. In other words, there are a number of administrative realities that must be considered in order for programs to be delivered to learners in a timely and effective manner. To effectively address such institutional issues, a program designer must take the time to clarify his or her own philosophy of program design. This clarification of personal philosophy must then combine with a clarification of agency philosophy. Obviously there will be differences between the personal and agency philosophies of program design. Understanding such differences provides a starting place for design negotiations so that the eventual programs designed can satisfy both parties in the design loop (designer and agency). Without such clarification and negotiation, the programs designed are likely to either foster a sense of frustration in the designer or foster dissatisfaction among the agency administrators. In the real world (in contrast to abstract discussions in classrooms or professional conferences), successful online educational programs must be designed in a win-win environment.

DOI: 10.4018/978-1-61520-865-4.ch006

The task of educational program design and educational program delivery is fraught with ethical issues that must be both anticipated and resolved. Such anticipation and resolution requires several crucial steps for designers. First, program designers must understand the institutional or agency context into which their planned educational program will fit. Agencies and organization vary widely in terms of their view of education and training and its relative status and function within the broader organizational environment. How will your agency or organization view the product of your design effort? Second, program designers must understand how to both negotiate and navigate within their own institutional realities. In other words, administrative systems must be understood and used to insure that budget considerations, personnel, and student support services all work together in a mutually supportive manner. Within these administrative systems, program designers must learn to interact effectively with institutional or agency management to help agency decision makers understand the value and potential of the online courses being designed. Certainly program designers must know how to obtain funding and other forms of institutional support for their efforts. Planners must also be sure that instructional faculty are recruited and trained. Learners at a distance require multiple learner support services, such a registrations, advising, financial aid, technical support, and learning assessment. In this chapter we will examine a number of administrative issues that impact on program designers and provide some practical suggestions to increase your effectiveness as designers within the administrative context into which your programs must fit.

PROGRAM DESIGNERS MUST LEARN TO THINK MORE LIKE ADMINISTRATORS

While the focus of most this book is upon the various sills involved in the task of designing effective online educational programs, many program designers are in positions where they have coordinating responsibilities for educational and training programs beyond the ones they personally design. If you find yourself in such a position, you know what it means to be responsible to oversee the delicate interplay between individual educational programs, i.e., seek to control the effects programs have on one another. In such a role you also need to be attending to the interacting variables of people, procedures, and work (Handy, 1985). In other words, although educational designers, you must also think and act like educational administrators. Most of you have probably seen situations in which the best-designed programs have failed due to administrative issues, not teaching and learning issues.

Donaldson (1990) has suggested five helpful principles for effective program coordination that can help you as a program designer to begin to think like an educational administrator and more effectively provide the proper leadership to your program design effort.

1. **The Helicopter Effect:** To be effective, program designers must be willing to rise above the day to day issues of designing a particular program and gain a bird's eye view of the broader context into which their program will fit. Such non-program specific issues would include seeing the agency culture, the competing programs, and the learner context.
2. **Power and Influence:** Often designers possess very limited formal power or authority in their agencies. Because they are dependent upon persons over whom they have little or no control, designers must learn to rely on influence and leverage to accomplish their goals. Management research and theory suggests that influence in organizations can be gained by three main strategies: status, expertise, and inter-personal skills. The status of a position grows as more people in an organization come to see the position as important. Designers must discover ways to communicate the value of what they do (i.e., designing educational programs) for achieving the goals of others, such as the value of well designed programs to improving the safety record of a shop or reducing the loss due to faulty skills. Expertise refers to acknowledged proficiency in valued activities. As the program designer demonstrates effective programs over time, the organization will come to value his/her expertise and tend to be more willing to be influenced by his/her recommendations and counsel. Interpersonal skills are critical to develop networks, communicate information, and manage conflicts. The more effective these skills, the more influence the program planner has within the broader organization despite limited formal authority.

3. **Uniformity and Diversity**: Balancing uniformity and conformity is a crucial coordinating skill. The organization needs uniformity in procedures, policies, and processes to maintain efficiency. Yet organizations also need diversity to have the flexibility to best respond to different learners and changing needs of learners. Too much uniformity limits ability to be flexible, a critical element in developing effective and marketable programs. Too much diversity can result in inefficiency and ineffectiveness, undercutting the viability of the organization offering programs.
4. **People, Systems and Procedures, and Work:** Related to the previous point, program designers in their coordination efforts must learn to manage three interacting variable--people, systems and procedures, and work and structure. Recruitment of learners and staff must be integrated with procedures for teaching, evaluating, and monitoring the learning programs, which in turn must be integrated with budgets. Change at any point impacts all other points. For example, deciding to use a new delivery method such a online learning also impacts upon the staff chosen, the technologies required, the anxiety level of support staff, etc.
5. **Information Nerve Center:** The program planner must learn to serve as an information nerve center. Develop your information sources and share strategically throughout your agency. This will foster support for your program and increase you value (status) within agency.

Personal Reflection Questions

1. *Consider a recent program design project in light of the five program coordination principles suggested by Donaldson. To what degree were your coordination efforts reflective of these five principles?*
2. *How might applying these principles have made a difference in the program outcomes?*

CLARIFYING YOUR OWN PHILOSOPHY OF DESIGN

People design educational programs, including online programs, from a variety of assumptions regarding such things as the proper purpose for education and training, the proper role for the teacher/instructor, the proper role of the learner, and the true nature of the teaching/learning process. There is no escaping the fact that the approach you take to planning programs is rooted in philosophical assumptions. Notice how a number of educational theorists have underscored this reality:

"Adult educators must acquire and be committed to a unified framework of basic beliefs about adult education to guide their efforts in program planning." -Edgar Boone (1985).

"Philosophy is the guiding principle behind practice as an adult educator." -Elias and Merriam (1995).

"In applying the interactive program planning model, program planners need to know what they stand for as educators and trainers. More specifically, they need to be able to identify their beliefs and values and determine working philosophies about the program planning process." -Rosemary Caffarella (2002)

While program planners operate from a set of pre-suppositions about a number of important issues related to program planning, such presuppositions are often not examined carefully enough by program planners. Yet such an examination is central to the development of consistent practice. Patrick Boyle (1981) suggested that such presuppositions revolve around four issues.

- First, the program planner must determine his/her beliefs about the purpose for the education they design.
- Second, the program planner must determine his/her beliefs about the learner and learning. On other words, what is the proper role for the learner in the process and what is the nature of effective learning?
- Third, the program planer must determine his/her beliefs about the nature of teaching and the proper role for the program planner. In other words, are the teachers to be the authorities, the experts, or simply facilitators? What is the proper level of relationship that should exist between the teacher and the learners? How collaborative is the teaching/learning process?
- Finally, the program planner must determine his/her beliefs about the process of program planning. Should it be a linear or cyclical process? What level of collaboration should exist between various groups in the program (learners, instructors, designers, agencies, etc)?

Program designers need to know where they stand ideologically as educators and trainers. They need to identify their beliefs and values and determine working philosophies about program planning. Clearly education programs can and do take a variety of forms and serve a variety of purposes. Some of these differences in form and purpose are primarily pragmatic, i.e., different settings and program contexts naturally lead to a variety of program purposes. Some of these differences in form and purpose are primarily philosophic, i.e., educators can differ dramatically in their underlying beliefs about proper purpose for education and the proper structure for teaching and learning efforts. A helpful summary of some the major philosophical differences in education and training has been suggested by Elias and Merriam (1995).

1. **Behavioral Education Philosophy:** From a behavioral standpoint, the primary purpose of education and training is to teach people to comply with certain standards or expectations set by societal leaders, professional experts, and/or employers. Behavioral education emphasizes teacher control, management-by-objectives, behavioral change, lockstep learning, and technical training. Generally, behavioral education/training relies on step-by-step teaching methods where one skill must be mastered before another is started, and incorporates lots of practice with feedback and (positive and/or negative) reinforcement. A behavioral philosophy of adult education is more closely aligned with technical/skill training, job performance, and military training than interpersonal communication skills or collaborative learning. A behavioral approach to adult education includes an emphasis on measurable outcomes of learning.
2. **Liberal (Arts) Education Philosophy:** The primary purpose of a liberal philosophy of education and training is to provide a broad-based, general education rather than a specialized or vocational education. The emphasis in this philosophy is on liberal learning, organized knowledge, and the development of intellectual capacity and thinking skills. A key outcome of a liberal (arts) education is the ability to integrate new knowledge with enhanced intellectual abilities and a conceptual understanding of ideas and values. "Academic excellence" is a cornerstone of liberal education.
3. **Progressive Education Philosophy:** The primary focus of progressive education and training philosophy is educating people

to live responsibly and resolve problems cooperatively within a democratic society. Essential elements of progressive education philosophy include learner-centeredness, emphasizing real-life experience in the learning process, creating communities of learning, and encouraging active inquiry and interactive learning. A primary role of the teacher in progressive education is that of a "coach" who provides guidance and cooperatively assists the natural capacities of the learner.

4. **Humanistic Education Philosophy:** Humanistic education and training philosophy suggests that learning and education can actually transform people, helping them to reflect upon and perhaps change their "world view," develop their full human potential, and become more self-directed, self-confident, and fulfilled in life. Humanism emphasizes freedom and autonomy, mutual trust, interpersonal relationships, self-directedness, and self-esteem. The primary focus of humanistic education is to support and facilitate the personal growth and development of each individual learner. Learners are expected to fully participate in all phases of the learning process, from needs assessment and planning to learning assessment (if appropriate). Teachers' values that are humanistic in nature include trust, acceptance, respect, friendship, self-directedness, democratic climate, flexibility, diversity, learner-centeredness, and positive support. A basic assumption of humanistic educational philosophy is that human nature is essentially good, and that people are constantly growing and improving.
5. **Radical Education Philosophy:** Radical adult education philosophy views education and training as a primary force for achieving social change, or transforming society. A primary theme is awareness and understanding of the influences of cultural, political, and economic factors on individuals within a society. Radical education advocates political consciousness and social action, emphasizing knowledge as power and fostering a partnership between teachers and students. This philosophy strongly supports individual freedom and autonomy.

Personal Reflection Suggestion

1. *One way to consider how ideology/philosophy impacts on approaches to program planning is to consider the following scenario: Your company has recently decided to offer professional development programs for mid-level managers in the agency. Consider the similarities and differences in approach to such an educational intervention based upon differing philosophical assumptions as held by streams of education ideology above:*
2. *Reflect upon your own personal philosophy of program design, particularly regarding your basic assumptions about human nature, role of the learners, role of the teacher, and purpose of adult education.*

SOME OTHER INESCAPABLE ADMINISTRATIVE QUESTIONS FOR PROGRAM DESIGNERS

Although we will have been examining the process of program design in the various chapter of this book, it is important to stress that the task of design is filled with important administrative questions at nearly every point in the educational effort, from the first idea for the program itself through the evaluation of program outcomes. Boyle (1981) suggests a number of core issues, or questions, that must be answered when designing education programs. Many of these issues link to the discussion above on ideology and philosophy.

1. **Involvement:** How involved should the learners and other stakeholders be in the designing of instruction?
2. **Needs:** Who's needs will drive the programs? Learner, company, organization, society, etc.
3. **Evaluation:** Who should evaluate outcomes of learning efforts? Learner, program designer/instructor, outside consultant?
4. **Content Control:** Does designer have "right" to impose their values, attitudes, beliefs on learners? Is it acceptable to have "hidden agenda"?
5. **Program Support:** Who should "pay" for program? Organization, divisions, learners, government, etc.
6. **Instructional Focus:** Should programs be directed to individuals or groups – issues of level of self-directedness.
7. **Program Flexibility:** How flexible is the program to address socio-cultural differences and learning style differences in learners?
8. **Mandate:** Will learners be forced to attend training and what will be done to address motivation and resistance in mandated learners?
9. **Quality:** How will quality be measured and when is "enough" enough? (cost-effectiveness vs. quality)

In a similar vein, Moore and Kearsley (1996) proposed seven questions they felt needed to be addressed at the onset of the course design which include:

1. What content should be included or left out;
2. What is the best way to sequence and organize the material;
3. What are the best media to use to present the material;
4. What kind of teaching strategies should be employed;
5. How can learning be measured most appropriately;
6. What feedback should students receive about their progress; and
7. What methods should be used to create the materials.

Personal Reflection Question

Consider the issues highlighted by Boyle and by Moore and Kearsley above in light of your own personal philosophy of education and in light of your agency's implicit beliefs about educational or training programs. Use a recent educational program within your agency or organization to help focus your thoughts on these issues.

CONFRONTING INESCAPABLE ETHICAL ISSUES WHEN DESIGNING PROGRAMS

Reflecting upon our own personal beliefs and values inevitably leads to a consideration of the ethical issues in program planning. Caffarella (2002) discusses common ethical dilemmas and issues which many program designers encounter and suggests four important tasks that in order to adequately address ethical issues:

1. We need to examine your own beliefs about program design. It is critical that you understand and affirm your beliefs and values about program planning. This helps you to "know" and anticipate what you can and cannot do in the process of planning a program.
2. Help your organization or educational unit to develop definitive statements of the beliefs of your organization and then share them with program participants and other stakeholders.
3. Identify any codes of ethics or statements of beliefs of professional groups or other groups that are part of the planning process. These statements should be brought into the planning process as warranted.

4. Identify the values of the community and wider society in which designers work. This can be a very difficult task especially when there are competing and constantly changing beliefs and values in the society or community.

Clement, Pinto, and Walker (1978) suggest that six ethical problems emerge for many program planners. First, they believe a lack of professional development on the part of the programmer constitutes questionable practice. Program planner must be committed to their own continuing professional development in order to increase the effectiveness of the program they design and thus improve the value for others devoting time attending their educational offerings. Second, an ethical compromise occurs when program planner betrays confidences of others, such as when confidentiality is broken in needs assessments. Third, program planners who seek to promote/market their programs by unjustified promises as to outcomes break an ethical line. "Cure all" programs simply don't exist. Fourth, failure to give credit is a frequent ethical problem for program planners. Much plagiarism of content without proper citation occurs as program planners design training and leave the impression the content is drawn from their personal insights. Finally, abuse of learners can violate ethical standards. For example, at times some very questionable practice occurs in the midst of extreme programs such wilderness survival or stress/crisis management workshops. Singarella and Sork (1983) warn against the frequent error of sharing needs assessment data with those outside the learning situation, or sharing evaluation data as a form of performance assessment for jobs. People do not necessarily do the same in measured tests as they do in actual worksite activity. Martel and Colley (1986) also suggest that far too much fraudulent advertising is done with educational programs. Also they question the efforts to justify programs solely on the basis of their profit potential.

Reflection Question

Reflect upon a time when you faced one ethical dilemma identified above in planning education programs. Consider what was done to resolve the situation and whether Caffarella's suggestions would have lead to a different strategy of approach.

MAPPING YOUR PROGRAM'S CONTEXT

Understanding the context of educational programs is an important part of effective program design. Houle (1972) stressed that every program takes place within the framework of a specific situation and is profoundly influenced by that fact. Contextual analysis involves two steps for any program efforts: "mapping" the internal context and then "mapping" the external context. Let's examine these two steps a bit more.

Mapping the external context involves turning attention to a number of environmental factors that could influence program development. For example, what do you know about the nature or characteristics of the targeted learners? Are there other organizations or agencies providing competing educational programs to your target learners? Are there new or proposed changes in laws and/or regulations that could impact on the learners and your organization, e.g., changing OSHA standards?

Boyle (1981) suggests doing a social systems analysis as part of understanding the external context for your program, particularly if working in a community agency or educational institution. Such an analysis involves getting demographic information on income levels, occupations, educational backgrounds, age, gender, race, etc. of potential learners. He also suggests identifying key leaders and influencers in a community, both formal leaders and informal leaders. Cookson (1998) suggests programmers pay attention to many factors when seeking to understand the external context, including demographic attributes of potential learners, attributes of the economy, such a employment levels and economic outlook, and the political and dominant tendencies of the region. Such external factors are important for program planners and they must make an effort to keep up to date with these conditions. Reading papers and listening to news, joining professional associations, and creating advisory committees are some key strategies to maintain a grasp on important external factors.

Mapping the internal context involves grasping the goals, resources, and training context of your organization to insure that the goals of training program agree with organizational goals. Essentially such internal mapping gives the programmer a political astuteness when dealing with the agency or organization. The internal context involves a number of structural, political, and cultural factors. Structural factors include missions, goals, objectives, procedures, and other administrative frameworks. Political factors include coalition building, power relationship between units, and the politics of funding. Cultural factors include the history and traditions of organization, the values, rituals, and symbols of the organization. A number of issues should be examined regarding the internal context, including:

1. The strength of organization commitment to education or training. What is the degree of priority afforded education and training within an organization?
2. The preferred approach to instructional design and delivery in the organization. What is the normal variety of Technology used or the sophistication of technology used?
3. The locus of authority to make program planning decisions. Who actually makes the final decisions regarding program planning issues?
4. The source of financial support for programs. Will the organization subsidize the educational program or will it need to pay its own way through fees or tuition?
5. The availability of instructional resources. Do you have the staff to teach the programs developed, or do you need to go outside to hire others? Do you have the facilities internally for the programs or will outside facilities need to be contracted?

Reflection Question

1. *Consider program context issues for a program you are currently designing. Reflect upon the background of the program problem/idea (the context of the problem or idea) and describe the source of the need driving the program (people, responsibilities and tasks, organization, community).*
2. *Do you have any documentation for the nature and extent of the problem?*
3. *Do you understand the institutional and personal context for the program.*
4. *Finally, can you describe the target population: age, grade, reading level, attention span, occupation, previous experience, motivation level, health, interests, socioeconomic status, attitudes toward school or work, previous performance levels, language, ethnic/cultural background, gender.*

SUGGESTIONS TO IMPROVE PROGRAM STAFFING AND ON-SITE COORDINATION

While staffing needs can take a number of forms in education programs (administrators, designers, advisors, clerical help, instructors, etc), the discussion in this section will be focused upon the instructor/facilitator staffing needs. At the outset let me warn you that the best-designed educational program can be ruined by the wrong choice in instructor/facilitator. Conversely, many short-comings in your design can be moderated in impact on the learner by an effective instructor/

facilitator. Thus the choice of instructor/facilitator is a critical decision for the program designer. While it is not unusual for the program designer to also be the instructor/facilitator in many education settings, understanding the nature of effective staffing is a critically important skill for all program designers.

Caffarella (2002) suggests nine criteria to consider when obtaining instructors, including content knowledge, competence in the processes of instruction, ability to respond effectively to the background and experience of the learners, belief that caring for learners matters, credibility, enthusiasm and commitment, personal effectiveness, enterprise knowledge, and the ability to teach from the heart and spirit, as well as the mind. In a similar vein, Knowles (1980) suggests the following criteria in selecting instructors/facilitators:

1. Instructors must not only have knowledge, but must be successful practitioners in their subject or skill.
2. Instructors must be enthusiastic about their subject and about teaching it to others.
3. Instructors must have an attitude of understanding and permissiveness toward people (i.e., good people skills).
4. Instructors must be creative in their thinking about teaching methods, willing to try new approaches to foster greater learning.
5. Instructors must possess professional credentials necessary for validating the program content.
6. Instructors should approach adults differently than youth in their teaching approach (i.e., have some grasp and acceptance of adult learning principles).

The selection of instructors/facilitators, drawing upon the criteria suggested above, usually requires some sort of interview/screening process. An interview should explore the applicants attitudes toward teaching, learning, adult education, and non-traditional approaches to learning. Certainly discussing the experience of the instructor in both teaching and the topic of the program is necessary. Ideally the program planner should have an opportunity to observe the potential instructor in a teaching situation. Program planners must also accept the necessity of a thorough check of the potential instructor's references.

The work is not finished with the selection of instructors. You must also develop the proper working relationship with the instructional staff. Donaldson (1990) provides some sound advice when working with your instructors/facilitators after choosing them. First and foremost, clearly communicate all expectations. This includes all agency policies and procedures linked to teaching programs. Be sure to be clear on pay, expenses covered, and types of support routinely provided for their teaching efforts. Of course all content and quality expectations should be clarified. Second, discover practical ways to involve the instructor/facilitator in the life of your agency. The instructor will be representing your agency to the learners. They need to understand how their particular course or workshop fits into the broader course offerings of your agency. Third, be sure the instructor are not in positions of teaching those who report to them. Seldom can supervisors and subordinates toss aside their work roles when they enter the classroom. The potential for compromises and negative impacts in the work setting are great if this rule is ignored. Fourth, view the instructors/facilitators as resources to be developed. Since much time is expended in recruiting and selecting instructors, your agency directly benefits from their professional development. Certainly providing help in better understanding the adults as learners and adult teaching methods will pay dividends for everyone concerned.

In the case of online learning programs, it is critical that instructors/facilitators hired to teach be proficient in the skills of teaching online. In many cases this will require some staff development efforts to insure instructional staff have the necessary skills to perform effectively within an online environment.

Reflection Question

1. *What influence do you have as a designer over the instructors chosen for your programs?*
2. *If you influence this decision, are you insuring that contracted instructors have he both the content expertise and the teaching skills to effectively achieve your program goals?*
3. *What steps are you taking to maintain the proper on-going communication with instructors?*

A FEW WORDS ABOUT PROMOTING YOUR ONLINE PROGRAM

All the best design work will avail nothing if you can't recruit learners to your program. For designers working outside the traditional education settings (K-12), participants generally must be recruited into their programs. The ability to wisely promote and market your program is central to overall program effectiveness. Struther and Klus (1982) suggest that program promotion deals with the actions required to inform the right people that an event is to take place and to inform them in such a manner that they will want to participate. In other words, promotion is the marketing function of program planning. Struther and Klus go on to suggest six essential principles in effective program promotion. Let's examine each of them.

1. The promotional materials must reach the target audience: Unless you can actually connect with the group you wish to recruit to your program, any promotional effort is wasted. For example, you may decide that a newspaper ad is a good, cost effective choice, but if you are trying to recruit into a literacy program, the likelihood of your targeted learners reading the newspaper is low.
2. The promotional materials must get their attention: People receive many advertisements in the course of their daily life. Many (most) are never paid attention to and end up ignored and/or in the waste basket. You must design and transmit your materials in a way that will get some attention from the potential participant.
3. The target audience must understand the message delivered: Be sure to develop your promotional materials in terms that are easily understood by your potential participants. Be sure to avoid jargon and language that is too technical. Be sure the materials clearly explain exactly what the program is designed to achieve.
4. The promotional materials used must appeal to learner needs: People will be motivated to attend what they perceive is useful. Most adult learners are very pragmatic and utilitarian in their educational efforts. One benefit of an effective needs assessment is that the findings can be drawn upon to improve promotional efforts for the programs.
5. The promotional materials must persuade the learners that your program is the best way to meet these needs: Once you clarify the needs and have gotten the potential learner's attention, you must communicate why they should choose your program over other similar, competing programs. Certainly the credibility of the instructor and agency offering the program is linked to this point.
6. The promotional strategy must be cost effective: The critical importance of all aspects of instructional costs should be clear should be clear to all program designers. The previous 5 principles must be achieved within a reasonable cost. The cost of promotion must be figured into the overall budget and effectives the registration fee for the program.

Three critical variables affect the overall promotional/marketing strategy chosen. The first variable is price. Potential learners must be both able and willing to pay the amount you choose to charge for your program. Ability to pay is linked to personal income and other subsidizing sources (such as grants or employer benefits). Willingness to pay is tied to a wide range of personal and social factors. Studying the targeted learners (in the situational analysis done at the beginning of the program planning process) should help to uncover information linked to ability and willingness. A second variable is geography. The traveling distance to the program does impact on the promotional decisions. Will you be targeting learners within your agency, within your city, within your region, or on a national/international level? A third variable is competition. The greater the number of competitors for your program, the more it will cost to promote the program.

When deciding upon a promotional method, many options are available. The obvious strategy is to choose the one that will reach the most potential participants for the least cost. Yet this strategy must be constrained by the six principles previously identified from Struther and Klus (1982). The tool chosen must reach the target audience, get their attention, meet their needs, and be perceived as the best answer to their need. Struther and Klus, suggest four reasons for communication failure in promotion.

1. **Insufficient information:** The promotional material did not effectively answer the how, what, when, where, why, and how questions of the potential participants.
2. **Inadequate dissemination:** The promotional material did not get to the potential participants because of too small a mailing or poor choice of media.
3. **Misdirected information:** Bulk mailing are often delayed in delivery. Those receiving mail in an agency are not sure to whom the mailing should be directed.
4. **Failure to get attention:** The materials delivered (whether in print or other forms) simply did not grab the attention of the potential participant. There could be many reasons, including bad design, too much information, etc.

Simerly (1990, 1989) identified top marketing/promotion mistakes in education agencies and suggests three are particularly important for agencies and organizations to avoid. Consider them carefully when developing your promotional strategy for your program plan (and future plans).

1. Don't offer discounts for early registration and penalties for late registrations: Many must go through a chain of command in their agencies to get approval to attend training. The inevitable delays in getting such approvals should not be penalized. Also, penalizing people for late registration encourages people NOT to register, undercutting your program and defusing the effect of your promotional efforts. On a related note, it is generally a bad strategy to create cancellation penalties for late withdrawal. Most adult education is offered by service-oriented agencies and such penalties can create anger and a backlash when offering future training opportunities.
2. Never mail any direct-mail brochure unless it contains final, complete copy, and asks for a registration: Many of the potential participants will never see more than a single promotional tool for your program. Be sure the one they see has everything they need to know to register for the program.
3. Never wait until the last minute to promote the program: Always begin the promotional effort early enough to insure adequate time for the potential participants to adjust schedules and commitments to attend the program. An 8 to 12 week lead-time is usually fine for smaller scale programs. Large conferences need a longer lead-time.

Finally, the best marketing/promotional strategy for education programs is satisfied learners. Past success in programs provides a strong word-of-mouth support for future programs. Conversely, a learner who had a bad experience in one of your previous programs will remember that bad experience for a long time. Not only will they refuse to attend your current offering, they are likely to discourage others from attendance as well. The bottom line is that effective promotion is a cumulative process that draws upon past effectiveness as a strong motivator for current enrollments. No amount of expenditure in the present is likely to overcome existing negative experiences. Thus the best promotional and marketing strategy is to prioritize the effective design of the educational program and draw upon good faculty to deliver the program.

Program promotion leads naturally to considerations of recruitment. Obviously, recruitment is more critical in voluntary programs, such as seminars organized by community-based organizations or industry training programs funded by grants. In these cases, the survival and continued success of the program depends on participant recruitment. On other hand, recruitment may be less important in mandatory programs, such as sexual harassment avoidance training that is mandated by the US Equal Opportunity Commission. But even in such mandatory programs, program designers are required to justify the return on investment and thus the need to recruit and retain participants. The question then is: how can program designers improve the recruitment of program participants?

Simerly (1990) suggests that we can look at recruiting as involving public relations, marketing and/or promotion. Public relations is the process of promoting the image and goodwill of an organization and consists of activities undertaken to project a favorable image of planned learning activities in a program in general. The main purpose is to foster general awareness of planned learning and to promote positive attitudes toward the program sponsor and the sponsor's services. This image of planned learning and of the sponsor should be visible to actual and prospective learners in everything the organization does. Galbraith, Sisco and Guglielmino (1997) suggest that a typical public relations plan can consist of the following elements: defining the mission statement, determining program goals, analyzing publics, identifying benefits to the constituencies, and deciding on public relations strategies. There are a number of strategies and tools to consider in the development of a public relations plan. These include news releases, speakers' bureaus, special events, and public service announcements.

Personal Reflection Suggestion

1. *To what extent are you involved in the recruitment of learners and/or the marketing or promotion of the programs you design?*
2. *In light of some of the preceding principles, how differently would you approach the promotion of the last program you designed?*

SOME THOUGHTS ON DEVELOPING LEARNER SUPPORT SERVICES

A final administrative issue that program designers must consider in order to accomplish the most effective programs possible is to insure proper provision of learner support services. The importance of such services is underscored in many research studies (Brindley, 1995; Sewart, 1993; Tait, 1995; Thorpe, 2002). Certainly it stands to reason that effective learner support services will affect the reputation and credibility of an educational institution in a competitive market for learners. Research confirms that responsive, flexible, and integrated learner support systems decrease both learner dissatisfaction and failure (Brindley, 1995). Buchanan (2002) has demonstrated that inadequate learner support systems impact negatively on the institution's brand in the marketplace, create loss of enrollment revenue to other competing institutions offering similar programs, but with better support systems, and ultimate leads to high levels of attrition or drop-outs.

Keast (1997) identifies four distinctive types of learner support for distance learners, including administrative support, instructional support, technical support, and counseling and tutorial support. McCraken (2004) suggests a five-fold categorization of such learner services, including reliable technology and technological support; instructional, business, and student support systems; on-going communications with faculty and support staff; career counseling and transition assistance; and finally, interactive learning opportunities. Moore (2003) suggests that learner support systems create a "back-up safety net" that is intended to handle unexpected difficulties that either could not be anticipated by course designers or difficulties that can only be dealt with on a case-by-case basis. Rumble (2000) suggests learner support services take on two forms: "compensatory services" that are designed to overcome students' "learning difficulties" vs. "comprehensive services," which are integral or built in the programs design.

Personal Reflection Suggestion

1. *To what extent have you considered the issue of learner support services in your program design model.*
2. *Consider some instances when educational or training programs have been adversely affected by the lack of a "back-up safety net" (to use Moore's phrase) of learner support services. What services seem important to the effective implementation of an educational design project in which you are currently involved?*
3. *In light of some of the preceding principles on learner support, what changes should be negotiated within your agency?*

REFERENCES

Boone, E. J. (1985). Developing Program . In *Adult Education*. Englewood Cliffs, NJ: Prentice-Hall.

Boyle, P. G. (1981). *Planning Better Programs*. New York: McGraw-Hill.

Brindley, J. (1995). Learners and learner services: The key to the future in open distance learning . In Keough, E. M., & Roberts, J. M. (Eds.), *Why the information highway? Lessons from open & distance learning*. Toronto, Canada: Trifolium Books, Inc.

Buchanan, S. (2002). *Learner support in an online graduate program: A case study*. Unpublished master's thesis, Carleton University, Carleton, Canada.

Caffarella, R. S. (2002). *Planning Programs For Adult Learners: A Practical Guide For Educators, Trainers, and Staff Developers* (2nd ed.). San Francisco: Jossey-Bass.

Clement, R. W., Pinto, P. R., & Walker, J. W. (1978). Unethical and Improper Behavior By Training And Development Professionals. *Training and Development Journal*, *32*(12), 10–12.

Cookson, P. S. (1998). Examining The External Context . In Cookson, P. (Ed.), *Program Planning For The Training And Continuing Education Of Adults: North American Perspectives*. Malabar, FL: Krieger Publishing House.

Donaldson, J. F. (1990). Managing Credit Programs In Continuing Higher Education. [The Guide Series, University of Illinois.]. *Urbana (Caracas, Venezuela)*, IL.

Elias, J. L., & Merriam, S. B. (1995). *Philosophical Foundations Of Adult Education* (2nd ed.). Malabar, FL: Krieger Publishing Company.

Galbraith, M. W., Sisco, B. R., & Guglielmino, L. M. (1997). *Administering Successful Program sfor Adults: Promoting Excellence in Adult, Community, and Continuing Education*. Malabar, FL: Krieger Publishing Company.

Handy, C. B. (1985). *Understanding Organizations* (3rd ed.). New York: Penguin.

Houle, C. O. (1972). *The Design Of Education* (2nd ed.). San Francisco: Jossey-Bass.

Keast, A. (1997). Toward an effective model for implementing distance education programs. *American Journal of Distance Education, 11*(2), 39–55. doi:10.1080/08923649709526960

Knowles, M. S. (1980). *The Modern Practice Of Adult Education*. New York: Cambridge University Press.

Martel, L. D., & Colley, R. M. (1986). Ethical Issues In Marketing And Continuing Education. *New Directions For Continuing Education, 31*, 91–101. doi:10.1002/ace.36719863109

McCraken, H. (2004). Extending virtual access: Promoting engagement and retention through integrated support systems. *Online Journal of Distance Learning, 7*(1).

Moore, M. G. (2003). Editorial - Learner Support. *American Journal of Distance Education, 17*(3), 141–143. doi:10.1207/S15389286AJDE1703_1

Moore, M. G., & Kearsley, G. (1996). *Distance education: A systems view*. New York: Wadsworth.

Moore, M. G., & Kearsley, G. (2005). *Distance education: A systems view* (2nd ed.). Belmont, CA: Wadsworth.

Rumble, G. (2000). Student support in distance education in the 21st century. *Distance Education, 21*(2), 216–235. doi:10.1080/0158791000210202

Sewart, D. (1993). Student support systems in distance education. *Open Learning, 8*(3), 3–12. doi:10.1080/0268051930080302

Simerly, R. (1989). The Strategic Role Of Marketing For Organizational Success . In Simerly, R. (Eds.), *Handbook On Marketing For Continuing Education*. San Francisco: Jossey-Bass.

Simerly, R. (1990). The Top Ten Marketing Mistakes And How To Avoid Them. *Adult Learning*, 22–25.

Singarella, T. A., & Sork, T. J. (1983). Questions of Value and Conduct: Ethical Issues For Adult Education. *Adult Education Quarterly, 33*, 244–251. doi:10.1177/0001848183033004005

Struther, G. B., & Klus, J. P. (1982). *Administration of Continuing Education*. Belmont, CA: Wadsworth.

Tait, A. (1995). Student support in open and distance learning . In Lockwood, F. (Ed.), *Open and Distance Learning Today* (pp. 232–241). London: Routledge Falmer.

Thorpe, M. (2003). Collaborative online learning: Transforming learner support and course design . In Tait, A., & Mills, R. (Eds.), *Rethinking learner support in distance education* (pp. 198–211). London: Routledge Falmer.

Section 3
Developing Differentiated Instruction:
The "Tool Box"

Chapter 7
Preactive Stage:
Needs Assessment

Chapter 2 defined the four course types as: *foundational courses, skills based courses, analysis/synthesis courses and hybrid courses* and the focus of each. This chapter will look at the phases that the online instructors and designers engage to plan their online courses in the preactive (or the planning) phase. Defined as work conducted prior to the course beginning, the preactive phase includes the needs assessment, establishing objectives within the three learning domains of cognitive, psychomotor and affective, preparation to teach, lesson planning which includes a design for interaction and dialogue, formative and summative evaluation, LMS (Learning Management System) preparation, and technological requirements. Preactive stages of teaching include first understanding the type of online course and the implications and ramifications to all concerned in the development and delivery of the course. The preactive program is crucial and a little challenging, as the online instructional designer in many cases must plan to meet learner needs without knowing who they are and what their individual needs may be.

DOI: 10.4018/978-1-61520-865-4.ch007

As stated the course developer first needs to define the type of course: *foundational courses, skills based courses, analysis/synthesis courses or hybrid course* that he/she is going to teach online. This will help guide the designer to plan the lessons, activities and the interactions for the learners. After defining the category of course, you can now begin to understand the needs of the course and the needs of the students who are going to be taking the online lessons.

Each of the four course categories has specific goals and objectives that need to be attained by instructors and students. By understanding these course goals and needs, we can more appropriately design pedagogies that can assist in meeting student, instructor and institutional needs.

The *foundational course* targets the base or core knowledge of a professional area that will be built upon and utilized throughout a discipline as well as the fundamental information found in some college and university liberal arts courses. The goals are to provide the students with a solid foundation of knowledge. The *skills based course* focuses on the development of the necessary mental and/or physical skills needed in the professional area. The *Analysis/Synthesis* course teaches students to analyze a situation and engage in critical thinking or problem solving that is vital to higher order thinking and the ability to function in a profession. The *hybrid course* incorporates components from each of the other three course types that are necessary in preparing students to engage in all aspects of a profession.

NEEDS ASSESSMENT PHASES IN THE FOUR COURSES CATEGORIES

As teachers and instructional designers, one cannot let the media or the platform that you are using to establish what and how we teach. You need to take control of your online teaching to assure that it is needs-driven and not platform-driven. Many people who engage in online teaching believe that it is the online format that drives what and how things are taught and that the perceived limitations guide the pedagogies employed. It is through the use of needs assessment of all stakeholders involved in the educational process that you understand what and how things should be designed.

PURPOSES OF NEEDS ASSESSMENT

Conducting a need assessment is the initial step in most models of instructional design and a very important step (Rothwell, 2004, p. 57) as it establishes the direction for the preactive and active online teaching phases. A significant competency for the instructional designer is to "conduct a needs assessment" (Richey, Fields, and Foxon, 2001, p. 48-49) although most educational courses do not conduct a needs assessment as they conform to a set of outside standards that may be grounded in a needs assessment. The objectives of a needs assessment are twofold: 1) to identify needs of the learners not being met by the curriculum and 2) to form a basis for revising the curriculum in such a way as to fulfill as many unmet needs as possible (Olivia, 2005). The purpose of a needs assessment is to understand the needs of everyone involved or the stakeholders in the online educational process. A stakeholder is any one or group that has a vested interest in the education or training. These stakeholders may be the learner, the administrators at an educational institution, the instructor and the employers in a profession. Each of these entities have requirements that need to be addressed in the preactive and active teaching phases to assure that the program is viable for all concerned. The instructional designer also needs to consider the situational context of the education and training.

STRATEGIES FOR NEEDS ASSESSMENT

The online instructional designer in the preactive phase must ask several questions regarding each of the stakeholders to better understand his audience. Learner needs must be addressed through several lenses. What are the learner needs? What is the background of the learners? Where and how will the learner use the knowledge, skill and the analysis/synthesis problem solving that is to be learned in the course? What is the student's access to technology (i.e., software, bandwidth Internet access)? What are the technological capabilities of the learners in regard to their ability to use and understanding technology for learning? What is the learner's access to the necessary learning platforms? Having a deeper understanding of the answers to these questions will better prepare the developer to design online learning lessons that are relevant in content and appropriate methodologies. Knowing your audience and the learners becomes part of the differentiated instruction planning process. By understanding the learners and their needs, you can provide a variety of learning opportunities that are specifically targeted at the learners.

The *educational institution* offering the program or course of study may also have needs that must be addressed. Many educational institutions have accrediting bodies that mandate standards. What are the standards of any accrediting bodies that need to be met? The standards may necessitate goals, objectives and outcomes as well as success rates. These need to be understood upfront and built into the design process. Institutions may also have limitations with regard to resources and any financial implications that play a role. Class sizes and the number of online faculty members that are able to provide online education and costs associated with the learning management platform are also institutional factors. The institution may have a strategic plan that targets specific goals and objectives of the online programs that need to be taken into consideration. The online instructional designer needs to have an understanding of any of these issues that may affect their online planning in the preactive phases.

The *instructor* has needs that also must be addressed. What if any technology support need does the instructor have? Do they need any additional access to software or hardware upgrades to allow them to affectively navigate and teach in the online Learning Management System (LMS)? If they are going to work and teach from home, do they have a large enough broadband high speed Internet connection to allow them access to online lesson and student files? There are also faculty time issues that may need to be addressed. Workload issues should not be underestimated (Brown, 2002). What are faculty time considerations for preactive and active phases of teaching online? Bartolic-Zlomislic and Bates (1999) found that instructing in the online format was more time consuming than traditional face to face teaching due to the larger amount of reading and writing and the interaction necessary via discussion boards and email contact. The time commitment for faculty to do an effective job of online teaching and to provide the appropriate levels of student interaction both with the group and with individual students can be formidable. Does the online instructor understand this time commitment and is he/she able to devote the time to teach the online course effectively?

Another *instructor* need may be in the area of training and development for providing online pedagogies. For example, if a faculty feels that they need to provide or develop a streaming video or to develop a voice narrated PowerPoint lecture, is there training available to assist them in the production of these pedagogies? Is there training for the learning management system or for any new software that may need to be employed for the betterment of the learning opportunities? Addressing instructor needs in the preactive phases provides the opportunity to deal with issues prior to the course initiation making it more likely that the instructor will maximize student learning opportunities.

There may also be needs of the *profession.* Many professions have governing organizations that establish standards and set criteria for entry into a profession and for the education and training by an institution. These serve as expectations and guiding values of performance in the areas of content and contact hours for training and education. They can also serve as minimum standards of practice that must be taken into consideration when program and course scope and sequences are developed. What are the standards and are they constant or are they dynamic? Have they changed or are they changing in the near future? If they are going to change, is it relevant to address them in the current program?

There is also a *situational analysis* that needs to be considered in a needs assessment. Where and how will learners apply new knowledge and in what possible venues? An example may be the teaching of an instructional design course or an instructional methods program may seem universal as the basic concepts and tenants are consistent in the ISD models. However, if you were teaching a group of nurse educators how to develop instruction versus a group of elementary teachers, it may be approached differently. The needs of the nurses and where and how they are going to apply the knowledge and skills attained is different than where and how a group of elementary educators would apply the course concepts. The basic foundations of the curriculum are consistent; however the application is unique to the two professions.

Additionally, the instructional designer needs to assess the mission of the sponsoring organization and assure the training is in line with the overall mission? What are the resources of the organization? How will the knowledge and skill of the course be used in conjunction with other courses? How will the knowledge and skill be utilized in the professional setting and in what context? Each of the answers to these questions can again guide the designer in establishing appropriate curriculum and online learning materials and pedagogies.

Online needs assessment techniques may include surveys, interviews, focus groups, literature reviews and reports which are the same as conducting any instructional or research based project. The instructional designer needs to look at the questions to determine the appropriate needs assessment methods and strategies. From the question, the designer can then choose the appropriate data collection technique necessary to adequately address those needs. This assessment process is similar to any quantitative or qualitative research project. Some questions are best answered with a review of existing documents (i.e. existing organizational policies, accreditation requirements or written standards) others are best answered by interviewing organizational leaders, learners, or instructors. Some questions may require the use of a larger survey type assessment tool to gain the proper information. The proper tool is at the discretion of the instructional designer. The key to gathering more complete and appropriate data is to triangulate needs assessment techniques. This requires that the designer use a variety of needs assessment techniques and tools to address the questions. If the designer simply focuses on one method, he may not receive the entire picture of information necessary to make an informed decision. Triangulating allows him to apply several methods that validate the information assuring a more accurate picture of the true need of a given educational or training need for all concerned.

NEEDS ASSESSMENT TOOLS AND TECHNIQUES

Needs Assessment is crucial to improving the impact of programs. Educational programs are expensive to design and deliver. We must be sure that the program is actually addressing a real need existing in the learner or the time and effort is wasted. Identifying needs is the critical root of all effective programs. How can an educational program be developed if you are not really sure what the learner actually needs? How can an educational program be evaluated/measured without knowing what it was intended to produce?

The term "Needs" is used in very different ways. It can mean a gap in performance or competence. Experts or legal authority set a standard and "need" means some measured/observed gap or deficiency in the learner in regard to this established norm. "Need" can also refer to a felt or expressed desire or interest. Desires or wants that have been measured or expressed to program designers, but not arising out of gaps that have been measured. At other times the word "need" refers to basic developmental needs that are linked to tasks that occur at various points in adult development. The key is that we must determine what we mean by the word "need" before we can begin to look for "needs." This is because the definition determines the data needed and because the data determines the tools needed.

Based upon your definition of "needs", determine the type of information, or data, you will need to identify the "needs" that actual exist in the targeted learners. Will you need information or data that grows out of learner or expert observations and measurements? If yes, then you will need quantitative data that usually takes form of numbers, test results, statistics. Will you need data that grows out of learner or expert perceptions? If yes, then you will need qualitative data that usually takes the form of interviews, focus groups, etc. The program planner must choose the "tools" that will yield the type of information or data needed to discover the actual needs. Whatever the tools decided upon, it is always a good idea to triangulate the tools. Data from several sources that overlaps increases validity of findings and conclusions, but realize that needs assessment is crucial, but expensive.

Some "TOOLS" for Needs Assessment

Research show that most organizations rely on the "big 4" tools to fulfill the needs assessment process:

1. Management or Government Directives: In other words, new regulations and/or management dictate determine the "need" driving the educational program. Thus the "need" is not really uncovered by needs assessment tools. Yet even when such directives drive a program, a program planner or course developer should consider doing an actual needs assessment, if not to identify the need, then to better clarify existing learner levels. The strength of this form of "needs assessment" is strong management support and clarity of program purpose. A weakness is that the program designed may not be address the actual "need" in the targeted learners.
2. Standardized Tests: This approach to needs assessment uses established diagnostic tools to uncover gaps in knowledge and skills in the targeted learners. The use of "pre-tests" is a common way to discover gaps in knowledge or skills. The strength of this form of "needs assessment" is that it is easy to use and standardized. Many tests are available from which to choose. A weakness is that many have validity and reliability concerns.
3. Analysis of Records: This approach to needs assessment looks at pre-existing documents such as work records, management reports, accident records, etc. Such work-related data provides insights into possible areas needing educational interventions. The strength of this approach is that it doesn't require additional measures and usually the programmer has ease of access. The weakness is that such an approach is very limited in focus (due to the nature of records available) and may not reflect current realities.
4. Questionnaires: This approach to needs assessment is the most frequent "tool" chosen for needs assessment. The strengths of this approach are that questionnaires reach many potential learners at little cost. Questionnaires avoid face-to-face expressions of views and thus avoid possible embarrassment and retaliation (a real fear in workplace learning contexts). Answers to questionnaires are easy to review and report. The weakness of questionnaires is that they are very difficult to construct in a way that provides valid and reliable results. Most questionnaires tend to channel responses from learners and thus provide a somewhat limited basis for decisions about programming. Another weakness is that many questionnaires are not given to a well chosen sample of potential learners and thus produce somewhat skewed info.

Beyond these four approaches, a number of other "tools" are useful for needs assessment in a variety of settings to gain both qualitative and quantitative data regarding needs (remember to triangulate).

1. Informal Interview: This is an unstructured method of obtaining answers to various questions and gaining information on various

topics. This tool is used to measure perceptions of learners or experts. The tool gathers qualitative information about needs and allows for open-ended responses and offers the change to explore unforeseen issues. The limitation of the approach is that it requires excellent interviewing and interpretive skills. Data analysis can be complicated and time consuming.

2. Personal Interviews: Gather information through direct verbal interaction between individuals in face-to-face or telephone conversations. Such an approach also measures perceptions of learners and experts and provides facts, opinions, and specific information about needs. Interviews are often used to measure specific attitudes and interests. Interviews can also be designed to allow for open-ended responses. The limitations are that this approach requires a standardized approach/interviewing schedule to obtain comparable data. It also tends to be time consuming and thus expensive.
3. Focus Groups: Gather information through direct verbal interaction between individuals in small group situation. This tool also measures perceptions of learners, experts, etc. Focus groups are essentially a group interview and thus reflect similar weaknesses as interviews, but do provide a different quality of information (whole of group input is greater than sum of the parts).
4. Nominal Group Technique: This is a form of focus group decision-making in which all suggestions related to a topic are recorded and ranked. This tool is used when contributions need to be encouraged and synergistic results from group involvement or commitment are desired. A limitation is the tool is that not all people will participate fully in the ranking process and the process can be quite time consuming. An example of nominal group technique is brainstorming discussed below.
5. Brainstorm Storming: This is a form of focus group approach in which group members (usually in a small group) spontaneously generate various ideas or descriptions of needs, with a facilitator providing support. This approach is used when quick responses are desired or needed, such as creating an initial list of possible educational needs. The limitation of this approach is that spontaneous responses may not always be accurate and some people may not want or be able to participate.
6. Advisory Council Input: This is an approach to needs assessment that asks an outside group to serve in an advisory capacity to the program planner (sometimes referred to as Professional Advisory Committees or PACs). The programmer then obtains advice, insight, or factual information from a group of people knowledgeable about an area or organization in order to evaluate ongoing or completed educational activities for the purpose of determining new needs. The limitation of this approach is that advisory council members may not truly represent all the areas of interest of the targeted learners for a program.
7. Consultants or Outside Experts: This approach to needs assessment draws upon professionals for advice when assessing needs or evaluating performance. While often providing useful data, this approach has weaknesses when used alone. Relying solely on an outside expert for advice on needs may reveal only that person's view or built-in bias. The targeted learners' real needs may differ considerably from those suggested by experts.
8. Games and Simulation Devices: This approach uses role-playing and is facilitated by some sort of board game or other device that allows for self-observation. Simulations help to determine a participant's knowledge about certain topics. A core problem with

games and simulations is that viable games or devices that will maintain participant interest are difficult to find or create, despite the marketing ploys used to market such tools

9. Competency Models: This is an approach to needs assessment that is essentially a diagnostic process involving three steps:
   - Development of a model of desired behaviors or competencies (through expert opinion)
   - Assessment of current practice & performance
   - Assessment of gaps
     - This tool is often used to identify needs before designing large scale programs, such as professional certification programs. While this tool generates a lot of useful data, it is a very costly approach and usually reserved for large scale programs.
10. Questionnaires: This approach involves a survey form, usually mailed, and is used to obtain a broad analysis of needs, interests, or opinions from a sampled group of potential learners. This approach is often limited in effectiveness because research reliability can be quite low at times. The rate of return frequently is quite low, while open-ended responses or added comments may be difficult to interpret.
11. Diagnostic Forms: This is an approach, where respondents, individually or groups, check on a form and/or prioritize answers, interests, or perceptions of need from a list of statements. A pre-test/post-test tool is example.
12. Interest or Attitude Inventory: This is a tool used to determine what participants or potential participants are interested in or their attitudes toward some area of concern. The problem is that interests/attitudes can change over short periods of time.
13. Content Analysis: This is the objective, systematic, and quantitative description or analysis of the contents of written materials to determine any trends or weaknesses indicative of educational needs. This tool is used for the analysis of materials representative of a group when past information can suggest current needs. The problem is that historical information may not portray current needs, it may be impossible to gain access to certain records, and the analysis process can be quite time consuming.
14. Critical Incidents Assessment or Task Analysis: This is an interview with a supervisor, judge, or someone knowledgeable about an individual to determine specific behavior patterns considered critical to a skill or behavioral area. It is useful in studies of leadership ability or potential. It can also be used for determining qualifications of individuals for instruction and in determining individual job behavior. It also has function to examine training needs in relation to job performance. There are inherent limitations as it may be difficult to obtain the cooperation of busy supervisors or persons in authority and it can be quite time consuming.
15. Peer Evaluation: This is the evaluation of behavior by an individual's peers to provide feedback on perceived training needs. It has value in assessing certain aspects of human behavior and job performance. It does however require trained observers with considerable skill and sensitivity if it is to produce reliable results as peers may not always report information accurately.
16. Supervisory Rating or Performance Appraisal: This is the ratings of an individual made by someone in a supervisory role. It is used to analyze individual performance, or training needs through the determination of performance gaps that can be interpreted as educational needs. Supervisors however may not always provide cooperation and this

method may provide a limiting single view of any issues.

TRANSLATING NEEDS INTO EDUCATIONAL LANGUAGE AND CONTENT

A core question that must be addressed by all program designers is how to design an educational intervention (program) to actually address the "needs" uncovered through Needs Assessment Tools (those we decided could best be met through educational interventions)? The proper answer is that educators must learn to "translate" the "NEEDS" into educational language as they seldom emerge in terms or language that lends itself to educational design. We must turn the needs into language conducive to curriculum development. This process of "translating" is also called "establishing objectives". Unfortunately, far too often objectives are developed simply to create "accountabilities" or "measurable behavioral outcomes". This is an unfortunate result of Behaviorism gone amuck. Objectives are intended to help us link needs to programs - this is the critical reason we develop objectives. Obviously this can't happen when curriculum is developed and **then** some objectives are developed to satisfy authorities.

There are a number of core elements in the "Establishing Objectives" sub-process. First, we must determine which "NEEDS" to actually address. This is an issue of program priorities and was discussed when we examined "needs assessment". Second. we must "translate" the chosen "NEEDS" into statements regarding the knowledge, skills, attitudes that must be gained in order to best meet the uncovered "NEEDS". Third, we must determine what broad areas of content are necessary to cover to achieve the knowledge, skills, and/or attitudes components of the established objectives. Let's examine each of these a bit more.

Most uncovered needs have knowledge components that explain, or operationalize, the need. Knowledge components refer to "thinking", the facts, information, and thought processes essential to performing a job or task. Such "knowledge" can involve knowing certain facts, comprehending concepts, applying what is known to practice, and synthesizing information from various sources. We must translate discovered needs into objectives by first asking what "knowledge" is required to address the need identified.

Most uncovered needs will also have skill components that define the skills that must be combined with knowledge to successfully address the need. These skills are issues of behavior or performance, the ability to behave in ways associated with successful job performance. Such skills can involve observing appropriate skills (observational learning, imitation), being able to perform the skills (practice), and turning skills into habits or automatic responses. We must translate needs into objectives by asking what "skills" are required to address the need identified.

Finally, most needs will also have attitude components that define the feelings that must be connected to knowledge and skills to successfully address the need. These attitudes are perceptions and perspectives we want to see in the learner, or feelings about performance adopted and voiced to others. Such attitudes can involve paying attention to training, valuing learning or training, and adopting new value systems and beliefs (like moving toward quality from quantity). We must translate needs into objectives by asking what "attitudes" are required to address the need identified.

Our first step is to try to "flesh" out each specific need according to the knowledge, skills, attitudes needed to satisfy the need. If you are not a content expert for the training, use interviews with content experts to try to identify appropriate knowledge, skills, and attitudes dimensions of the various identified needs. Once the knowledge, skills and attitudes have been established, the next step is to expand them into broad learning objectives. To do this, we must refine and expand the knowledge, skills, attitudes we have identified previously for each "need" through the use of descriptive verbs. Such verbs can be useful ways to clarify what we mean by a knowledge, skill or attitude. Examples of such verbs include the following:

- **Facts, Terms, Etc:** to arrange, to name, to define, to order, to duplicate, to recognize, to label, to recall, to match, to repeat, to memorize, to reproduce, etc.
- **Comprehending Concepts:** to classify, to recognize, to describe, to report, to discuss, to restate, to explain, to review, to identify, to sort, to tell, to locate, to translate, etc.
- **Synthesis & Application:** to apply, to operate, to choose, to practice, to demonstrate, to prepare, to schedule, to illustrate, to solve, to interpret, to use, to analyze, to differentiate, to appraise, to judge, to predict, to distinguish, to synthesize, to estimate, to value, to diagram, to test, to formulate, to write, to evaluate, etc.
- **Skills:** to balance, to stretch, to reach, to catch, to move, to use, to stop and restart, to measure, to set up, etc.
- **Attitudes:** to listen to, to reply, to attain, to perceive, to answer, to assume, to be alert to, to follow along, to support, to show tolerance of, to approve, to participate, to obey, to continue, to organize, to believe, to identify with, etc.

After expanding through verbs, we continue to "flesh-out" the learning objectives by determining the broad content tied to each of the expanded learning objectives. The key here is to think through what specific content is necessary to achieve each of the learning objectives you have identified and fleshed out for your program.

We've already seen how developing educational objectives from identified needs is really an issue of "translation work". The translating involved turning the needs into educational language through identifying the knowledge, skill, attitude components of each need, refining the objectives through the use of action verbs, and expanding the objectives through identifying underlying content linked to each objective. The final step involves fuller expansion of the content to be delivered through the curriculum. The content identified under the objectives (see final form) must be expanded in order to develop an educational program. Each of the content issues identified when establishing objectives must be expanded upon to discover the specific data needing to be known under the objective. This is where content experts can be handy and where further study on the part of the programmer is needed.

Once the identified content has been expanded, the program planner is ready to develop a rough outline of content needed for the program. This is an initial rough outline of content. As the program is further refined, the outline may expand or reduce, or get into a slightly different order before the design phase is complete. The goal at this stage is to summarize the broad content needed for the training intervention and getting it into an organized array. This step is where you get rid of overlaps between content intersecting various objectives (frequent situation). It is also where you get "hit" with all you are trying to address to meet the needs. Frequently it is here that you begin to decide on pre-requisites for training to reduce the material needed to be covered. Frequently it is here that you go back and become more realistic about what can actually be covered in your program.

NEEDS ASSESSMENT IN THE FOUR COURSE CATEGORIES

Placed within the context of the four course categories, *foundational courses, skills based courses, analysis/synthesis courses and hybrid courses,* the needs assessment can be operationalized to ground each of these courses to meet all concerned. The instructional designer needs to first identify the type of course that is going to be conducted, then conduct the needs assessments in light of that course. Applying the needs assessment schema to the four course types provides yet another lens to align the needs of all stakeholders with the specific course structure.

Needs Assessment and the Foundational Course

Foundational courses require course developers to develop the fundamental knowledge and in some cases skills. What are the fundamental concepts that need to be included? The online instructional designer needs to ascertain what content is foundational and how and when the learner will use this information. What information and content does the educational institution believe is vital? What does the profession and/or any accrediting bodies establish as foundational content? Much of this information can be derived through a review of existing documents that outline the professional directives and in some cases mandated by accreditation standards or education and training standards. This can be found through professional organizational web sites or through the published standards in accreditation documentation. Breaking these down can assist the instructional designer to first meet the needs of the profession.

Next the instructional designer needs to understand the situational context of the foundational course. In conjunction with the rest of the curriculum, how is the foundational course positioned within the curriculum? What and how will the participants utilize the foundational content and knowledge in future course work? If this is not ascertained, the instructor runs the risk of not providing the proper and complete foundational content that other courses and instructors rely upon for further knowledge and skill development. This may foul the programmatic scope and sequence of content. If the foundational course does not provide the complete body of information, then subsequent courses and instructors will need to provide this foundational information detracting from time dedicated to achieving their objectives. This can address the institutional needs and instructor needs.

The learner needs are addressed in a foundational course in a number of ways and through addressing several questions. What are the learner needs in achieving the foundational course objectives? The instructional designer needs to understand who and what the backgrounds of their learners are. This way they can tailor the foundational course to their needs. What foundational information does the learner already possess, if any? Where and how will the learner use the content in the course? What pedagogies can be provided given the student's access to technology (i.e., software, bandwidth Internet access) and technological capabilities?

One of the ongoing needs that are specific to the foundational course is assisting the student to understand the value of the information being learned. The information provided in a foundational course may appear to stand alone and the student may not understand the application or importance of the information being provided. They may not fully understand the situational context of the content to future courses or the application within the profession. It becomes important for the instructor to position the information so that the learner understands the value of the information and why it is important. (This will be discussed in greater depth under the Affective Domain section in this chapter.)

Needs Assessment and the Skills Based Course

As defined in Chapter 2, a skills based course is a course that provides physical and cognitive skills necessary for a course of study and/or to function within a profession or situation. Some examples may be those courses or trainings that focus on the cognitive (mental) or physical skills in nursing clinical, computer programming or the cognitive skills needed to conduct research. At first glance, the instructional designer may believe that skills cannot be taught or evaluated online and may limit their inclusion in the online course or program of study. The use of a skills based course needs assessment (which may require assessment through observation or task analysis) can assist in the preactive phase to guide the design of the online pedagogies and break through any misperceived ideologies surrounding teaching skills online.

What physical skills need to be included? What mental skills need to be included? The instructional designer at this point needs to simply address the skills that are needed and not view the perceived limitations of the online pedagogy at this point. Pedagogical decisions can be made at the time that we operationalize the needs into objectives. Again the designer needs to assess what skills the educational institution believes is vital? What skills do the profession and/or any accrediting bodies establish as essential? Much of this information can again be derived through existing professional documents and accreditation or education and training standards. First listing these cognitive and physical skills begins to put them into perspective. Breaking these down can assist the instructional designer to first meet the needs of the profession and then allow them to design appropriate online pedagogies to meet the skill goals and objectives.

The instructor needs in a skills based course are to be evaluated from both the technological capabilities and from the assessment of the instructor's skill in an area. Does the instructor possess the necessary skills to teach them? Does the instructor possess the necessary understanding of technology and technology based pedagogies to teach them online? The designer and the instructor, *who may be one and the same or may be two different people,* need to also assess the online and technological resources that are available for designing online pedagogies. Much of the time required to develop online teaching pedagogies goes into the production of online materials. In the needs assessment there is a need to align instructor technological and skills abilities with the available resources. The instructor also needs to conduct a personal inventory and decide what additional technological training is needed and then locate the training to assist them. This is again not a static process but a rather dynamic practice as technology is in constant change and new and exciting technological capabilities are always being developed. Even those instructors and designers who are technologically savvy need to stay current to new technological and online opportunities.

The instructional designer needs to understand the situational context of the skills based course. In conjunction with the rest of the curriculum, what skills and knowledge have already been taught and learned in other foundational courses as well as other skill based and analysis synthesis courses within the curriculum. What and how will the participants utilize the physical and cognitive skills both in future learning situations and application within the professional setting? Again a focus on the application of the skills will offer the student insight into the value of the skills to be learned.

Needs Assessment and the Analysis/Synthesis Course

Analysis/Synthesis Courses as defined in Chapter 2, are used to teach students to analyze a situation and engage in critical thinking and problem solving (Fuller and Kuhne, 2008). These problem solving skills are valuable in helping participants in an educational or a training situation to think and develop the ability to analyze new information and to be able to synthesize or apply the knowledge in new situations. This is vital as most knowledge and the application of that knowledge is not static but ever changing and dynamic in most professions. The needs assessment in an analysis/synthesis course is different as the knowledge and skills may not always be as tangible as in the foundational or the skills based courses. The objectives attained are in learning the knowledge and skills but are more involved in using higher order thinking processes to apply the content in different venues that the student may find themselves working.

The instructional designer needs to again ascertain what the learner has already been exposed to in the areas of knowledge and skill and what additional foundational knowledge is necessary. The instructor/designer also needs to understand how the learner will apply the analysis and synthesis of the content. This affords greater insights and a greater likelihood that the content will meet the needs of the participants involved in the online education and training.

The ability to analyze and synthesize information and content is a skill set in and of itself and one that the educational institution or in a training situation, an organization may have need for participants to attain. The designer needs to assess what the specific analysis and synthesis skills are that are necessary for the learner to attain. The professional standards need to also be assessed to understand what skills in this area are required for success.

Instructor ability to design pedagogies and to facilitate instructor to student and student to student interactions in both the synchronous and asynchronous arena is a vital online skill. This is an instructor skill that needs to be developed. The ability to facilitate a discussion in a face-to-face program is important. This same ability in the online arena is even more paramount. The interactions in the analysis synthesis type course are designed to have the student interact with the material in such a way to scrutinize all angles of the content and application. The careful facilitation through discussion boards or virtual chat rooms directs and guides the students to completely analyze and synthesize the material. The instructor needs to be able to properly guide the students through all aspects of the analysis and synthesis through careful facilitation, using guiding questions and probing pedagogies. As Beaubine (2002) discusses, the instructor needs to perturb the system. The instructor again needs to take a careful personal assessment inventory to develop these synchronous and asynchronous online facilitation skills.

Needs Assessment and the Hybrid Course

A hybrid course as discussed in Chapter 2 includes a combination of the foundational, skills and analysis/synthesis courses and the nature of the course necessitates a blending of techniques to facilitate online learning through instruction, interaction and assessment. The first thing for an instructor to realize in a hybrid course is that it has components and qualities of the first three courses. There may be elements of the course that are foundational. There may be skills based components that are incorporated and there may be sections of the content that require analysis/synthesis. The instructional designer needs to identify which elements of the content are where in the program and then integrate the needs assessment as with the other course types. Careful attention needs to be taken in assessing all elements of the hybrid course to assure that the needs of all stakeholders: the learners, the institutional administrators, the instructor and the professional employers, as discussed previously are met.

Additionally as discussed in Chapter 2, the concept of hybrid learning also takes on the elements of blended learning or a combination of face to face and online. This again can be a very powerful way to learn as it includes the positive elements of both the traditional face to face and the self-directed nature of online learning pedagogies. Needs assessment is vital in a blended or hybrid course to understand what elements of the traditional and online are to meet each of the stakeholder's interests. Many times the institution structures a blended learning for administrative reasons such as classroom availability or cost factors. The instructional designer needs to understand the institutional needs first and then combine the answers with the data from the other needs assessment questions to maximize the learning opportunity.

In addition to addressing the learner needs as discussed in this chapter, the instructional designer needs to assess what components of the course will be best served in the online and what will maximize learning in the face to face component to provide the greatest level of clarity in teaching (Wlodkowski, 2008). The decisions of what to include in the online and what to present in the traditional can go a long way to providing this type of instructional clarity. Instructor issues also play a role in conjunction with the institution to collaborate on scheduling online and face to face components, especially if there is a classroom scheduling consideration. These issues also have impact on the scope and sequencing of online and face to face teaching and learning. This generally takes some coordination with the registrar or those charged with room availability. Once all the needs have been established the objectives can be set for the different course types.

Personal Reflection Suggestion

1. *How has needs assessment been approached in your organization?*
2. *What implicit beliefs exist in the division regarding the definition of "need" and the type of data needed to identify needs.*
3. *Is there a preferred tool or approach to identifying needs?*
4. *Where could better needs assessment help in recent program development efforts?*

REFERENCES

Akengin, H. (2007). Opinions of prospective social studies teachers on the use of information technologies in teaching geographical subjects. *Journal of Instructional Psychology*, *35*(2), 126–139.

Bartolic-Zlomislic, S., & Bates, A. (1999). Investing in online learning: Potential benefits and limitations. *Canadian Journal of Communication*, *24*(3), 349–366.

Bernard, R. M., Abrami, P. C., Lou, Y., Borokhovski, E., Wade, A., & Wozney, L. (2004). How does distance education compare with classroom instruction? A meta-analysis of the empirical literature. *Review of Educational Research*, *74*(3), 379–439. doi:10.3102/00346543074003379

Brooks, J. G., & Brooks, M. G. (1993). *In Search of Understanding: The Case for Constructivist Classrooms*. Alexandria, VA: Association for Supervision and Curriculum Development.

Cavanaugh, C., Gillan, K. J., Kromrey, J., Hess, M., & Blomeyer, R. (2004). *The effects of distance education on K–12 student outcomes: A meta-analysis*. Naperville, IL: Learning Point Associates.

Cavanaugh, C. S. (2001). The effectiveness of interactive distance education technologies in K–12 learning: A meta-analysis. *International Journal of Educational Telecommunications*, *7*(1), 73–88.

Cradler, J., McNabb, M., Freeman, M., & Burchett, R. (2002). How does technology influence student learning? *Leading and Learning with Technology*, *29*(8), 46–56.

Delgado, A. R., & Prieto, G. (2003). The effect of item feedback on multiple-choice test responses. *The British Journal of Psychology*, *94*, 73–85. doi:10.1348/000712603762842110

Fuller, R. G., & Kuhne, G. W. (2008, January). Fostering Meaningful Interaction in Health Education Online Courses: Matching Pedagogy To Course Types. *International Journal of Information and Communication Technology Education, 4*(1).

Hobbs, V. (2004). *The promise and the power of online learning in rural education*. Arlington, VA: Rural School and Community Trust.

Hunter, M. (1982). *Mastery Teaching*. El Segundo, CA: T.I.P. Publications.

Kinney, M. (2008, July 17). What the Army Taught Me About Teaching. *Inside Higher Ed*. Retrieved January 1, 2009, from http://www.insidehighered.com/views/2008/07/17/kinney

Knowles, M. S. (1984). *Andragogy in action*. San Francisco: Jossey-Bass.

Krathwohl, D. R., Bloom, B. S., & Masia, B. B. (1964). *Taxonomy of Educational Objectives, the Classification of Educational Goals. Handbook II: Affective Domain*. New York: Longman.

Kulhavy, R. W., & Stock, W. A. (1989). Feedback in written instruction: The place of response certitude. *Educational Psychology Review, 1*(4), 279–308. doi:10.1007/BF01320096

Moore, M. G., & Kearsley, G. (1996). *Distance Education: A systems view*. San Francisco: Wadsworth Publishing Company.

Mory, E. (1992). The use of informational feedback in instruction: Implications for future research. *Educational Training Research and Development, 40*(3), 5–20. doi:10.1007/BF02296839

Narciss, S. (1999). *Motivational effects of the informativeness of feedback.* Paper presented at the annual meeting of the American Educational Research Association, Montreal, Quebec, Canada.

Olivia, P. F. (2005). *Developing the curriculum*. Boston: Pearson Education Inc.

Olt, M. R. (2002). Ethics and distance education: Strategies for minimizing academic dishonesty in online assessment. *Online Journal of Distance Learning Administration, 5*(3).

Richeki, R., Field, D., & Faxon, M. (2001). *Instructional design competencies: The standards* (3rd ed.). Syracuse, NY: ERIC Clearing on Information and Technology.

Rothwell, W. J., & Kazanas, H. C. (2004). *Mastering the instructional design process: A systematic approach*. San Francisco: Pfeiffer.

Tallent-Runnels, M. K., Thomas, J. A., Lan, W. Y., Cooper, S., Ahern, T. C., & Shaw, S. M. (2006). Teaching courses online: A review of the research. *Review of Educational Research, 76*(1), 93–135. doi:10.3102/00346543076001093

Walker, C. (n.d.). *So you've decided to develop a distance education class.* Faulkner University. Retrieved from http://technorhetoric.net/6.2/coverweb/de/walker/index.htm

Waxman, H. C., Lin, M.-F., & Michko, G. M. (2003). *A meta-analysis of the effectiveness of teaching and learning with technology on student outcomes*. Naperville, IL: North Central Regional Educational.

Wesley, P. W., & Buysee, V. (2001). Communities of practice: Expanding professional roles to promote reflection and shared injury. *Topics in Early Childhood . Education, 21*(2), 114–124.

White, C. (2002, November). Creating a world of discovery by thinking and acting globally in social studies: ideas from New Zealand. *Social Studies*, 262–266. doi:10.1080/00377990209600176

Wiggins, G., & McTighe, J. (1998). *Understanding by design*. Alexandria, VA: Association for Supervision and Curriculum Development.

Zhao, Y., Lei, J., Yan, B., Lai, C., & Tan, H. (2005). What makes the difference? A practical analysis of research on the effectiveness of distance education. *Teachers College Record, 107*(8), 1836–1884. doi:10.1111/j.1467-9620.2005.00544.x

Chapter 8
Preactive Stage:
Behavioral Objectives and Lesson Planning

ALIGNING NEEDS ASSESSMENT WITH BEHAVIORAL OBJECTIVES

Once all needs assessment schema have been conducted and analyzed as discussed in the previous chapter, the instructional designer can set the objectives. Even if a course or training is one that has been conducted previously, a needs assessment is necessary to assure that the content is meeting all the stakeholders prescribed needs. Most content is not static and requires a reevaluation to be certain that the information and the methodologies being taught are relevant to current practice and needs of all stakeholders.

To establish objectives for a course or training, the instructional designer first needs to focus the results of the needs assessment, to understand what the online training and/or education should accomplish. In other words what are the final goals or outcomes that need to be achieved by the online program? The instructor and designer should step back and look at the list of needs and then envision what the learner's performance should look like at the end of the education or training. What knowledge, skills, abilities and attitudes should the participants be able to leave the online training being able to do and apply? The designer at this point should create a listing of all that the education should achieve.

With the needs assessment having been completed and the instructional designer understanding and having a vision of the needs of all stakeholders and how they integrate with the specifics of the four course types, the objectives can be established and operationalized. To operationalize the learning objective is to look at the each of the needs lists as established and then to have that listing culminate in a set of well defined the objectives. In the online teaching and learning environment this means to establish the objective that is necessary to meet the needs assessment without consideration to any perceived online pedagogical limitations. The objective is established and then the proper pedagogy to address that objective can be developed. The designer at this point should not consider the online pedagogies or the perceived limitation of teaching online. Many online instructors will develop their objectives based upon perceived

DOI: 10.4018/978-1-61520-865-4.ch008

boundaries of the online arena. The instructional designer should not place any perceived restrictions to the online teaching, trying to design an online pedagogy and then writing an objective to fit. The objectives should be established first then the appropriate online pedagogies can be determined to meet those objectives. Don't allow the use of an online learning platform to drive the objectives. Set the objectives then design the online pedagogies.

There are some educators and trainers who believe that creating a set of objectives or as some define behavioral objectives (as we are defining the behavior that we wish the participant to leave the program having attained) is just semantics and not worthy of their time. Many instructors just design their content from what they think or what is felt to be important. This is false thinking as the objectives are an outgrowth from the needs assessment and serve as the cornerstone for the rest of the preactive phase. If the objectives are properly crafted, the rest of the preactive phase of planning and designing online lessons becomes clear and everything can fall into place.

Bloom's Taxonomy

Once the needs assessment is completed and the designer is satisfied that all information has been gathered, he can begin the process of developing and establishing the objectives for the program. In planning and developing the objectives for each of the four course types, the designer must take into consideration how they will integrate with the different learning realms or as Bloom (1956) and Krathwohl, Bloom, & Masia (1964) developed, the three domains of learning. Bloom discusses three domains of learning that are not only applicable in the traditional face to face setting but also in the online environment (Figure 1). The three domains are cognitive, psychomotor and affective. Each of these plays a significant role in establishing the objectives in the four online course types.

Figure 1.

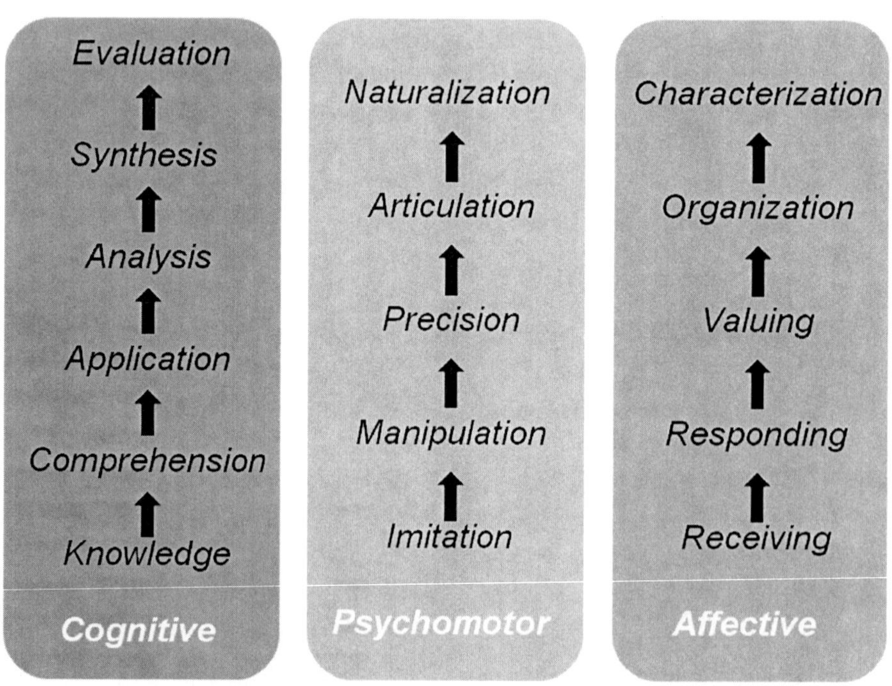

COGNITIVE DOMAIN

The cognitive domain deals with knowledge, concepts, information and facts. It involves the emphasis from simple recall to complex synthesis and the creation of new ideas. The cognitive deals with six levels: knowledge, comprehension, application, analysis, synthesis and evaluation (Figure 1). Each of these levels is hierarchical in nature and is designed to build upon each other to achieve the most appropriate level of learning for the student.

Knowledge is the lowest level of the cognitive domain that generally involves memorization of information and facts required for instant recall. In the online course, these are considered the lowest level and serve as the foundation for scaffolding information and skills. One might have an objective in a foundation course that students are able to define key terms. The memorization of these terms is important not for rote learning but for use with higher order thinking skills. They can serve as foundational. Key verbs that are used to help the instructor to design pedagogies and understand if these objectives are being met are: identify, define, list, name and recognize.

Comprehension is at the next level in the cognitive that allows students to understand and interpret received information. This level focuses on the ability to understand the meaning behind information and concepts. In a nursing course it is the ability to interpret blood pressure and pulse and their effect on the heart and other body systems. It is more than simply knowing what a blood pressure is but begins to apply the concept at a higher level. Key terms that are used at this level are: summarize, describe, evaluate, explain, interpret.

Application is the third level in which students are to relate the concepts that they are to learn in a real life situation. The application of the concept becomes important as the student is to apply the information in new and unique situations. Students in a finance class will take the concepts of financial interpretation and apply them in different circumstances and have the ability to understand market trends and economic data. Key terms used in the application level are: explain, calculate, apply, and demonstrate.

Analysis is the level that requires students to take something that is whole and break it down into its parts. By breaking something down into its pieces, the student is able to thoroughly understand the construction and formation of a thing. In an online research class a student needs to be able to read through research articles and interpret the information (application level) and have the ability to analyze the research or break it down into its parts to determine the value of the information and to know if that information is valuable or not to their setting. This is an important skill, one that requires a higher order thinking process. Key terms in this level are: discriminate, outline, identify, differentiate, and distinguish.

Synthesis requires that the student is taking parts and building a whole. This works generally in harmony with objectives written at the *analysis* level. Here students can take the components that they previously analyzed and apply them or use them in a different venue. This is a higher order of thinking that allows them to further interpret concepts and information and apply them in a new or different situation. The research student above who has interpreted the information that he obtained through analyzing a research article is now able to synthesize and apply those concepts in his own research design. This becomes important for the student as they are now able to use the information that has been learned at other levels and put into application. This helps the student to begin to see the value of the information and works in harmony with the affective domain (which will be discussed in the coming sections). Key terms used are: organize, determine, create, compose, design, prepare, devise and formulate.

Evaluation is the highest level that works again with the affective domain as it places a worth on the information and concepts or knowledge that has been learned and applied. The student is able to justify why and how the information is applied in new and different situations. They use judgment and evaluation of situations and circumstances, actions and outcomes for personal understanding and application of the knowledge, concepts and information in their own life situations and venues. This is then more likely that they will retain the information as it becomes real to them. Key terms that assist the designer and instructor are: examine, assess, evaluate judge, justify, compare, appraise, contrast and critique.

The higher the level that can be achieved in the cognitive domain, the greater the retention and the deeper the learning is likely to occur. It is however up to the student to place that value. It is the instructor and the designer's role to develop objectives that will maximize the opportunity for students in the online courses and trainings to reach these individual learner goals.

PSYCHOMOTOR DOMAIN

The psychomotor domain emphasizes physical movement, coordination, manipulation and/or control of objects, principally through motor control. In the online arena and using the four course types model, there are also mental skills that emphasize the ability to manipulate, coordinate and control the application of concepts. The psychomotor domain also has hierarchal levels as does the cognitive. In the cognitive domain, the different levels are scaffolded to build on each other but can stand alone as the terms used define the level of achievement for each objective. In the psychomotor domain, the different hierarchical levels are directly linked and the overall goal with each skill objective is for the learner to achieve the highest level with each objective. The psychomotor domain has five levels: imitation, manipulation, precision, articulation and naturalization. Let's take an example to explain the value of this. If you have ever taught someone to drive a car you can appreciate and understand the psychomotor domain. As drivers, most of us have achieved what Bloom would term the *naturalization* of the driving process. When we get in our car, we rarely think through each step of getting from one place to the other, starting the car, putting the car into gear, accelerating, when to signal, when to break, steering, looking in our mirror etc. These are all things that have become second nature over the years of driving. The new driver however thinks of every step and is working toward becoming *you* as a driver, someone who is naturalized in the process. To get to this point the learner needs to work and learn the skills in each of the five levels first to finally achieve the naturalization process.

Imitation is the level at which the student is able to mimic what is demonstrated by instructors. The instructor serves as a model of how the skill is to be performed. This requires that the instructor model the proper way to conduct the skill. This also requires that the instructor pay attention to the text book ways to conduct the skill so as to not demonstrate inappropriate or unintended habits. In this realm, the learner will do exactly what is modeled for him as this becomes the only example for duplication.

Manipulation is the ability to work with a skill and begin to perform the skill through following instructions and beginning to perform the skill through practice. Students may begin to internalize and making the skill their own. Practice is the key as they have not yet mastered but they are learning through trial and error and understand when the skill is being conducted correctly and more importantly when it is being done incorrectly.

Precision is the level at which the student begins to refine the skill and develop accuracy with the process of conducting the skill. The level to which they become accurate with the skill is related to the amount and quality of the time that they can practice.

Articulation is the level where the student is able to coordinate multiple components of the skill fitting all elements together to function as one. Precision for all of these skill steps has been achieved and fits it into their surroundings with proficiency.

Naturalization is the final level of the psychomotor domain in which the learner can perform the skill naturally, without much thought to the process. This is the overall goal with any physical or mental skill. The student, when presented with a situation where the skill must be put in place, finds that he/she knows what to do and does it without much thinking.

Whether teaching a cognitive or a physical skill, most teachers are happy if they are able to assist their students to achieve at the precision level. This is likely due to the limited instructional time that they have with the learner. They set the stage for the learner to develop a level of precision so that they are able to move on and eventually develop the articulation and naturalization levels of skill performance. When a new driver takes his driving test he has hopefully developed somewhere between the precision and the articulation levels enough to successfully pass his physical driving exam. It is unlikely at this point that he is naturalized. This will take some time. Naturalization is dependent on the complexity of the skill and the number of components that must be integrated together. The online environment may not suffer the same time limitations that the traditional face-to-face classroom does as the learner is operating in their own time frames and may devote more time and effort to learning the skill.

AFFECTIVE DOMAIN

The affective domain as presented by Krathwohl, Bloom, & Masia, (1964) is the domain that emphasizes emotional feelings, attitudes and why the student should value the knowledge (cognitive domain) and skills (psychomotor domain) that are being learned. If the affective domain is not given the same importance and consideration as the first two, the danger is that the learner will simply learn the material to satisfy course outcomes assessments such as a test and then promptly forget the knowledge and/or skill. The highest levels as described above in each of the other domains cannot be attained unless the affective domain is given the same significance in the teaching and learning process. The affective domain provides the learner with the reasons and shows where the knowledge and skill can be applied in their life. In other words where are they going to use this? The utilization may be different from learner to learner, but the instructor and designer is providing the opportunity to afford this. This is consistent with the tenants of the constructivist concept that focuses on and emphasizes the learner making meaning of what is being learned, as well as consider the concept benefits. According to Cameron White (2002):

Constructivism encourages a more student–centered focus to teaching and learning, whereby students are responsible for making sense of their own learning, with the help of perceptive teachers and the use of powerful strategies ... Constructivism really comes down to the teacher's building on what the students already know and encouraging them to become more responsible for their own learning, while integrating the essential skills of critical thinking and problem solving (p. 264-265).

According to Akengin (2007) technology allows students to engage in the process of learning, which coincides with the basic tenets of constructivism (p. 128). Akengin (2007) goes on to say that, "use of technology in constructivist learning environments is both significant and necessary in order to create interactive learning environments".

The Affective domain could be described as the *forgotten domain* as many instructors focus on the cognitive and psychomotor, but as time becomes limited they fail to allot time to this area. Another reason that many instructors and designers fail to focus on this area is that it is not as measurable as the other two. The objectives in the cognitive and the psychomotor are easily measured with a knowledge exam or project assessment or through a skills demonstration. The affective domain is not as tangible and the assessments are less definitive; however it works in harmony for the instructor and student with the psychomotor and cognitive domains. In viewing the components of the affective domain, some crossover to the psychomotor and the cognitive domains are evident as this synchronization is present. The Affective domain consists of five levels of interest and value from simplest to most complex: receiving, responding, valuing, organization and characterization.

Receiving is the first level and the most basic as it focuses on the importance of learning and strives for a willingness to focus attention on the learning. In the online the students willingness to center attention on the weekly activities and to interact with the material, the asynchronous and synchronous communication is an example of this. Measurable words that assist the designer are: listen, observe, focus, concentrate and inquire.

Responding is the next level that involves the willingness to actively participate in the online learning process. It also focuses on the learner's motivation and satisfaction in participation in the learning. This could be described as *student presence* in the online arena. Not so dissimilar to instructor presence, student presence is the level of interaction that the student is demonstrating in the online learning platform. The key terms that the designer uses in this level are: answers, assists, complies, participates, discusses, performs, practices, presents, reads, recites, reports, selects, writes.

Valuing is the third level which involves the value that a learner places on the behavior or the object being learned. Through the internalization of the concepts and skills this ranges from a simple acceptance to a higher level commitment. The internalization is demonstrated in the learner's outward behavior surrounding the learning. For the student this can become motivational. The key words used in this level are: appreciate, value, differentiate, justify, select, proposes, shares and demonstrates.

Organization is the forth level which is more complex integrating different values and belief systems about the learning and the conflicts that may arise. The learner prioritizes their beliefs through the process of comparing and contrasting elements of the learning to understand how they relate. This analysis and synthesis process serves the learner to reconcile the differences that exist and to culminate a personal value system surrounding the learning. Key words that are used are: compare, defend, synthesize, recognize, organize, integrate, combines and generalizes.

Characterization is the highest level and once reached directs the learner behavior. This characterization drives future acts and reactions in a manner that is consistent with their personal value systems. By working with the values and attitudes at this level the student integrates the knowledge and skills into their own value system that directs their actions in a highly consistent manner. Key words at this level are: act perform, practice, demonstrate and influence. It should be noted that while many of the key words used at each of the levels appear to be redundant to other domains and levels, it is the intent of the instructor as to which domain and level they are integrated that is important in the preactive phase.

A Revision of Bloom's Taxonomy

In 1995 a group of curriculum theorists, cognitive psychologists, and testing and assessment experts met to revisit and revise the original work of Bloom's Taxonomy (Anderson et. Al, 2001). This meeting resulted in modifications to the original work of Bloom (1956). While much of the original framework described above was held consistent, some changes occurred. The summary of changes is depicted in Figure 2. The significant changes are the addition of the word "understand" which previously was seen as unmeasurable. The authors felt that over the forty years since the inception of the taxonomy that the term had taken on many connotations to educators. Wiggins and McTighe (1988) believed that when you truly understand something you can explain, interpret, apply, will have perspective, can empathized and have self-knowledge about it. One other significant change is the reversal of evaluation being the highest level of the taxonomy. In the revised version, it has been relegated to the second position behind "create" which is synonymous with the ability to "synthesize" from the original work. These changes overall may appear minor in nature, but reflect what the authors believe is the upgrading of the taxonomy to reflect the needs of the times. The efficacy of the revised work is yet to be realized over the 1956 version. However, both versions serve to assist online educators in creating effective objectives and lessons.

LINKING THE THREE DOMAINS TO THE FOUR COURSE TYPES

Linking the three domains of learning to the four course types aids in adding clarity in developing objectives to fit each of the courses and meet the needs of all stakeholders. This serves as a type of design engine that can provide the designer and the instructor with a level of clarity that can then be passed onto the learner as the course unfolds. As has been stated each of the courses has a specific direction that is enhanced by integrating the clarity of the three domains. The following Venn diagram chart (Table 1) helps to bridge the three domains with the four course types illustrating the overlap and assimilation of each.

WRITING OBJECTIVES

While some instructors may not see the relevance of objectives, writing objectives may be the most

Figure 2.

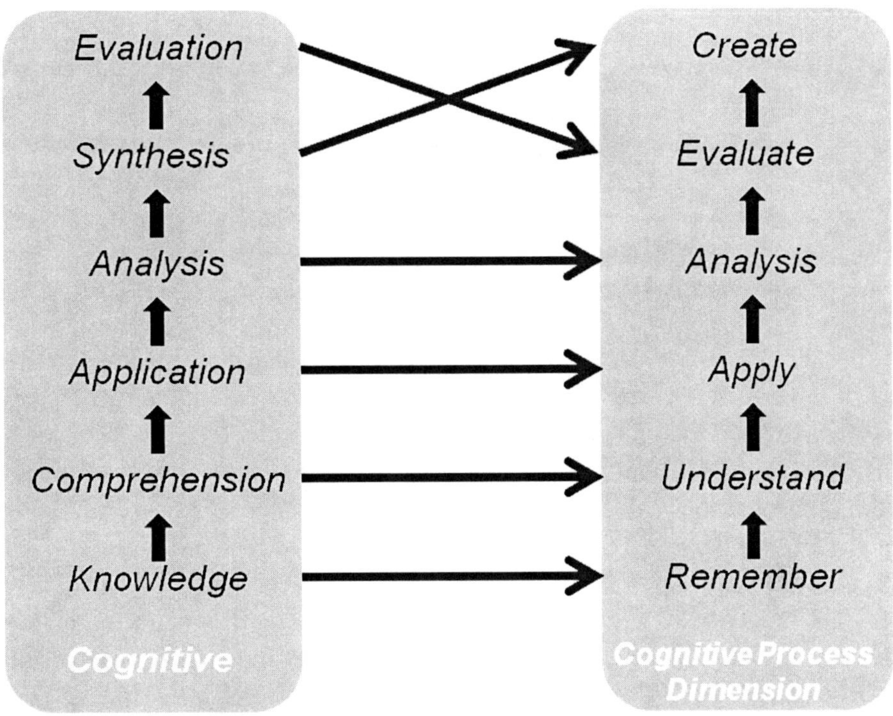

Table 1. Venn diagram chart

Domains/Course	Foundational Courses	Skill Based Courses	Analysis/Synthesis Courses	Hybrid Courses
Cognitive Domain	*Initial presentation of concepts and information vital to the program of study and the discipline*	*Within each skill based course there is information, concepts and knowledge that are necessary for the understanding of the skill and to assess whether the skill is being performed properly and in the correct venue. Focus also centers on where and how to apply the mental and physical skills*	*Background information, concepts and knowledge of particular sides of issues is vital to properly analyze situations and to synthesize of put them into new context. It is also vital to have the base information to properly problem solve and make proper decisions based all the information, knowledge and concepts.*	*Integrates the knowledge, concepts and essential information into each aspect of the foundational, skill and analysis/synthesis components of the course.*
Psychomotor Domain	*Within each foundational course, there may be basic mental or physical skills that provide the foundation for future courses. This may be writing skill or computer skill or other.*	*The skills taught in a skill based course work through the hierarchy of this domain to assist the student toward naturalization of both mental and physical skills to be used outside the boundaries of the course.*	*The analysis/synthesis works with a level of mental and physical skill to collect and gather information vital to a proper analysis of information with the ability to combine it into the learners own world. The goal in this course is to assist the student toward a naturalization of this process combined with the career, profession or venue of the information*	*Works to integrate the naturalization of the mental and physical skills in the analysis/synthesis, foundational and skill components of a the course.*
Affective Domain	*The goal in the foundational course is for the student to perceive the worth of the concept, knowledge and information being learned and where this will be utilized in the future (courses and profession). This provides the basis and reasoning for the learner to retain the information.*	*In the skills based course, learners need to understand why, where and how the skill will be applied and employed for the motivation to attain the skill and to understand where it will be employed.*	*The goal here is to help the learner explore all aspects or sides of issues for the them to compare and contrast ultimately influencing their own thinking and to make their own meaning to the analysis and synthesis of ideas (constructivist).*	*Focuses to bring all understanding of what skills, foundational information and the ability to analyze and combine them all into their learning and practice and the ability to understand where it will be utilized and why it is all of value to the learner.*

important step in the preactive phase of online teaching. If the designer has properly identified all the objectives that need to be included in the learning process, the rest of the preactive and active teaching phase becomes clearer and the process takes on a higher level of consistency. This better assures that the instructor designs lessons and assessment tools that are aligned with the needs assessments conducted and the overall intent of the online learning.

Course and program objectives are sometimes called behavioral objectives as they describe the desired behavior that the student should be able to exhibit at the end of the educational experience. They serve as a foundation for the rest of the online lesson plan and can serve as a logical flow of ideas which can generate online lesson pedagogies and assist in designing evaluation tools to measure student learning and attainment of the stated objectives. The objectives serve to guide the instructor during the planning in the preactive phase and assists in the completion of the rest of the plan and the design of learning activities and connections with the course content. It also assists the learner in having a better idea of what he/she is to learn and what is expected of him/her. This necessitates that the objectives and the outcomes of the education be posted online and communicated to the student at some point.

The objectives must conform to the following criteria:

- Written for the student
- Are measurable (i.e., use measurable terms)
- Are clearly stated and specific to be useable
- Includes Conditions of Performance (given or withheld)
- States Standards of Acceptable Performance (time, quantity and quality)

Objectives must be *written for the student* and should describe student behavior and not instructor behavior. By focusing on the student the instructor assures that the objective will reflect what the student will be like and learn by the end of the lesson. Writing for the student allows the designer to center the objectives squarely on student knowledge and skills attainment and on the desired outcomes and provides a level of clarity to the preactive phase. Many instructional designers will begin their objectives with "the student will be able to…" and then complete the sentence with the rest of the objective. This student based prefix to each objective guides the designer to focus the objectives on student outcomes and not instructor behavior or activity such as "the instructor will give the students a list."

Objectives must be *measurable*. For the objective to be of value to the instructional designer, it must be stated in measurable terms. These terms as described above in the three domains of learning, provide the direction for the remainder of the lesson. Measurable words are action verbs that describe what the learner should do. They will d*escribe the three domains of learning*, or they will *demonstrate* something in the scope of the online learning. They will be able to *examine* or *judge* or *compare* and *contrast* elements of the learning. These measurable words serve as a cornerstone for developing the lesson pedagogies and tell the designer what he is planning and measuring through the final assessment. It provides a logical roadmap for the designer and the instructor to follow. If this level of clarity is not present, then the designer runs the risk of not developing instruction that meets the needs assessment and may focus on something different that may not have been intended.

Objectives *must be specific and clearly stated* to be of value. Some objectives can appear to be functional but are not specific enough for the designer to know what the desired outcome may be; therefore he may not be able to use the objective to design learning activities nor assessment tools. The objective must be clearly written for the purpose to be of value and specific for the pedagogies to become clear.

Objectives must state the *conditions of performance*. This is what the instructor will give the student or withhold from the student in the learning process. The conditions of the objective can actually assist in defining the knowledge and skill to be obtained in certain circumstances. If you give a student a calculator you have defined the skill and knowledge that will unfold. However if you withhold the use of a calculator, this would require that the learner conduct the math on their own without an electronic aid which also defines the knowledge and skill to be attained as mental or physical. In the online learning environment, the instructor may provide a particular scenario or situation for discussion or they may withhold certain information that would require the student to analyze a situation. This can not only define the objective more clearly but can also differentiate the level of the domain to be attained. These are questions the designer should ask themselves.

What will the learner be provided? What will the learner be denied? Are their behaviors you are specifically trying to avoid and do the objectives deal with this.

Not all objectives will have a condition of performance. Many objectives have conditions of performance that may be implied. Example: if you wanted to have a student take a blood pressure you might include a statement that the student will be given a blood pressure cuff. This does not necessarily need to be stated as it becomes obvious and hence can be implied in the objective. Some instructors will attempt to insert a condition that may state, that after a lecture or after the student reads posted text material or given an instructor created and narrated PPT, the student will be able to.... The online instructor should avoid using things like the student will be provided with a PPT or will be given an article. These all border not on the goals and objectives that we want the student to accomplish but instructor behavior and are hence not necessary. The objective should describe student behavior and not the pedagogical opportunities. Choice of the instructional or teaching methods to achieve the objectives will come after the objectives are established.

The *standard of acceptable performance is* the final criteria for writing objectives. This establishes how well the student must perform and establishes the benchmark for success for both instructor and student. Standards of acceptable performance can fall into three types: time, quantity or quality. If one were to focus on an objective dealing with key boarding skills an objective may read: the student will be able to key 50 words per minute (quantity) for 5 minutes (time) with less than 3 errors (quality). Some performance objectives may not have all three and they again may be implied. In performing skills we generally want them to be conducted with 100% accuracy. If this is true, then it becomes implied. If you were teaching Accounting online and wanted a learner to be able to properly complete and develop a balance sheet given a worksheet of account balances (conditions) you would most likely not want that done with anything less than 100% accuracy. Using the 100% in this case becomes unnecessary as it is implied. If however in the needs analysis portion of the preactive phase, you have identified standards adjudicated by an outside agency that establish a standard of 86% accuracy or higher, then we should certainly build that in as it states the benchmark minimum standard to be attained by the learner. The key with writing objectives is to keep them simple and not to use extraneous words that could complicate the true intent of the objective. Keeping it simple makes them more useable when completing the remainder of the instructional plan in both the preactive and active teaching phases and ensures that the intent of the needs assessment is realized.

Writing Objectives in the Three Domains of Learning

In writing objectives you want to assure that they meet the needs of the stakeholders in the needs assessment. This requires that the designer analyzes the listing of needs in each area and then synthesizes those into objectives in the three domains. Let's look at an example. If we have an identified need that an accrediting body mandates that a particular program of study includes research methods and that the learners need to have knowledge and skill regarding quantitative and qualitative methodologies, a portion of our objective listing might look like this:

Cognitive Domain

- The student will be able to design focused research questions.
- The student will be able to determine and describe independent and dependent variables.

Psychomotor Domain

- The student will be able to calculate a two-tailed ANOVA and interpret the data using (given) SPSS software.
- The student will be able to perform electronic database searches using Boolean operators, in a manner that reflects understanding of key word searches, terminology, and the relationship among terms and concepts.

Affective Domain

- The student will be able to defend which statistical equation should be employed to prove a hypothesis and disprove a null hypothesis.

Let's assume that in the needs assessment portion of the preactive phase, you identified that participants need to be able to take a patient's blood pressure. An example skill objective might read something like:

- The student will be able to demonstrate the proper steps and procedures for taking a blood pressure.

In the online environment, one may believe that this is not an attainable objective as educators and trainers have certain "mental models" (Senge, 1990) about online education that might preclude us from moving forward in the design process. At this point that is not something that should be considered. The goal at this stage is to capture the need and to craft an objective that will match it. Then the instructional designer can consider the pedagogical options and opportunities to teach and evaluate the objective.

As has been stated, once the objectives have been written for all domains and cover all the identified needs for all stakeholders through the needs analysis, two things can be done. The instructional designer can design the online pedagogies that will serve to achieve those objectives and he can also design the evaluation process in both the summative and formative arenas. Since both are based on the written objectives it matters little which is done first in the preactive phase. In the next chapter we will focus on the development of the lesson plan and developing the evaluation process by operationalizing the behavioral objectives discussed in this chapter.

Personal Reflection Suggestion

Think of a course that you would teach online. Of the four course categories, which is it? How have or would you utilized objectives in the development of this online course? How can you address the three domains in this course, cognitive, psychomotor and affective? How are the objectives different in the four course categories?

LESSON PLANNING

Once you have listed and established the objectives the designer can now plan for the teaching and learning activities that will help the learner to achieve them to the level of success stated in the objectives. Lesson planning in the online arena can take on one of two methods. The instructional designer can utilize an offline plan first then develop the online activities from the plan or he can develop the online plan and activities directly into the shell prior to making that course shell available to the students. It is advisable however to create the content offline so the developer can maintain a stable copy of all materials and plans.

Whichever method is utilized the principles are the same. Lessons and activities must integrate clarity, learner engagement and active learning. Much of the course development process integrates the levels of interaction discussed in Chapter 4.

The designer in the preactive phase must plan for this active engaged learning by focusing on how the interaction with content, the instructor, other learners and the technology will be planned and developed. In order to provide clarity, lessons must be chunked (broken down into easily understood segments) and organized in a manner that can be easily understood and followed by the learners. This can take on a number of strategies and formats. Some instructors if teaching in a 15 week format will organize their lessons by the week. Others will use a two week method. If the online education or training does not have time constraints, instructors can utilize a competency model that allows the learner to work at their own pace. Lessons are then organized based on a logical break down of information and skills to be attained. Many times the lesson design utilizes a scaffolding technique where one lesson builds upon the previous lesson's knowledge, skills and values developed.

Introductory Focus

One of the first things that the lesson needs to do for the student is to provide an introductory focus. Madelyn Hunter (1982) discusses this in her lesson plan model as the design of an Anticipatory Set. An anticipatory set or introductory focus is a tool that is used to begin the lesson. It serves as a motivational tool that will help to get the student's mind focused on the learning and allows them to anticipate what is coming in the lesson. In the traditional classroom setting this may be a 2-5 minute activity designed to focus the learner's thinking. It can be a series of questions, or the review of a short video clip, the reading of a news story to illustrate not only an overview of the lesson but why it is important. In the online, this introductory focus can take on the form of an initial section in the weekly lesson posts that could be titled *Focus*. This is in addition to a weekly announcement although the introductory *Focus* can be included in the announcement. The weekly *focus* is part of an *expectation position*. It establishes what the lesson is about and helps the online learner develop a mindset of where the lesson is going and what they are going to learn and do. It can be an activity or a series of questions to focus students' interest which can be linked to previous material learned, that will set the tone for the instruction to come in this lesson. It can be as simple as telling students what this lesson is about and what will be done or it can include an opening activity that establishes a certain thinking pattern in the participants. It can relate to previous learning in this course or *foundational course* material from prior class work. If successful, the anticipatory set should help the online student get mentally and physically ready for the lesson.

Procedures

The procedure section of the plan is the actual instructional activities or pedagogies that are aligned with the established objectives. By reading the objective the designer can logically see a number of pedagogies that may be utilized to aid the learner to achieve the goal. Let's take an example. If you have the objective as listed above that *the student will be able to develop and describe independent and dependent variables* in a quantitative research study course there are some logical choices of activities and text that can assist the learner to understand this and can be built into an online lesson plan and course shell. A designer could reference and assign text book readings and post text material that describe independent and dependent variables. The designer could utilize a series of examples that demonstrate the independent and dependent variables. This can be presented asynchronously or in a synchronous virtual chat if the instructor deems appropriate. He/she could then add a series of activities submitted through email or for posting on a discussion board that would have the students utilizing sample research questions or scenarios to design independent and dependent variables. This could ultimately culminate in an exercise that would require the learners to set their own research ideas, with questions and then define the independent and dependent variables either for submission to the instructor via email or posted on an asynchronous discussion board. This most likely would serve to build or scaffold on previous lessons and continue building over several sessions.

Establishing expectations in online learning requires the instructor to provide both clarity and empathy (Wlodkowski 2008) so that students can understand what they are to do and how they are going to learn it. In the preactive phase, the instructional designer needs to be certain that what they are posting and designing has that level of clarity for the student receiving the information. The designer needs to be empathetic to student needs by putting themselves in the student's position, thinking how the student on the other end of the computer is going to receive and interpret the information through the learning platform.

Kinney (2008) states that too often, instructors fail to adequately communicate our expectations to our students. We make assignments for a reflective or analytical paper, but the students may not truly understand what is needed and required for success. They may ask "What should be in the paper? What are areas that need to be addressed? Should this include information from the literature and if so what articles? How will this be graded? " Four things that instructors can do to assure that their students understand: provide clear concise but detailed online instructions, provide a rubric that describes and details the assessment criteria, encourage email contact to clarify any potential misunderstanding on the learner's part and provide a model of an exemplary paper. Some instructors may be reluctant to provide a model paper as they feel that it may preclude or deny some levels of student creativity, however it will go far to increasing clarity for the students, easing student anxiety which will allow them to focus on the paper and increase their own creativity and assure that the assignment becomes more aligned with the outcomes established in the objectives.

Lesson Closure

The Lesson Closure to the weekly lesson plan is an important summarizing activity to review what was learned in the lesson. The closure of the lesson should actively engage students to reflect on the learning that occurred in the online lessons and content activities. A strong closure involves key review questions that the teacher poses to generate student thinking so that the key learning that took place is summarized by students. This helps them to focus on what was important and to internalize what was learned. It can also help them to understand what if any work they still need to accomplish to attain the objectives. For the online, this can again be done in a couple of manners. Instructors, who drive the interactive closure, can conduct this in an asynchronous discussion board. It can be part of the weekly discussion or can be a series of posts attached to the end of a weekly discussion. The instructor can pose a question and guide the students through a reflective dialogue to conclude the weekly objectives and bring closure to the content. It could also be designed as a series of emails that accomplish similar areas or a culminating weekly assignment posted or emailed to the instructor. This closure can additionally serve as a bridge to the next lesson if it is part of a scaffolding process.

The instructor must model what they want the learner to do. This is of high importance in the online learning environment. If the instructor wants student online participation and what was discussed as *student presence* in a course, then the instructor must also practice presence. We as instructors must always model even in the online learning environment as our students are always watching what we do and emulating our behavior. To assure that this occurs, it must be built into the planning process.

In the next chapter we will build on the objective writing and lesson planning by looking at the evaluation process and how it becomes an integral process in formative and summative assessment. We will also look at the process of program evaluation. This is similar to the needs assessment techniques discussed in chapter 7 but conducted after the course or training has been conducted. In chapter 9 and 10 we will look at a number of pedagogical opportunities that can be employed to both meet the objectives that are established and assist in building the active engaged learning that is described in the lesson plan procedures section.

Personal Reflection Suggestion

In your online lesson planning, how have behavioral objectives played a role? How can you provide what Wlodkowski (2008) discusses as clarity at all sections of your online lessons? How will your lesson plans be different for each of the four course types?

REFERENCES

Akengin, H. (2007). Opinions of prospective social studies teachers on the use of information technologies in teaching geographical subjects. *Journal of Instructional Psychology*, *35*(2), 126–139.

Anderson, L. W., Krathwohl, D. R., Airasian, P. W., Cruikshank, K. A., Mayer, R. E., & Pintrich, R. (2001). *A taxonomy for learning, teaching, and assessing: A revision of Bloom's taxonomy of educational objectives*. New York: Longman.

Bartolic-Zlomislic, S., & Bates, A. (1999). Investing in online learning: Potential benefits and limitations. *Canadian Journal of Communication*, *24*(3), 349–366.

Bernard, R. M., Abrami, P. C., Lou, Y., Borokhovski, E., Wade, A., & Wozney, L. (2004). How does distance education compare with classroom instruction? A meta-analysis of the empirical literature. *Review of Educational Research*, *74*(3), 379–439. doi:10.3102/00346543074003379

Brooks, J. G., & Brooks, M. G. (1993). *In Search of Understanding: The Case for Constructivist Classrooms*. Alexandria, VA: Association for Supervision and Curriculum Development.

Cavanaugh, C., Gillan, K. J., Kromrey, J., Hess, M., & Blomeyer, R. (2004). *The effects ofdistance education on K–12 student outcomes: A meta-analysis*. Naperville, IL: Learning Point Associates.

Cavanaugh, C. S. (2001). The effectiveness of interactive distance education technologies in K–12 learning: A meta-analysis. *International Journal of Educational Telecommunications*, *7*(1), 73–88.

Cradler, J., McNabb, M., Freeman, M., & Burchett, R. (2002). How does technology influence student learning? *Leading and Learning with Technology*, *29*(8), 46–56.

Delgado, A. R., & Prieto, G. (2003). The effect of item feedback on multiple-choice test responses. *The British Journal of Psychology*, *94*, 73–85. doi:10.1348/000712603762842110

Fuller, R. G., & Kuhne, G. W. (2008, January). Fostering Meaningful Interaction in Health Education Online Courses: Matching Pedagogy To Course Types. *International Journal of Information and Communication Technology Education*, *4*(1).

Hobbs, V. (2004). *The promise and the power of online learning in rural education*. Arlington, VA: Rural School and Community Trust.

Hunter, M. (1982). *Mastery Teaching*. El Segundo, CA: T.I.P. Publications.

Kinney, M. (2008, July 17). What the Army Taught Me About Teaching. *Inside Higher Ed*. Retrieved January 1, 2009, from http://www.insidehighered.com/views/2008/07/17/kinney

Knowles, M. S. (1984). *Andragogy in action*. San Francisco: Jossey-Bass.

Krathwohl, D. R., Bloom, B. S., & Masia, B. B. (1964). *Taxonomy of Educational Objectives, the Classification of Educational Goals. Handbook II: Affective Domain*. New York: Longman.

Kulhavy, R. W., & Stock, W. A. (1989). Feedback in written instruction: The place of response certitude. *Educational Psychology Review*, *1*(4), 279–308. doi:10.1007/BF01320096

Moore, M. G., & Kearsley, G. (1996). *Distance Education: A systems view*. San Francisco: Wadsworth Publishing Company.

Mory, E. (1992). The use of informational feedback in instruction: Implications for future research. *Educational Training Research and Development*, *40*(3), 5–20. doi:10.1007/BF02296839

Narciss, S. (1999). *Motivational effects of the informativeness of feedback*. Paper presented at the annual meeting of the American Educational Research Association, Montreal, Quebec, Canada.

Olivia, P. F. (2005). *Developing the curriculum*. Boston: Pearson Education Inc.

Olt, M. R. (2002). Ethics and distance education: Strategies for minimizing academic dishonesty in online assessment. *Online Journal of Distance Learning Administration*, *5*(3).

Richeki, R., Field, D., & Faxon, M. (2001). *Instructional design competencies: The standards* (3rd ed.). Syracuse, NY: ERIC Clearing on Information and Technology.

Rothwell, W. J., & Kazanas, H. C. (2004). *Mastering the instructional design process: A systematic approach*. San Francisco: Pfeiffer.

Tallent-Runnels, M. K., Thomas, J. A., Lan, W. Y., Cooper, S., Ahern, T. C., & Shaw, S. M. (2006). Teaching courses online: A review of the research. *Review of Educational Research*, *76*(1), 93–135. doi:10.3102/00346543076001093

Walker, C. (n.d.). *So you've decided to develop a distance education class*. Faulkner University. Retrieved from http://technorhetoric.net/6.2/coverweb/de/walker/index.htm

Waxman, H. C., Lin, M.-F., & Michko, G. M. (2003). *A meta-analysis of the effectiveness of teaching and learning with technology on student outcomes*. Naperville, IL: North Central Regional Educational.

Wesley, P. W., & Buysee, V. (2001). Communities of practice: Expanding professional roles to promote reflection and shared injury. *Topics in Early Childhood Education*, *21*(2), 114–124. doi:10.1177/027112140102100205

White, C. (2002, November). Creating a world of discovery by thinking and acting globally in social studies: ideas from New Zealand. *Social Studies*, 262–266. doi:10.1080/00377990209600176

Wiggins, G., & McTighe, J. (1998). *Understanding by design*. Alexandria, VA: Association for Supervision and Curriculum Development.

Zhao, Y., Lei, J., Yan, B., Lai, C., & Tan, H. (2005). What makes the difference? A practical analysis of research on the effectiveness of distance education. *Teachers College Record*, *107*(8), 1836–1884. doi:10.1111/j.1467-9620.2005.00544.x

Chapter 9
Preactive Stage:
Lesson and Program Evaluation

EVALUATION OF THE ONLINE LEARNING PROCESS

There are two types of evaluation that are conducted in the online program. The first is the evaluation of learning and the second is the evaluation on the effectiveness of the course. This chapter will discuss both.

As previously mentioned, when the instructional designer has completed the objectives he/she can plan the lesson and establish the evaluation process to measure the course outcomes. Evaluation in the online as in the face-to-face course involves both the summative and formative. *Summative evaluation* is evaluation that takes place in that end of a lesson or series of objectives. It can be described as a formal type of evaluation as it measures the sum of all learning that has occurred at the end of a period of time or at the end of a competency based lesson. It is utilized to measure the degree to which the objectives have been met and to assess student learning for posting grades and in some instances to provide certification of knowledge and skill attained. In the online environment it can take the form of online exams, projects or skills exams (Figure 1)

The *formative* evaluation takes place during the formation of learning, as the lessons and the online course progresses. This is evaluation that takes place by the instructor to understand if the student is grasping the concepts and developing the skills and if the objectives are taking place. Some instructors in the traditional setting call this "checking for understanding." It is also referred as an informal evaluation as it occurs during the process of learning from week to week through the interactions that occur through observations and questioning through assignments, emails, through threaded discussions in the discussion boards (asynchronous) or in virtual chats (synchronous).

The question always arises as which of these, the summative (formal) or the formative (informal) is more important. Some feel that the summative, which happens at the end, is what matters as it is quantitative and truly measures the knowledge and skills that have been learned. If the student however has not attained the necessary knowledge and skill

DOI: 10.4018/978-1-61520-865-4.ch009

Figure 1.

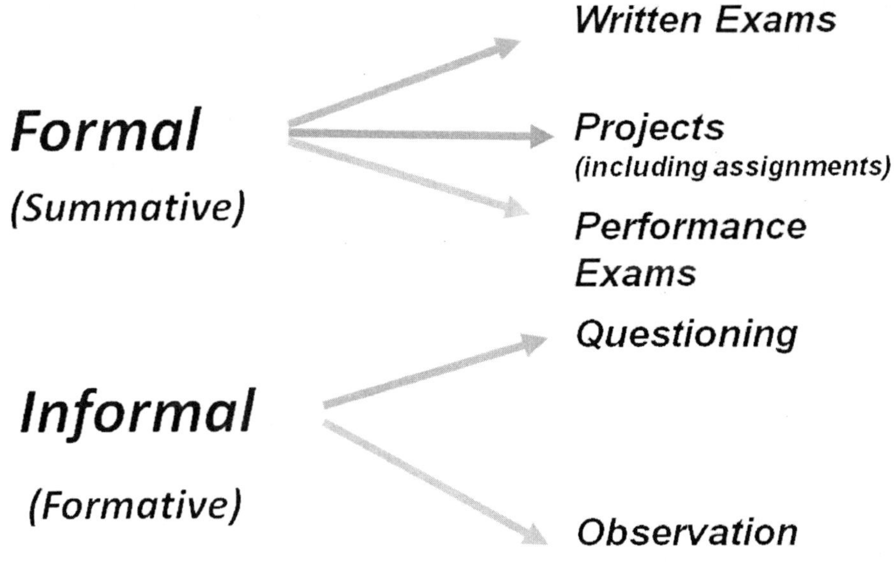

then there is nothing that can be done other than have the student retake the online course and try again. Others believe that it is the formative as the instructor can assess whether learning is occurring during the teaching and learning process and make the necessary adjustments as learning progresses. The real answer is that they are both important and both vital in assuring that skills and knowledge are attained. It is important that we measure the final learning through exams, skill demonstrations and papers or projects to know whether students have achieved the desired levels of success and if our pedagogies were of value to help them get there. It is just as important however that the formative be incorporated so that we can have an ongoing assessment throughout the course to know if the pedagogies are being effective and guiding the student toward the desired learning. If they are not then we can make the necessary adjustments and try different activities or interactions that may be better. If they are, then we move forward with the plan as designed and continue to monitor.

SUMMATIVE EVALUATION

Summative evaluation can be the trickiest for educators to deal with in the online arena. The idea of the online graded assignment makes some educators nervous that we are really not getting the same evaluation as that provided in the face to face. Many instructors worry about the academic integrity of the online exam or grading the online paper. This is not so different than the issues faced by classroom teachers long before computer and online education became part of the lexicon of opportunities. Olt (2002) describes four issues with the use of online summative assessments:

- The instructor's inability to identify that the student is actually the person completing the evaluation instrument.
- The instructor's inability to control the student's use of unauthorized materials while completing the evaluation (text book, notes, Internet, libraries, etc.).
- The possibility of student collaboration.

- Technical difficulties such as computer crashing, learning platform issues, student access, etc.

Much of the research supports that distance education in the form of online learning is at least as effective as traditional classes in terms of learning outcomes and often more effective (Bernard et al., 2004; Cavanaugh, 2001; Cavanaugh, Gillan, Kromrey, Hess, & Blomeyer, 2004; Cradler, McNabb, Freeman, & Burchett, 2002; Hobbs, 2004; Tallent-Runnels et al., 2006; Waxman, Lin, & Michko, 2003). In a meta-analysis of distance education studies, Zhao, Lei, Yan, Lai, and Tan (2005) reported an overall conclusion of equal effectiveness when all studies were taken into account but noted that in more recently published studies distance education was found to be more effective than face-to-face education.

There are several options for summative evaluation in the online environment that an online instructor can utilize for assessment. They can use quizzes throughout the course and end of course *exams* to assess content knowledge, *projects and papers* turned in at the end of a course and mental and *skill assessments* that assess physical and mental skills.

Online Exams

The summative process for some is and can be the most controversial element of the online arena. Many focus on the concept of a traditional in class examination process and the inability to have the same level of control in the online. The use of online exams is an area that can make new instructors to the online teaching and learning, approach distance education with a bit of skepticism. They may not feel that the online exam is as valuable as the question of academic integrity and the inability to control student security comes into play. There are two options that the instructor can utilize. One option that has been used by many students and educators is to have the student visit a remote testing center where the exam is administered and proctored. This can be established by the educational institution or set up by the student with the institution validating the site. The costs can be built into the course fees or passed on directly to the student by having him pay the remote site directly. In either case the educational institution validates the process by directing what personnel and which institutions can be used as a remote testing site. Many times this is another educational institution, a university, college or local high school that is geographically located near the student. The originating educational institution is provided the testing institution's contact name and validates their credentials and willingness to participate in the examination proctoring. They send the exam through regular mail or through electronic means. The remote testing cites administers the exam, sign some form of affidavit and forwards the exam back to the instructor for grading. This for some is an alternative, but it can be time consuming and cumbersome to coordinate.

Another alternative is to design the exam as a take home exam posted through the LMS. Most LMSs have testing options and exam builder systems where the instructor can construct the exam directly into the course shell. The LMS has many control parameters that can be built into the exam process. The instructor can launch the exam directly in the course shell by setting the dates and times for the exam to be released (or viewed by the student). They can also set time limitations for how long and how many times a student may view the test. So for example an exam can be set to be open from 9 to 10 AM or allow access over the course of several days and allow only one attempt. In other words the student can't just open it, look at the questions that need to be studied and answered, then come back later to take the exam. This limited time element requires that the student understand the information before taking the exam. However it is well understood that he will have access to text information and notes or handouts used in the course as a resource. Questions can be worded so as not to just be simple recall of information points and elements of the objectives. The instructor has a variety of question options in most online exam builders that allows short answer, formula questions, fill in the blank, matching, multiple answer, multiple choice, short or longer answer, true/false or will allow uploaded questions from exam pool or a file.

Many of the LMS options can automate grading that will provide immediate feedback to correct or incorrect answers or provided directly at the end. Other questions such as short answer or long answer require interpretation and grading from the instructor. Once the exam has been graded either through automated means of the LMS or by the instructor, the grade is automatically posted in the online grade book for the student to see and review the exam which can be part of the learning process to validate what was known and provide feedback as to what was not known.

The key element of success here is the idea that the online environment provides the learner the ability to review their own learning process and their achievement of their goals. When learners compare their performance at the end of a learning experience with their performance at the beginning of the experience they enter a period of rediagnosis of learning needs (Knowles, 1984, p. 49). This allows students to see the evaluation process differently as one that helps and guides them toward the course goals as well as to their own goals of learning.

Projects and Papers

In addition to exams, there are also summative options in the forms of projects and papers. These types of projects may involve higher order learning and work to achieve higher end levels within each of the three domains of learning. Projects can take on the form of student presentations, group work, and written papers. Presentations can be accomplished through the evaluation of a student posted presentation or a group presentation (cooperative learning will be discussed in Chapter 9) in an asynchronous discussion board where the student or student group prepares and posts a PowerPoint or Word file that has student researched and developed information and then the student leads an online threaded discussion facilitating ideas and concepts. The presentation can also take on a synchronous form where the student leads a real time discussion through the online chat or synchronous discussion board function innate to most LMSs. Utilizing a preposted rubric (Table 1) for the presentation provides the students with an understanding of what is required and the instructor has a tool to evaluate consistently.

Another option is the written paper. This takes on a new level of self-directed learning in the online environment and provides the student the opportunity to delve deeper into the study of a particular subject that is either student or instructor prescribed. The instructor can evaluate an assigned paper through the traditional manners although the options for grading and evaluating papers take on a new dimension in the LMS platform. The instructor can receive the paper electronically through the LMS by setting this up through an assignment drop. In most LMS platforms there are a variety of options to set up that will allow feedback. The student will drop the paper in an assigned area for the instructor to view. When the instructor views this, he can open it on his computer and through word processing grade and attach comments both as text and in some word processors post an innate digitally recorded message. This can provide feedback to the student to learn better paper writing skills. The instructor graded paper with comments can then be posted for the student to view along with a posted score in the grade book.

Another dynamic available to the grading of electronically submitted papers is the use of a monitoring program that can check for plagiarism. Academic integrity has long been an issue in both face-to-face and online courses. In the traditional,

Table 1. Presentation rubric

	1	2	3	4	Total
Organization	Audience cannot understand presentation because there is no sequence of information.	Audience has difficulty following presentation because learner jumps around.	Learner presents information in logical sequence.	Learner presents information in logical, interesting sequence.	
Content Knowledge	Learner does not have grasp of information; learner cannot answer questions about subject.	Learner is uncomfortable with information and is able to answer only rudimentary questions.	Learner is at ease with expected answers to all questions, but fails to elaborate.	Learner demonstrates full knowledge of content material and addresses questions with complete answers and explanations and elaborates beyond expectations citing literature and research.	
Graphics	No graphics utilized	Learner occasionally uses graphics that rarely support text and presentation.	Learner's graphics relate to text and presentation.	Learner's graphics explain and reinforce content information	
Mechanics	Presentation has four or more errors.	Presentation has three errors.	Presentation has no more than two syntax errors.	Presentation has no syntax errors	
Enthusiasm	Little interest demonstrated	Some enthusiasm	Occasionally shows enthusiasm	Learner demonstrates a strong positive enthusiasm about topic	

there are few options other than the instructors own knowledge of the literature to assure that students are turning in their own work. With the use of online electronic submissions, the instructor can submit the electronic version of the paper through anyone of a number of plagiarism software programs. Some of these can be set up to operate directly through the LMS with the students actually posting the paper directly into the software. The instructor then receives a report to review. Software such as *Scan My Paper, Turnitin, Gatt Plagarism* software to name a few are available and will match the student's work against a number of literature based data bases, Internet sites, and papers already submitted through their systems. These data bases, by their own accounts scan billions of sources and are constantly updated. This affords the instructor a view of the paper to assure original work and to help understand if the student has properly cited references in the creation of the paper. This can be an invaluable tool that has generally not been used in the traditional classroom where students submit a hard copy of their work for grading. Again the use of a rubric like the example below (Table 2) will go far to adding the level of clarity for students and for consistency of instructor grading.

FORMATIVE EVALUATION

Formative evaluation of the students learning is an ongoing process throughout the teaching phase. The needs analysis discussed in this chapter is not a static process conducted solely during the preactive phases but is dynamic and ongoing throughout the active teaching phases. Each week the instructor will have planned different online lectures, access to content and activities to generate interaction and allow students to manipulate and work with the content to see application. Much of this will have been developed and built

Table 2. Written paper rubric

High Low	
Achieves Goal of the Written Assignment • Paper focuses on appropriate assignment topic and theme • Follows all assignment directions • Follows appropriate writing style (i.e., APA, MLA, ICMJE, etc)	4 3 2 1 ❑ ❑ ❑ ❑
Develops Concepts and Ideas • Paper establishes a focus and defensible thesis • Develops a strong introduction and conclusion • Provides strong support from appropriate research literature	4 3 2 1 ❑ ❑ ❑ ❑
Paper Organization • Organizes major concepts are developed and logically organized throughout the paper • supporting ideas are developed consistently • Provides smooth transitions from concept to concept	4 3 2 1 ❑ ❑ ❑ ❑
Syntax • Paper is free of grammatical errors • Paper uses proper sentence structures • Follows proper English language rules	4 3 2 1 ❑ ❑ ❑ ❑
Research Citations • Uses reliable sources • Uses proper research quotes to support and build on major thesis points • Provides proper analysis and synthesis of referenced concepts as evidence to support thesis • Properly cites quoted text	4 3 2 1 ❑ ❑ ❑ ❑
Comments:	Total Score:

into an LMS course shell in the preactive phases. This is not the end of the pedagogical analysis. As the course progresses, the instructor needs to monitor the progress and understanding of the student toward the course and lesson objectives. If all is progressing as planned during the active phase through each session, then no changes may be necessary. However, if the instructor starts to identify areas or students who are not absorbing key components in the online lessons and sessions, then the instructor needs to consider changing pedagogies that will meet student needs and help them to achieve the course goals and objectives.

Formative techniques in online learning or checking for understanding can be conducted and observed in a number of ways generally through ungraded evaluation. When providing feedback and formatively assessing student success toward the objectives, it is important to focus on the student's work and their level of understanding of the material. This is demonstrated through the interaction in discussion boards, synchronous discussions, posted work and through email communications. Providing feedback in these online areas is beneficial to both the instructor and to the student. It helps the instructor to understand what is going on and if there are needs for change. It assists the student in understanding if they are making progress toward the stated goals and their desire to achieve.

Feedback can be defined as "knowledge of one's performance provided by an external agent" (Delgado and Prieto, 2003, p. 73). In this case it is an online instructor who is providing the feedback to assist the student toward achieving the course goals. From the aspect of the behaviorist, feedback is primarily concerned with reinforcing correct responses (Kulhavy and Stock 1989; Mory, 1992). From a cognitive perspective "feedback is regarded as a source of information necessary for verification, elaboration, concept development, and metacognitive adaptation" (Narciss, 1999, p. 3). The constructivist view of feedback attempts to understand the student's current thinking about the topic and should be used as a tool to enhance both the student's learning and the teacher's understanding of the student's current understanding (Brooks and Brooks,1993). The constructivist sees the learning process as one that allows the student to build his own reality of the information. The feedback process is designed to enhance this progression. Moore and Kearsley (1996) support this but also add that lack of sufficient relevant feedback is one of the most common sources of dissatisfaction and frustration for distance learners (p. 119). The key element here is for the instructor to be highly interactive and contact and respond to the student within a reasonable period of time. Generally this is within 24 hours

Kulhavy and Stock (1989) describe feedback as a progression of three cycles: Cycle I, consists of an assignment being presented to the learner where the learner processes the assignment and provides a response. Cycle II begins with feedback being presented by the instructor and processed by the learner to generate response corrections as may be needed. Cycle III culminates with the original assignment presented again as an exam item, which is processed and responded to by the learner to produce a posttest response. This process allows the instructor to guide the learner through the thought process necessary to achieve success in a way that has a discovery learning format rather than a telling process.

There are many options in an LMS to provide feedback and formative assessment. The use of discussion boards is an excellent tool to assist in the student achieving the specific goals and focus of each type of course. It allows each student individual attention and focus on their learning and it allows each of the other students to learn from each other as they all have view of the feedback. If there is a need to limit the view of all students for individual confidentiality, then another medium such as email, file exchange or phone conference can be used. The discussion board can be used in a *foundational course* to assist the student in achieving the fundamental principles and understanding through the affective domain as to why they are learning these concepts and where they will be used in future courses and professional practice. In a *skills based* class the discussion board can serve as a platform to provide feedback on both mental and physical skills. Students can again learn through monitoring and interacting with each other and monitoring the feedback from the instructor.

In an *analysis/synthesis* course the feedback is used to guide the learning of all ideals and to assist in viewing all sides of any issue that may be controversial. Feedback in this type of course is a delicate balance as the implications for these courses are for the instructor to understand that there may be multiple views of a situation that require exploration by the participants to fully realize the depth and breadth of the concepts. The obvious nature of these types of courses is for students to explore all aspects of the topic and then draw conclusion based upon the information presented and explored. The online instructor in this type of course must take care not to be too authoritative as stated above, otherwise he will shut down the exploration and the insights that can be gleaned from students interacting and dialoguing about opposing viewpoints. Instructors will find that taking an authoritative stance and letting participants see their opinions on an issue will close dialogue or they will find that students will simply repeat or "parrot" the instructor's view on the issue (Fuller and Kuhne, 2008). This is in direct conflict of what the instructor may wish to accomplish by allowing students to analyze and synthesize all views of the problem or issue. Dialogue among participants provides regular opportunities for reflection and inquiry (Wesley & Buysse, 2001) and requires the least intervention in the discussion boards of all the course types.

The *hybrid* or blended learning approach courses can integrate each of the different course components as they arise. The following chart (Table 3) serves as a listing of feedback tools to be considered in the preactive development of student online interaction with instructor and content.

Personal Reflection Suggestion

Consider the online courses that you teach or could teach. How would you establish formative evaluation in each of the four course types that you teach online? Are their better techniques that you can utilize? How would you develop summative evaluations in each of the four course types that you teach online?

Table 3. Formative assessment techniques

Technique	*Description*	*Goal*
Questioning	*Questioning through email, discussion board, synchronous chats or phone can be designed. A variety of questioning techniques can be employed from simple recall questions to higher level analysis questions and finally justification type questions that allow learners to build on their responses and assignments.*	*The goal is to elicit student intent, understanding and can serve to guide the student to a particular direction and understanding.*
Emailing students	*The instructor will take a discussion offline to deal with students one on one. This can be a series of email initiated by the instructor or the student when additional information or clarification is deemed need by either.*	*To create a dialogue that will allow the student a forum to ask questions and for the instructor to assess and understand where the student is and what he may need. It also allows the student the platform to ask individual questions and seek clarification.*
Asynchronous Discussion board observations	*Provides feedback to student responses and ideas posted. It also allows the instructor to assess student ideas and understanding of concept, skill and problem solving skills.*	*Feedback should be designed to stimulate thoughts and ideas and assist the student to see all sides of an issue as in a analysis/ synthesis class*
Individual Phone conferences	*Individual phone conferences (one mechanism to take it offline) Can be requested and scheduled by instruct, student or both.*	*The goal is to put a real voice in real time to explain and provide one on one feedback and clarification to address student concerns and needs as were identified in the LMS. This level of clarification can be needed from time to time and can go far to ease student anxiety and get them back on track for success. This also allows them to make a connection with their instructor and illustrates a level of empathy on the instructors part.*
Group phone conference bridges	*Group phone conferences can be scheduled throughout the term or duration of the education or training. These can be mandatory or optional and can be used to enhance interaction and provide real time clarity from instructor to learners.*	*This can afford the instructor the ability to assess the overall group understanding and provide a real time platform to provide clarity and feedback toward each of the four course goals. Similar to the individual phone conferences, this can ease student anxiety and refocus them for success as well as have them make a connection.*
Synchronous Chat discussions	*These are real time communications that are conducted on the LMS. They offer the opportunity for real time communication that allow the instructor to present information, the students to ask questions and for a formative assessment where the instructor can check for understanding and make corrections in student performance and understanding.*	*Again the goal is to assess the overall group understanding and to assess the need for clarity and feedback for the group and individuals. This can ease anxiety and provide the platform for flexible explanations of ideas, concepts and skills.*

THE PROGRAM EVALUATION SUB-PROCESS

Core Question: "What happened as a result of your educational intervention, or program?"

This question forms the essence of the concern in program evaluation. To simply offer educational programs without measuring the results borders on irresponsibility. You must be able to validate time and efforts in educational and training programs. Educators and trainers must have some understanding of learning outcomes in order to know how to improve programs and to know what additional educational interventions may be needed.

The unfortunate reality within adult education settings, educational or training, is that only a small percentage of the programs have anything but the most rudimentary of evaluation efforts, and many have no program evaluation process. Of the few that actually carry out evaluations, most do little more than collect "happiness indexes",(i.e., questionnaires) that quiz participants about their reactions to the training. Such questionnaires provide no real measure of learning outcomes.

Good evaluation is all about making wise judgments. At its most basic, evaluation is a four step process:

- Establishing criteria before program is delivered to best measure whether goals are met and learning outcomes are sufficient.
- Gathering evidence of outcomes, etc. to address adequately the criteria established above (some gather "evidence" without ever determining criteria).
- Systematically comparing the criteria and the evidence gathered (many gather "data" and never even look at it).
- Making a judgment about program's effectiveness. Our task is to make a value judgment!

There are many approaches to conducting program evaluation. One famous approach is the Kirkpatrick's model (1982, 1987), which proposes that the efficiency and effectiveness of education can be evaluated (or measured) at four different levels:

- Level 1: Measurement of participants' reaction to the training at the time of the training.
- Level 2: Measurement of participants' learning of the content of their training.
- Level 3: Measurement of participants' use of their new skills and knowledge back on the job.
- Level 4: Measurement of the company's return on the training investment.

Another widely used evaluation approach was suggested by Gagne, Briggs, and Wager (1988). They suggest that evaluation should focus on measuring changes in intellectual skills, cognitive strategies, verbal information, motor skills, and attitudes.

FOUR TRAPS TO AVOID IN EVALUATION

It is easy to get so preoccupied in daily issues of planning and coordinating activities, or with meeting demands for quantifiable data, that we get mired in poor evaluation practices. Here are four traps to watch out for: measuring what's easy, underestimating the learning embedded in evaluation, unexamined power, and reductionism. Let's look at each a bit further.

1. Measuring what is easiest to measure: A fundamental error committed by most adult educators is that of measuring what is easiest to measure, instead of measuring what is most important. It may be easy to measure and rank numbers, but can numbers represent what you really want learners to learn and which programs to focus on? Adult learners often complain about having to write papers to demonstrate knowledge so remote from their own interests that it will never be integrated into their personal learning. Focus your evaluation only on what truly is most important. The best instructors help focus themselves by determining the two or three things they really want learners to understand or be able to do at the end of each learning experience.

2. Underestimating the learning embedded in evaluation: How you choose to evaluate becomes an integral part of your program. A project, observation or test of adult learners is sometimes the most vital, permanent part of the learning experience, not only with respect to the content but also the processes of thinking and behavior. The reason is twofold. First, learners are at heightened points of emotional, physical, and cognitive awareness during evaluation, and thus very susceptible to learning. The way a test is structured, the wording, format, and sequence of the questions, causes learners to synthesize information in a particular way. Second, the evaluation is often the last part of the learning process that is mediated by an instructor. Thus, the criteria used to observe a performance, and the personal approach of the instructor in applying the criteria and giving the feedback, often results in the most significant learning. Evaluation isn't simply measurement. It shapes knowledge and affects how well adult learners respond to further or future learning.
3. The issue of power and politics: The evaluator carries the power in the learning situation. Learners know it, and this dynamic influences their relationship to the instructor. Three implications are worth noting here. First, if adult learners are used to wielding control and enjoying autonomy, they may resent being thrust into a situation where someone else has power and authority over them. This resentment may be acted out in questioning the instructor's expertise and resisting directives, or it may be expressed in learner satisfaction forms commonly filled out after a learning experience. The situation becomes more complicated when learners are asked to engage in activities that make them uncomfortable or are confronted with ideas that challenge their values and beliefs. Learners must surrender their own knowledge structures and sometimes their sense of self to enter an unknown realm of learning. Such learning can be threatening, and it reinforces the power position of the instructor. The second issue of power is that evaluators sometimes take their own authority so much for granted that they may forget to examine their own assumptions and choices. They need to ask themselves: Who says this performance or project is better than that one? Why is this concept more important than that one? Who am I to judge--and who do I allow to be my judge? The third issue is that because evaluation involves making decisions, and thus negotiating interests and values, it is necessarily influenced by the prevailing politics. Quite often, the politics of the powerful stakeholders shapes the end-use of evaluation.
4. Reductionism: A fourth problem is that the instruction can be reduced to only what is being evaluated. For example, a written curriculum program may be innovative and exciting, but antiquated evaluation can rob it of its vibrancy. Many adult educators and trainers lament that, in their programs or jobs, the tail wags the dog.

A STRATEGY FOR EVALUATION

Establish a "Purpose" For Your Evaluation

All good evaluations begin with a clear statement of purpose. Not all evaluations serve the same purpose. The purpose determines criteria and methodology. Four possible broad purposes could be chosen for any evaluation. Justification is the first. Some evaluations are done for the express purpose of justifying a program, to ourselves, our agencies, or outside funding sources. Such a purpose is also called "summative evaluation" in the literature. Improvement is the second. Some evaluations are done for the express purpose of improving our educational programs. Such evaluations can be done at the end, or while programs are in progress. Such a purpose is also called "formative evaluation" in the literature. Planning is the third. Some evaluations are done for the express purpose of future programming efforts, to learn something that could help in future program designs which may often be conducted in connection with one-time program efforts. Perspective is the fourth. Some evaluations are conducted to gain stakeholder perspectives on programs. Such approaches to evaluation focus less on learning outcomes and more about players. Sometimes (often) a combination of purposes can be called for in a program evaluation.

Establish a "Focus" For the Program Evaluation

There can be many different focuses for program evaluations. We must decide which ones are most appropriate for the purposes driving the evaluation (see previous point of purposes). The possible "foci" fit into two categories: Program-related issues (non-learning outcomes of training) and Learner-outcomes.

At least five program-related issues can be the targets of an evaluation. Economic inputs can be a focus when seeking to answer the question of costs in our programs. Such an evaluation gathers data about the budget for the program, actual expenses for the program, staff time invested in the program, and/or outsider time invested in the program. Development activities can be a focus when seeking to answer the question of what we actually did in the process of trying to implement this program. Such an evaluation gathers data about promotional activities, educational methods and technology, and facilitative activities. Participant data can be a focus when seeking to answer the question of what we know about the people who participated in this educational program. Such an evaluation gathers data about the number of participants, demographic and personal characteristics, retention, and persistence of learners. Instructor perspectives can be a focus when seeking to answer the question of what the instructors think about this program after their participation. Such an evaluation gathers data about their view of the level of the learners and teachability, the content, schedule, support services, and learning environments. Finally, learner reactions can be a focus when seeking to answer the question of what the learners think about this program after their participation. A "happiness index" is often used to gather data about learner opinions on the value of information or instructor, the learning environment, and support services.

Actual Learner Outcomes

Actual learner outcomes are the more normal focus of program evaluation efforts. Learner outcomes can be targeted at three levels, or orders. These orders of outcome correspond to the final three of Kirkpatrick's levels as discussed in the Caffarella chapter on evaluation.

- **1st Order Outcomes Of Learning** refers to the immediate learning as a result of training and usually reflects changes in Knowledge, Skills, and Attitudes (also known as KAS-changes). The common methods used to measure KAS changes include the use of control groups, pre-test/post-test approaches, and performance or paper & pencil testing.
- **2nd Order Outcomes of Learning** is also known as transfer of learning. Such an evaluation seeks to understand whether measured KAS changes in a classroom have transferred to the practice setting. The issue is how much of what was "learned" is being "used"? While this answer might be more desirable for many, the answer is much harder and more expensive to measure. Many variables beyond the training

itself affect 2nd order outcomes. The common methods used to measure 2nd order outcomes include the use of surveys and interviews with supervisors, peers, and subordinates at some time interval after training, such as six months or a year.

- **3rd Order Outcomes of Learning** refers to the "System Impacts", or long-term results of training on the "bottom line" of an agency, a business, or a society. Nearly everyone wants us to measure 3rd order outcomes, but such measures are even harder and more expensive to measure than 2nd order because the variables are greater than in 2nd order outcomes. Some common methods used to measure 3rd order outcomes include, reduced turnover of employees, reduced costs, improved quality measures, increased sales, etc.

The key to understand is that the higher the order of learning outcome, the more difficult and expensive it is to measure. The higher the order, the more difficult it is to attribute success or failure to the actual training program. Most organizations simply refuse to provide funds to really measure higher order learning outcomes. Rather than factual measures, trainers and educators, when pressed to speak to higher order outcomes of their efforts, often give a "gut-level" feeling and imply it is quantifiable, or use anecdotal evidence

Decide the Type of Data (Hard or Soft) Needed For the Evaluation Effort

To better understand the difference between hard and soft data, let's examine examples for each of the orders of learning outcomes. An example of "hard" data for learner reactions would be the percentage of the total group agreeing to register for further training due to satisfaction with the course. An example of "soft" data for learner reactions would be written reactions to perceived applicability of training. An example of "hard" data for KAS changes would be changes in scores on validated measures of knowledge, attitudes, skills, and aspirations skills, and aspirations. An example of "soft" data for KAS changes would be opinions on the extent of change in participants' knowledge, attitudes. An example of "hard" data for transfer of training would be direct observation of use of recommended farm practices over a series of years. An example of "soft" data for transfer of training would be retrospective reports by supervisors of their staff use of recommended practices. Finally, examples of "hard" data for system impact would be trends in profit-loss statements, life expectancies, pollution indexes, and satisfaction with health. An example of "soft" data for system impacts would be casual perceptions of changes in quality of health, economy, and environment.

Choose Your Evaluation Tools

The tools used in Needs Assessment are the very same tools used for Program Evaluation. The difference is what we do with the data and when we use the tool. Go back and review the "tools" from the Needs Assessment Section. Caffarella suggests using five approaches to evaluation are frequently used in adult education.

- **Objectives-based reviews** help to determine whether stated objectives of a program have been met. The focus of the objectives is on the participants' learning (with resulting changes in the individual, organizations, and/or society) and/or the program operations. Tools employed include observations, interviews, written questionnaires, tests, product reviews, and case studies.
- **Systems evaluations** provides feedback on the effectiveness of the program planning and execution process, the structure of the educational unit function, and the efficiency of the use of resources in relation to the

outcomes of educational programs. Tools employed include written questionnaires, interviews, and cost-benefit analysis.
- **Case Study Methods** give a "thick description" of what a program looks like from the viewpoint of participants, staff, sponsors, and/or other appropriate groups. It characterizes how a program has been implemented and received. Tools employed include observations, interviews, and organizational & community records and documents.
- **Quasi-legal Evaluation** determines program quality through adversarial hearings. Panels hear a range of evidence (for example, opinions, data-based studies, and belief statements) presented in a legalistic fashion. The judgments rest with a majority opinion of the panel members.
- **Professional or Expert Review** relies on a panel of experts making judgments, based on a predetermined set of categories and standards, about a program (such as program accreditation, formal program reviews). It most often focuses on the resources, processes, and outcomes of large educational programs.

Knowles (1980) suggested that reactions from participants are the easiest to measure and could best be gained by using interviews, representative councils (such as a group of students from the class), questionnaires (such as the typical "happiness index type), and instructional procedures such as buzz groups. Measuring KSA changes and transfer of learning proves more of a challenge, although he suggests seven approaches that hold promise:

- Standardized tests on attitudes, apptitudes, academic acheivement, skills, etc.
- Tailor made tests by instructor (pre-test/post-test)
- Performance Tests in the real world where a skill can be demonstrated.
- Case Studies:
- Student Products: Papers, projects, critical assessments, etc.
- Job Performance Records such as production reports, safety reports, etc.
- Instructor Evaluations through written reports

Knowles doesn't address how to find the third order outcomes, or system changes.

Collect and Analyze the Data

This step is where you collect the data with the chosen evaluation tools and then reflect on the meaning of the results. Unfortunately, much evaluation data is gathered and then is simply filed with little or no reflection on implications. Perhaps the classic case of this is when surveys are taken at the end of a class to measure student satisfaction. Most are given the most cursory of glances and then filed away as opposed to spending the time needed to draw the maximum benefits from any evaluation that is done.

Report the Data

One way to insure that some analysis is carried on evaluation data is to develop a report of the finding. Such a report can be sent to important players for accountability, such as agency administrators or grant supervisors. Certainly a written report should be developed for yourself as program planner to be filed with the rest of the information on the program.

SOME PITFALLS AND ETHICAL ISSUES IN PROGRAM EVALUATION

Although systematic program evaluations are desirable, and a necessary part of the program planning process, there are four major pitfalls. First, the outcomes of some online programs may be too complicated, and the number of variables affecting those outcomes too numerous to allow planners to demonstrate that a given program actually produced the desired changes. Second, current evaluation procedures, however scientifically rigorous, may not provide hard evidence that the more subtle, and at times the most important, aspects of the program have been achieved. This is particularly true for educational programs whose objectives are to foster changes in personal, organizational, and societal values and beliefs. Third, conducting systematic program evaluation costs time and money, neither of which some organizations and groups are willing to provide if they do not see any immediate value for evaluating programs. Fourth, when staff know that no action will be taken on the basis of evaluation findings, it may be better not to collect the data at all, because the evaluation process raises expectations on the part of participants and/or sponsors that changes will be forthcoming.

In addition to the above pitfalls, there are several ethical and political issues in evaluation.

1. Ensuring Truth in Claims, Data, and Recommendation: Evaluation is political. People's values, perceptions, and politics affect the process of evaluation. The 'truth' often depends on the nature of power and politics among the key players in the process. As such, there is no one "truth." Moreover, even empirical data always requires interpretation.
2. Confidentiality: Just like in research, maintaining appropriate confidentiality in evaluation is a major ethical issue and concern. Confidentiality involves protecting the identity of the participants in the evaluation, as well as ensuring that the results of evaluation are only given to those who are entitled to it.
3. Ensuring Customer and User Participation: There is growing evidence that for evaluation and its outcomes to be effective, it is important to involve those for whom the evaluation is intended. Lack of customer participation and ownership is often cited as one of the major reasons for ineffective implementation of evaluation recommendations.
4. Balancing Organizational and Individual Needs and Interests: There is often a tension between the organizational needs and the individuals' needs and interests. There are a lot of instances where evaluations are used to promote or impose organizational interests at the expense of the individuals. It is important to try to address both organizational and individual needs and interests.

Reflective Questions

1. Consider how program evaluation has been approached by your agency. What do you consider to be the strengths and weakness of their approach and why?
2. What do you see as the major difficulties in evaluating transfer of training or long-term impacts of educational efforts?
3. Consider a recent course you have designed, taught, or taken: How would you go about evaluating the class at each of the levels? (1st Order, 2nd Order, 3rd Order)

REFERENCES

Akengin, H. (2007). Opinions of prospective social studies teachers on the use of information technologies in teaching geographical subjects. *Journal of Instructional Psychology*, *35*(2), 126–139.

Anderson, L. W., Krathwohl, D. R., Airasian, P. W., Cruikshank, K. A., Mayer, R. E., & Pintrich, R. (2001). *A taxonomy for learning, teaching, and assessing: A revision of Bloom's taxonomy of educational objectives*. New York: Longman.

Bartolic-Zlomislic, S., & Bates, A. (1999). Investing in online learning: Potential benefits and limitations. *Canadian Journal of Communication*, *24*(3), 349–366.

Bernard, R. M., Abrami, P. C., Lou, Y., Borokhovski, E., Wade, A., & Wozney, L. (2004). How does distance education compare with classroom instruction? A meta-analysis of the empirical literature. *Review of Educational Research*, *74*(3), 379–439. doi:10.3102/00346543074003379

Brooks, J. G., & Brooks, M. G. (1993). *In Search of Understanding: The Case for Constructivist Classrooms*. Alexandria, VA: Association for Supervision and Curriculum Development.

Cavanaugh, C., Gillan, K. J., Kromrey, J., Hess, M., & Blomeyer, R. (2004). *The effects ofdistance education on K–12 student outcomes: A meta-analysis*. Naperville, IL: Learning Point Associates.

Cavanaugh, C. S. (2001). The effectiveness of interactive distance education technologies in K–12 learning: A meta-analysis. *International Journal of Educational Telecommunications*, *7*(1), 73–88.

Cradler, J., McNabb, M., Freeman, M., & Burchett, R. (2002). How does technology influence student learning? *Leading and Learning with Technology*, *29*(8), 46–56.

Delgado, A. R., & Prieto, G. (2003). The effect of item feedback on multiple-choice test responses. *The British Journal of Psychology*, *94*, 73–85. doi:10.1348/000712603762842110

Fuller, R. G., & Kuhne, G. W. (2008, January). Fostering Meaningful Interaction in Health Education Online Courses: Matching Pedagogy To Course Types. *International Journal of Information and Communication Technology Education*, *4*(1).

Hobbs, V. (2004). *The promise and the power of online learning in rural education*. Arlington, VA: Rural School and Community Trust.

Hunter, M. (1982). *Mastery Teaching*. El Segundo, CA: T.I.P. Publications.

Kinney, M. (2008, July 17). What the Army Taught Me About Teaching. *Inside Higher Ed*. Retrieved January 1, 2009, from http://www.insidehighered.com/views/2008/07/17/kinney

Knowles, M. S. (1984). *Andragogy in action*. San Francisco: Jossey-Bass.

Krathwohl, D. R., Bloom, B. S., & Masia, B. B. (1964). *Taxonomy of Educational Objectives, the Classification of Educational Goals. Handbook II: Affective Domain*. New York: Longman.

Kulhavy, R. W., & Stock, W. A. (1989). Feedback in written instruction: The place of response certitude. *Educational Psychology Review*, *1*(4), 279–308. doi:10.1007/BF01320096

Moore, M. G., & Kearsley, G. (1996). *Distance Education: A systems view*. San Francisco: Wadsworth Publishing Company.

Mory, E. (1992). The use of informational feedback in instruction: Implications for future research. *Educational Training Research and Development*, *40*(3), 5–20. doi:10.1007/BF02296839

Narciss, S. (1999). *Motivational effects of the informativeness of feedback*. Paper presented at the annual meeting of the American Educational Research Association, Montreal, Quebec, Canada.

Olivia, P. F. (2005). *Developing the curriculum*. Boston: Pearson Education Inc.

Olt, M. R. (2002). Ethics and distance education: Strategies for minimizing academic dishonesty in online assessment. *Online Journal of Distance Learning Administration*, *5*(3).

Richeki, R., Field, D., & Faxon, M. (2001). *Instructional design competencies: The standards* (3rd ed.). Syracuse, NY: ERIC Clearing on Information and Technology.

Rothwell, W. J., & Kazanas, H. C. (2004). *Mastering the instructional design process: A systematic approach*. San Francisco: Pfeiffer.

Tallent-Runnels, M. K., Thomas, J. A., Lan, W. Y., Cooper, S., Ahern, T. C., & Shaw, S. M. (2006). Teaching courses online: A review of the research. *Review of Educational Research*, *76*(1), 93–135. doi:10.3102/00346543076001093

Walker, C. (n.d.). *So you've decided to develop a distance education class*. Faulkner University. Retrieved from http://technorhetoric.net/6.2/coverweb/de/walker/index.htm

Waxman, H. C., Lin, M.-F., & Michko, G. M. (2003). *A meta-analysis of the effectiveness of teaching and learning with technology on student outcomes*. Naperville, IL: North Central Regional Educational.

Wesley, P. W., & Buysee, V. (2001). Communities of practice: Expanding professional roles to promote reflection and shared injury. *Topics in Early Childhood Education*, *21*(2), 114–124. doi:10.1177/027112140102100205

Wiggins, G., & McTighe, J. (1998). *Understanding by design*. Alexandria, VA: Association for Supervision and Curriculum Development.

Zhao, Y., Lei, J., Yan, B., Lai, C., & Tan, H. (2005). What makes the difference? A practical analysis of research on the effectiveness of distance education. *Teachers College Record*, *107*(8), 1836–1884. doi:10.1111/j.1467-9620.2005.00544.x

Chapter 10
Active Teaching Phases:
Foundational Pedagogies

In Chapters 7, 8 and 9 we discussed the process of preparing to teach by looking at the preactive phases of teaching that included: needs assessment, objective writing and development, lesson planning, and both formative and summative evaluation processes. In the next two chapters, we will be looking at the dynamics of teaching in the four different types of courses. The process of teaching in the online versus the traditional will be discussed along with the pedagogical opportunities of teaching online in *foundational courses, skills based courses, analysis/synthesis courses and hybrid courses.*

While understanding the dynamics of teaching in a traditional face to face course, many instructors have a difficult time understanding the differing roles in teaching an online course or training session. The role of the instructor in the traditional setting is to prepare a lesson and deliver the education or training to a group of individuals through lectures and in class activities, then assigning out of class work to be collected in some manner and graded. Much of the focus is on the instructor. As Pallof and Pratt (2002) argue, in order for a high degree of interactivity to occur in an online course, the roles of faculty and students need to change. Instructors need to be willing to give up what is repeated throughout the literature, as the "sage on the stage" mentality of being in total control, and allowing students to take an andragogical level of responsibility in offering learning activities. For some faculty and students, this initially offers an uncomfortable sense of role paradigm as teachers are used to teaching and students have a sense of instructor control in learning. In the online course the dynamics are different but provide a powerful technological platform for teaching and learning. A meta-analysis study conducted by the U.S. Department of Education found that, on average, students in online learning conditions performed better than those receiving face-to-face instruction (2009). This may be due to the nature of online learning that includes additional learning time and materials as well as additional opportunities for collaboration that produce the increased learning advantages. The study also noted that online learning is much more conducive to the expansion of learning time than is face-to-face instruction.

DOI: 10.4018/978-1-61520-865-4.ch010

Feenberg (1999) claims that "technology is not a predefined thing at all, but an environment, an empty space faculty must inhabit and enliven." This establishes the stage that teachers can use the same creative energies that is expected to engage a face-to-face classroom to enhance the online classroom. The question is how to make the transition from the traditional face to face to the online. Feenberg emphasizes the importance of this shift in mindset about how technology plays a role in education with the need for an attitudinal shift:

- Move from the belief that face-to-face is best to the belief that various environments support high quality learning
- Move from being "people oriented is incompatible with technology" to "distance education is people oriented."
- Move from "blaming technology when learning process breaks down" to "when learning process breaks down, evaluate teaching strategies."

To accomplish this, institutions need to make an investment in properly training and educating faculty and trainers as to the opportunities for deep learning that the online arena has for teaching and learning. Speck (2000) alludes to the need to link research in the efficacy of learning in online classrooms to the training of online instructors. Institutions need to invest in instructor professional development in not only the use of online platforms but how to prepare and teach online and the myriad of technology based pedagogies. It also means learning how to fuse the online platforms, producing engaging and active online learning materials such as: streaming videos and audio, developing learning tutorials, how to conduct synchronous and asynchronous communications and the proper ways to maximize the learning opportunities that exist.

PEDAGOGIES IN FOUNDATIONAL COURSES

In designing and teaching foundational courses, courses targeted to provide a solid learning foundation of the core information and concepts of a particular discipline, online learners must be engaged learners and not just passive recipients of foundational concepts. The online instructor must utilize the best methods to assure that the learners in the online course are active learners. Active learning, be it in the form of constructivism, progressive education, or behaviorism, can involve the multiplicity of interactive distance learning suggested to provide the opportunity for the student to interact with the teacher as soon as he/she finds the need for this interaction (Notar, et al., 2002). Students generally don't learn through just the posting of PowerPoint presentations or volumes of text to read or through just writing papers or answering text base questions from the readings. Participants learn through active involvement with the material. There are many opportunities to engage learners in the course and training materials beyond the posting of text to read.

To create a more active and engaged online learning environment is the key to online student success. Klemm (1998) described eight ways to enhance student engagement:

1. Require participation – consistency in participation will keep students on track in the course content
2. Form learning teams – cooperation and interaction among students will encourage further engagement and teamwork, often inflicting a feeling of responsibility to others
3. Make activity interesting – most importantly, keep activities active and appealing to multiple learning styles; reading is likely not the best way that all students learn.
4. Don't settle for opinions – opinions are okay to include, but do not let students rely

on their opinion for discussion responses; research and reading must be incorporated

5. Structure the activity – provide a clear timeline and definition of requirements and expectations
6. Require a deliverable – require a deliverable to give the students a 'goal' of such and the chance to receive specific feedback on their end product
7. Know what you are aiming for – and make sure the students know what you are aiming for; not simply participation but the ability to learn, apply, receive feedback and improve
8. Use peer grading – this may not always be appropriate but can help the students share ideas and perhaps inflict a competitive motivation

In the weekly lessons there are many pedagogical opportunities. However, these opportunities that the instructor builds into a course shell is not automated learning where the instructor posts things to do and walks away. The instructor needs to be ever present in the course and an integral part of the learning process. The instructor must model what they want the learner to do. This is of high importance in the online learning environment. Instructors need to model even in the online learning environment as our students are always watching what we do and emulating our behavior. If you want them meeting target deadlines for assignments and activities, you must also demonstrate prudence in grading and returning items in a timely fashion. If the instructor wants student online participation and ***student presence*** in a course, then the instructor must also practice presence.

PRESENCE

Presence, related to the concept of interaction, works to illustrate that students who feel they are part of a group or "present" in a community will participate more actively in group or community activities such as projects or online discussions. Presence has a social psychology basis, relating to how people interact using different media formats. Lombard and Ditton (1997) defined presence as the perceptual illusion of nonmediation which occurs when a person fails to perceive or acknowledge the existence of a medium in his/her communications environment responding as he/she would if the medium were not present. Because it is a perception, presence will vary among individuals given different situations and from time to time. This concept of presence is not only dynamic in the traditional sense of education and community but also in the online asynchronous environment. Rourke, Anderson, Garrison and Archer (2001) defined their community of inquiry model with three presence components: cognitive, social and teaching. This model supports the design of online courses as active learning environments or communities dependent upon instructors and students sharing ideas, information, and opinions. The critical component is that presence in an online course is a social phenomenon which manifests itself through the interactions among students and instructors. Teaching strategies should be developed and planned that foster presence.

Youngblood, Trede and DeCorpo (2001) define the role of the online facilitator as guiding discussions and responding promptly to student's questions. Faculty need to log-on frequently and monitor and redirect discussions as necessary. The role here of the instructor becomes that of facilitator more than the traditional teacher. In the foundational as well as the skills based, analysis synthesis and the hybrid courses the quality of facilitation is important. This can be defined as having a sense of humor, being dynamic and having the commitment and energy for being an online facilitator. The implications here are that while the instructor presence is different than face-to-face teaching, it is of equal importance to the success of online learning. The instructor must clarify expectations, initiate and direct online discussions, and provide a level of clarity that goes beyond the traditional face-to-face learning roles.

Beaubien (2002) described the personal factors that contribute to quality facilitation that can harness the power of online learning in five instructor characteristics: persona, presence, perturbing the system, positive feedback, and playfulness. The first is *persona*. A faculty member needs to let his values, beliefs, and preferences show through in his/her postings. Students need to see that the instructor has a real life and that he/she is revealing his/her real character. This can be accomplished through the instructor sharing his/her relevant experiences from both personal and professional lives which should transpire over the life of the course.

The second characteristic is *presence* which is a critical element in Web-based facilitation. Students need to feel that the instructor is online regularly and participating fully in the dialogue. The instructor does not need to be intrusive to the online dialogue but his/her presence needs to be known and that he/she is there. Short postings are good for the most part but the teachable moment should be capitalized upon to provide sufficient information and clarification as is necessary especially in the dynamics of the foundational course where the application of what is being learned may not be fully understood. It becomes the instructor's role to define these and pay attention to the affective domain of why and where this information and knowledge will be of value. Sometimes this can be accomplished through the instructor posing questions that will stimulate or lead the discussion in a direction. Modeling a high level of presence sets a positive norm for the class and encourages students to do the same.

The third characteristic is *perturb the system*. You cannot predict the future of the class, but the instructor can influence it. Beaubien perturbed the system by:

- Constantly keeping a high volume of work in front of students.
- Requiring constant effort on their part to keep current, introducing diverse and contradictory readings to challenge students' paradigms.
- Asking challenging questions that require complex analysis and synthesis to answer.
- Introducing challenging real-life examples and asking students to suggest action paths.
- Describing relevant consulting situations where I have failed marvelously and asking students what I could have done differently based on the material we are covering in class.
- Asking students to respond to points in other people's postings.
- Continuously encouraging higher levels of participation.
- Having students work on projects with tight time frames.

Positive feedback tends to bring out the best in people and motivate them to invest discretionary effort (Braksick, 2000; Daniels, 2000). Positive feedback can energize the system and increase interaction frequency facilitating both instructor and student presence. Being present online and conveying interest in the students' work provides a reinforcing environment for students. Simple responses like "good job" or "great ideas" or "thanks for sharing your insightful thoughts with the group" can have significant impact on participation levels. Hacker and Niederhauser (2000) argued that online student learning can actually be hampered by too little or too much feedback but do find that consciously communicating encouragement to the online student does provide motivation and assist with learning.

Playfulness is a great energizer. Having fun is a self-reinforcing activity that tends to increase levels of participation. The brain is never learning more than when it is having fun (McCorkel, 2002). It strengthens relationships and helps people to develop a sense of belonging and safety, part of Glaser's five compelling whys (1998). It lowers stress and fosters creativity as well as increasing online energy levels, it strengthens identity and increases team cohesiveness necessary for a community learning atmosphere.

FRAMING COURSE PEDAGOGIES

Many of the pedagogies that are offered in online courses are still text based, however with the growing acquisition of technology and the understanding of how to use it, more technologies and innovations are beginning to become part of the lexicon of online pedagogies and can become a significant part of each of the four course types. Instructors must have a level of empathy to understand how the student will receive and process the information presented. The instructor while sitting at their computer needs to put themselves in their student's place to realize if the method being employed will really have the desired effect to produce learning and achieve the desired objectives in a foundational class. There are many learning opportunities and pedagogies that can be employed as seen in Table 1. The chart summarizes common classroom pedagogies and strategies, and how they may be converted to online courses.

Online instructors attempt to capture what has worked in the traditional educational settings and transfer that to the online environment modifying pedagogies to transition into the technology format. Adapting teaching approaches that work for the learner is more important than knowledge and skill with technology (Wilson et al., 2003). Technology is not limiting and effective course design and pedagogy are required to achieve quality educational outcomes.

Converting face-to-face courses to the Web-based environment is not a simple piece-by-piece conversion process. Faculty need to re-think their goals, students or audience, subject matter, activities, assessments, and technology skills and equipment to determine the most effective online teaching and learning strategies. Instructional technology provides new opportunities for collaboration, simulations, tutorials, and other forms of synchronous and asynchronous interaction. Ideally, faculty who are teaching online courses will have experience as online learners prior to teaching online. If this is not the case, they should explore exemplary course examples to see some of the best practices in online course design prior to developing their courses.

There are many free Web-based applications available on the Web, such as You Tube, Slideshare, DimDim, and Skype. Faculty and course developers should be aware of the intellectual property policies of these applications. Some programs require students to set up accounts. In addition, most institutions are unable to technically support all these third-party applications. We use these tools in our online teaching, but recognize the limitations and back-up online content on a frequent basis.

Instructors must think of a course shell as a classroom filled with learning opportunities (Figure 1). In doing so the instructor must design the course shell to have a proper online ***feng shui*** or orientation. To keep a consistent feng shui in the preactive and active phases of teaching, instructors need to design think forward type lessons with meaningful titles that offer clarity for student understanding and provide a high degree of redundancy and consistency of structure so learning elements are clear. (Fuller, 2008). Clarity means the learners should be able to direct their attention exactly where it needs to go to learn the concepts that must be mastered. Having a similar look and common navigational and educational components such as syllabus, calendar, weekly organizational pages outlining activities, and an academic forum are important for students to have continuity (Champage, Hewitt and Short, 2002) and the necessary feng shui. This requires that lessons and modules are laid out similarly from week to week and lesson to lesson, so learners do not have to get used to a new format. Each weekly type of format allows the learners to think

Table 1. Traditional versus web-based design

Traditional	On line Opportunity
Case Study	Case studies are usually structured as text-based or video narratives with a format for students to explore the scenarios. The interaction may be team assignments, synchronous or asynchronous discussion, or individually written responses to analysis questions.
Debate	Online debates may be conducted using either synchronous or asynchronous communication tools. If using audio or video conferencing, each teams' position statement and rebuttal can be limited by timed presentations (as in the traditional classroom). If using the text-based discussion board, consider word limits to balance the arguments and assure focused concise presentations. A controversial topic with clear interaction guidelines and deadlines will enhance the debate as a learning activity.
Demonstration	Instructor demonstrations are often video recordings uploaded to the course management system, an institutional Website, or a third-party Website such as You Tube*. Large video files can also be distributed to students through DVDs/CD ROMs or can be set up as streaming videos. In addition to video, demonstrations may be presented through Microsoft PowerPoint slides that illustrate steps and procedures through photographs or images and text instructions.
Direct teaching	Direct Instruction refers to a method of delivery that maintains a high degree of rigor and structure providing students a pre-scripted set of directions by the instructor. It is a series of steps that the teacher provides followed by a series of practice opportunities to promote learning of concepts. This can be accomplished in the online through the posting of text based direct instructions or through the posting of narrated PPT presentations with specific instructions and animated graphics.
Discussion	Similar to on-ground courses, discussions have many purposes such as organizing, clarifying, analyzing, synthesizing, hypothesizing, and summarizing learning concepts. Synchronous: Elluminate, Adobe Connect, Skype*, DimDim*, Wimba or other virtual classroom tools allow for real time communication. Synchronous discussions are effective for relatively short, timely decisions, or questions with a small number of participants. Asynchronous: Asynchronous discussion forums are effective for reflective, critical thinking, and ongoing discussions. Asynchronous discussions are especially beneficial for English as Second Language learners who need extra time to compose their discussion contributions.
Evaluation: Formative	Classroom assessment techniques (CATs) are non-graded writing exercises to help instructors understand their students' progress in the course. In online courses, these exercises may include muddiest point(s), one-minute papers, summary paragraphs, paraphrasing, or student-generated test questions. CATs may be submitted through email, assignment link/box, or posted on the discussion board. For some CATs exercises, consider collecting anonymous feedback for more candid student responses. In addition, there are online quizzes and surveys which are an extremely valuable formative assessment tools. Quizzes provide opportunities for practice and feedback without consuming large amounts of instructor time. The course management system gives timely programmed feedback and often records student grades or participation in the gradebook. Midterm surveys collect student attitudes and impressions during the term, while there is still time to address important learning or communication issues.
Evaluation: Summative	Most learning management systems have exam tools that allow for multiple choice, matching, true/false, short answer, ranking, essay, and other forms of questions. Depending on the testing system, exams may be programmed for specific dates and times, time limitations, repeated or single attempts, scrambled exam items, and scrambled response options within multiple choice items. If competency based or certification exams are required, programs may contract with educational agencies. Many institutions, such as the University of Pittsburgh and Pennsylvania State University, have testing centers and established processes for proctored exams.
Group Exercises and Cooperative Learning	There are benefits to collaborative learning (also known as cooperative, team, small group, or study circles) tasks that require interdependence among the group members. Group assignments may include conducting an experiment, writing a report, delivering a presentation, preparing an argument, or analyzing a case study. Especially in online courses, group assignments should be clearly outlined so students understand their roles and responsibilities. Grading criteria and policies should also be clearly defined. In most learning management systems, communication and collaboration tools can be established for sub-groups or teams of learners. The small groups can use these tools to plan and develop their assignment, and instructors can monitor the progress without actively facilitating the process. A valuable technology tool for collaborative editing is a Web-based wiki, which allows all members of the group to contribute and edit a document. The wiki history allows all participants to see who contributed and what he/she contributed to the document.

continues on following page

Table 1. continued

Traditional	On line Opportunity
Guest Speaker	Guest speakers can present either asynchronously or synchronously using a variety of Web-based communication tools. A structured presentation may be recorded in audio, video, or as a narrated PowerPoint session. A less formal presentation may be organized as a question and answer session. Consider requiring the students to submit their questions in advance. This gives the guest speaker an opportunity to organize the questions into an effective format that meets the learning goals.
Journal	Reflective journals are metacognitive writing activities in which students reflect on their learning. Web-based blogs are popular tools for writing reflective journal or experiential learning entries because students can enhance their commentaries with images, photographs, links to other Websites, audio, and video.
Lecture	Some faculty and course developers post their lecture content as online text. Text is easy to create, requires low bandwidth to download, and is accessible to students who use assistive technologies. Text is often readily available from publisher course cartridges and CD ROMs. Publishers may also have mini lecturettes available in audio or video (podcasts or vodcasts). Instructors may also deliver their lectures in relatively short time frames with video, Web conferencing, and/or PowerPoint-type tools. A key consideration in recording lectures is to develop an engaging, interactive style, and to avoid the "talking head" phenomenon.
Library Visits	Many libraries offer virtual tours to explain the process for borrowing materials and searching databases/ collections. In addition, librarians often present virtual sessions on how to site references, avoid plagiarism, and evaluate Web resources.
Participant Presentations or Speeches	Participants can deliver their presentations by posting video, audio, text, or PowerPoint-type files. Students can post on a synchronous or synchronous conferencing/ Webinar system, or through the asynchronous discussion board of a learning management system.
Physical Activities	Through detailed instructions and demonstrations, students complete activities and report their personal results. These activities may include labs or physical exercises that students do in their homes. (See the examples in Chapter 12.)
Microsoft PowerPoint or presentation software	PowerPoint is a popular application used in many online courses because it is easy to use and relatively inexpensive. In addition to the Microsoft version of PowerPoint there are also open source software applications available on the Web such as OpenOffice. Faculty should be aware of the size of their PowerPoint files as multimedia-enhanced presentations can get quite large. Several software applications, such as Articulate, Adobe Captivate, and Camtasia Studio, incorporate PowerPoint slides with audio and automated delivery. SlideShare* is a free presentation sharing website which allows users to upload files for public or private viewing.
Problem based learning	Problem-based exercises are authentic, complex problems that unfold in stages and are often completed over a period of several weeks by small groups of learners. Each stage requires research to explore alternatives and make decisions. Students discussion problems either synchronously or asynchronously and submit solutions. The process of solving the problem is often more important than the final decision.
Research Papers and Projects	Research papers and projects are common assignments in online courses. Web search or evaluation activities are often integrated with research projects. Instructors may use writing workshops to help learners plan and develop their papers or projects. Plagiarism is a concern for many instructors, so they organize research assignment deliverables into stages that might include a thesis statement, outline, and annotated bibliography. Anti-l-plagiarism software (e.g, Turninin and Safe Assign) is available at many institutions.
Simulations and Role Play	In general, simulations are interactive multimedia programs that provide students with authentic opportunities to apply their skills. Simulations are available for operating businesses, making healthcare decisions, conducting lab experiments, and completing certification exams. An excellent source for free simulations and learning objects is the Multimedia Educational Resource for Learning and Online Teaching (www.merlot.org).
Student Success Strategies	
Social Interaction (Participant & Instructor)	Social interaction is diligently facilitated by the instructor through discussion boards, emails, and telephone availability. Faculty and course developers can establish an opening introductory activity such as "This is Me" activity to enhance interaction.
Time Management	A structured course with clear expectations promotes effective time management for students and faculty. Strategies include controlling the dissemination of information and facilitating student involvement through established timelines with schedules, calendars, and course maps.

continues on following page

Table 1. continued

Traditional	On line Opportunity
Specific Seat Time	One of the advantages of the online teaching and learning environment is the flexible schedule or the "learn anytime anywhere" focus.

ahead as to what is expected and required for success and learning to occur. Students need to know that they will not need to spend time trying to find out where things are each week but that there is a consistent weekly (or other time design) structure that flows from the posted syllabus or program agenda.

As the student enters the course shell, he/she should initially see the announcement page that tells him what is going to happen and what the focus is for this particular time frame and lesson as well as direct him on where to go and what to do. This can be provided through text or audio that describes the activities and provides instructions on where to go. Many systems allow the instructor to post a hyperlink to specific sections in the course. This saves the student time and provides clarity to operations. Consistency in structure should also allow the student to see in the weekly lesson the expectations of the lessons and the workload and that provide an outline of the due dates for weekly activities, assignments and discussion boards. There needs to be a fair amount of structure with open-endedness that provides a comfort zone for the students.

The instructor needs to build in an expanded level of clarity so participants do not miss understand text information with different levels of interpretation and understanding. In the online teaching and learning the instructor needs to expand the level of clarity that is offered between student and instructor. To accomplish this, the instructor must

Figure 1.

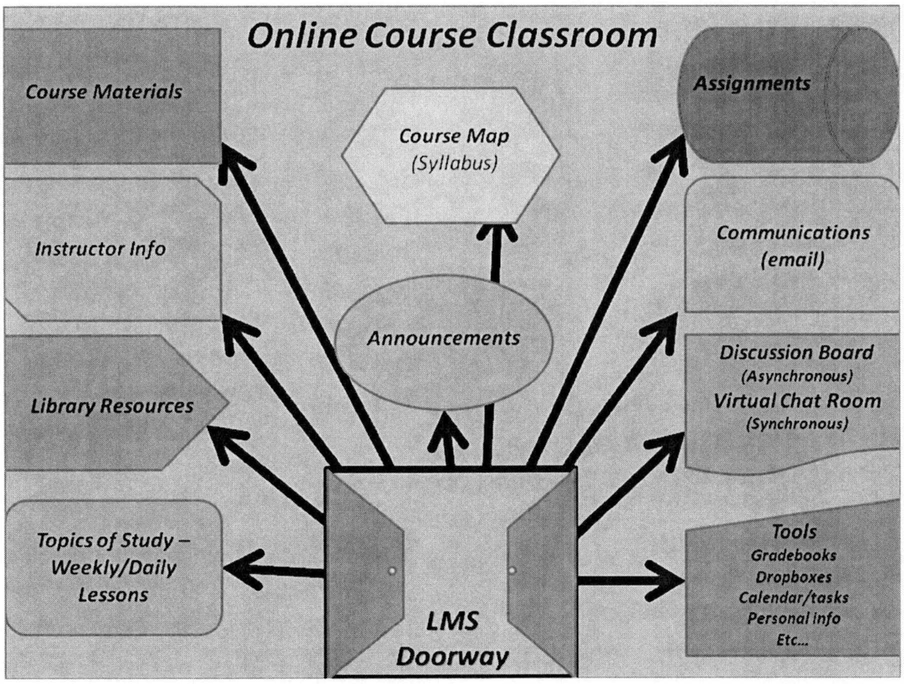

be empathetic to how the students will receive and interpret posted information. Consistency and uniformity of structure will go far to avoid confusion allowing the student to focus their efforts on the learning and not on the organization. For the student, the structure needs to become almost automatic in nature. One way to judge the level of clarity is for the instructor to look at their course shell design as they themselves enter the course. If the instructor is struggling with this course content and shell design, then the student will struggle as well. In having students feel more connected to the content the instructor must use an ongoing process to gain and maintain clarity. This can best be accomplished through clarity of the instruction and purpose as well as tying in the objectives so that students can understand the relevance of the content and the layout and design of the shell. For many instructors this is a developmental process to understand how to design course information and material best suited to achieve this goal.

Reflections

1. Take a look at your online courses. Do they provide a consistent structure that students can understand?
2. Are their areas that may be confusing to students in clarity of instruction or in the ability to understand and find materials.
3. How can you make your online courses more consistent and easier for students to understand?

FOUNDATIONAL COURSE PEDAGOGIES

As listed in Table 1 there are many pedagogical opportunities that can be employed in the foundational course. The limitations are only in the mind of the instructor as to how and what to include. The choice of pedagogy as previously stated should not be chosen based upon the perceived limitations of an online format but flow as a natural choice based upon the ability to meet the objectives. In this section we will look and discuss some different pedagogies that can be incorporated into online *foundational course* training and educational lessons.

COOPERATIVE LEARNING TECHNIQUES IN FOUNDATIONAL COURSES

Cooperative learning is based upon the work of Dewey (1916) in his book Democracy and Education. Dewey stated that the classroom should mirror the large society through teachers creating a learning environment that uses democratic procedures and scientific processes. Through cooperative learning students learn in a supportive environment from each other as much as they learn from the instructor and the material. By its very nature, much of online learning is cooperative in scope. Cooperative learning as currently defined emphasizes student learning through homogeneous and heterogeneous groupings where students learn through interaction with other students and through helping and guiding each other toward a stated goal. It is inherent in this type of learning that there are strong students teamed with weaker students with the goal that the stronger students will assist and guide the weaker student to make learning progress. The stronger student learns and retains at a greater rate through teaching and sharing. The intrinsic nature of online learning lends itself toward cooperative learning through discussion boards and the careful facilitation of students interacting on a weekly basis.

There are several cooperative learning opportunities that will engage students in active learning in the traditional face-to-face classroom. We will discuss these in terms of how they can be utilized in the online foundational classroom:

Jigsaw Method (Kagan, 1994) - Groups with up to five students are established with group members (designated as a home group) choosing or are designated some part of a lesson (chunked out by the instructor) to learn themselves and then teach the remainder of the group. To assist in the process, students from other groups gather together in expert groups to learn their sections deciding on what is important and how best to teach that particular subsection to the rest of the class. After learning the subsection materials, all expert groups return to their home group and present the material in a chronological order established either by the group or the instructor. In the online environment, the number of home groups and expert groups are based upon the number in the course. In most course platforms the instructor has the option of developing groups that can communicate online and via email separate from the entire group. In certain situations this Jig-Saw method can be modified to group the class into sections to research learn and develop presentation materials and then return to the larger group posting their group materials into a discussion board with each group presenting and leading discussions for the entire group. The instructor's role here is to monitor and inject in the discussion board where clarity necessitates. This can also be accomplished during a synchronous chat via the virtual chat functions or in another online platform such as Adobe Connect or Wimba where groups or individuals present to the entire group in a designated sequence to build the entire picture or knowledge.

Think-Pair-Share (Kagan, 1994) – is a widely popular tool that focuses students and allows them to come to a discussion armed with the tools and information to successfully participate in classroom discussions. This generally involves a three step process that is guided by the instructor. The first step involves participants individually analyzing a situation or a question that the instructor poses. In the traditional classroom participants will think silently and analyze a question individually writing down their ideas. The second step involves the pairing of participants to exchange thoughts and ideas. The third step entails the groups or pairs sharing their ideas with the whole group. The purpose of this in the traditional class is to avoid a superficial discussion that does not delve deep enough in the material to allow students to understand the purpose and the application of concepts (the affective domain). The shortcomings of traditional class are that discussions tend to be superficial by nature as students generally don't have the time to get deep enough into the discussion which can be generally dominated by a few while others choose not to say anything. The online environment does not suffer this dilemma. This cooperative method can be easily utilized in the online environment through the discussion board. Due to the feeling of anonymity, participants are more willing to post a thoughtful discussion board. As this is asynchronous and students are working and learning at their own pace they have time to analyze the material in the weekly lesson and then post a cogent thread that references the weekly materials and readings. The instructor can use the Think-Pair-Share in the nature of having students work individually and then pair them to discuss their ideas via email or an established group in the course shell and then post to the larger weekly topic discussion board or he can choose to eliminate step two in the process.

Group Projects and Presentations – In the traditional face-to-face classroom participants can be given an assignment that requires them to work as a team to develop and or present a concept. The students are provided with the assignment parameters and then are given class time as well as encouraged to work out of class to develop and present a group project. The projects can be in the form of a paper or a t presentation. It could be the analysis of a set of case studies or the solution to a presented problem. Many times this requires research through the literature to support ideas and findings. In the online course, group projects are just as opportunistic in posing a greater learning opportunity. Students can again be provided a group platform on the course shell or they can be encouraged to communicate via email or phone as may be deemed necessary. Through a division of labor, the students prepare a project in the form of a paper, or solution to a problem with steps and procedures or the presentation of a PowerPoint. This can be posted on a general discussion board for all in the class to review and comment upon through a specific discussion thread.

Group Investigations -operate very similarly to the Group project in that the instructor divides the group up into small heterogeneous units of 4-5 or whatever is appropriate for the task to be investigated and either assigns each group a topic or lets the group choose an area to study. The groups become responsible for the division of labor and gather and learns the materials. This culminates in the group reporting their findings through either an asynchronous discussion board or through the use of synchronous real time chat.

One of the major issues with both Group Investigation, and Group Projects and presentations is the division of labor and the fair and valid assessment provided participants (if a summative evaluation is being utilized). The complaint from students is that the division of labor is not always equitable and that a few in the group do the majority of work while others appear to glide along providing little to the project or investigation however receive the same grade. While a group grade is generally given for the work provided by the group a way to make the assessment more equitable is for the group to provide an assessment of the contributions made by all members of the team. This is done based upon established criteria set by the instructor and emailed individually by all group members. The instructor can then integrate the group's assessment of the team into the individual participant grades providing a fair assessment. Online participants understanding this at the onset of the project or investigation then know the value of their participation and how the assessment will be conducted.

Student Achievement Divisions (STAD) a technique that has traditionally been used in the face-to –face environment with great success provides learning opportunity in the online foundation class. This technique creates four to five member teams learning as a unit. The participants can utilize text based lessons or a series of text and streaming video or voice over type presentations. Coupling this with a worksheet format and other activity based devices that can include many of the investigative and project based activities discussed above, students work together to help each other learn the material. Communications again are established within the course shell as groups and monitored by the instructor. The instructor's role is not only to design the activities and set up the course shell but to interact with the groups for clarification and enhancement of content interaction. These can culminate in a form of weekly/biweekly tests or other summative evaluation tools to assure foundational information is being learned.

In the planning and incorporation of cooperative learning strategies, online instructors must consider whether the material is conducive to a cooperative activity and if the necessary time is available for students to interact, whether the geographical time zone differences are conducive to certain types of interaction, and whether specific instructions and or training are necessary to maximize the cooperative learning experience. Cooperative learning is like any successful technique, it can be overused. Any strategy, in fact, can be overused and lose its effectiveness (Marzano, Pickering, and Pollock, 2001, p. 91). The key with online instructional strategies is to mix them up, so that the learner is constantly being faced with new and different learning challenges. This can be motivational and maintain student interest.

Reflections

1. How have you utilized cooperative learning techniques in your face-to-face education or training courses

2. In your online courses, how have you utilized cooperative learning techniques?
3. Are there techniques that have been described here that you could incorporate into your online courses?

ONLINE DIRECT TEACHING METHODS

The use of direct instruction is a staple in many educational and training sessions. Direct Instruction refers to a method of delivery that maintains a high degree of rigor and structure providing students a pre-scripted set of directions by the instructor. It is a series of steps that the teacher provides followed by a series of practice opportunities to promote learning of concepts. It is a highly efficient method of instructional delivery that promotes the mastery of skills and knowledge outcomes.

First developed by Siegfried Englemann and Carl Bereiter through their work with disadvantaged children (Bereiter & Engelmann, 1966) direct instruction is grounded in behaviorism. The teaching and learning approach works with the idea that consequences for behavior both positive and negative strengthen the learning. This is contrary to Social Learning Theory (Bandura, 1986) which describes learning through the observation and interaction with others.

Direct instruction can play an integral role as an online instructional strategy in the foundational course as well as a skills based course. Through having students seeing the concepts demonstrated by the instructor, then practicing the concepts, the students in the online setting can master the concepts and skills to be learned and become active rather than passive learners. There are six basic steps or phases to using direct instruction online. They are first to 1) establish the goals and objectives, 2) Explanation/modeling, 3) provide guided practice opportunity, 4) provide feedback to the participant, 5) provide a comprehensive practice activity, and 6) evaluate knowledge and skill gained by the student.

Let's assume that we are teaching a foundational concept such as PowerPoint software online. While some may consider this a skills based course, it can also be considered foundational in nature as are many courses. There are many steps and procedures associated with learning the software. We want to teach the knowledge and skill that go along with changing the font of text on a slide. Let's look at the steps and phases in using the direct instruction strategy to accomplish this in a course shell:

Phase 1 Establish the Goals and Objectives

In the course shell the instructor can provide a lesson focus through listing the goals and objectives of the lesson, providing background info and explaining the importance or who cares. This can be similar to anticipatory set that allows the student an understanding of the goals. Below is an example of an objective and an introductory statement or focus that can provide clarity for the participants.

Example: At the end of this lesson students will be able to change the font in a PowerPoint.
Focus: This week we are going to look at how we change the fonts in a PowerPoint presentation. Fonts are an important part of how the viewers of a presentation receive our information. Different fonts can set the tone for different kinds of presentations. If we wanted to be more whimsical we might choose Comic San MS. If we wanted a more formal look we might use Arial or Times New Roman. We are going to look at the steps and procedures for changing font styles. Please follow along with the PowerPoint presentation below.

Phase 2 Explanation/Modeling

In the explanation/modeling phase the teacher correctly demonstrates the concept or skill correctly. This is presented as step-by-step information. This can be accomplished through a number of methods. The instructor can develop a PowerPoint that would demonstrate the steps with the use of graphics and arrows of the program with the use of voice over demonstrating and explaining all procedures. This is not so dissimilar to how an instructor would demonstrate and explain in a face-to-face class. This can also be accomplished through the creation of a streaming video. Please review Figures 2 through 4 that demonstrate the graphics that might be utilized.

Phase 3 Provide Guided Practice Opportunity

The instructor in this phase creates an assignment that requires the students to practice what they have just seen in the online demonstration. This initial practice allows the participants to initially work with the concepts just presented. The question is how would you create an initiate practice activity? What would you have the students do? In this instance the process is relatively easy. You could provide the student with a predeveloped PowerPoint you created or have the students create a few slides and then go in a change the fonts to Arial or Times New Roman or any other.

Phase 4 Provide Feedback to the Participant

Teacher checks to see if students are performing the concepts and skills correctly check for understanding and providing feedback to correct and incorrect performance. In the online this feedback is through posted or emailed work and communications. If the student is having difficulty with a concept, the instructor can provide online dialogue as to how better accomplish the task and provide clues to success. While this example concept of changing fonts is relatively simple, other more involved concepts may take more instructor interaction. If students were conducting literature searches through an online library, the instructor could provide the same type of direct instruction for the use of Boolean searches with a set of PowerPoint or text based instructions and

Figure 2. Step 1: highligh the text

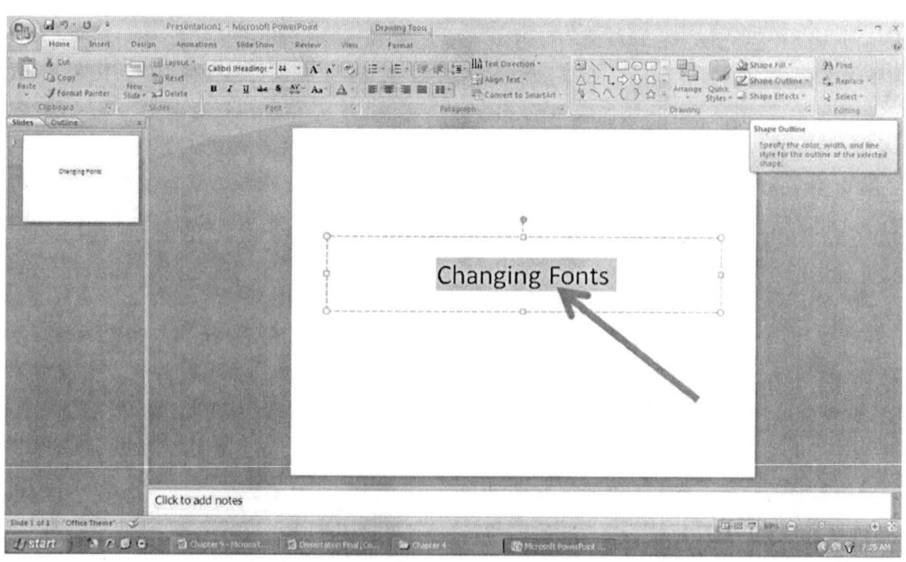

Figure 3. Step 2: on the 'home tab' click the drop down font menu

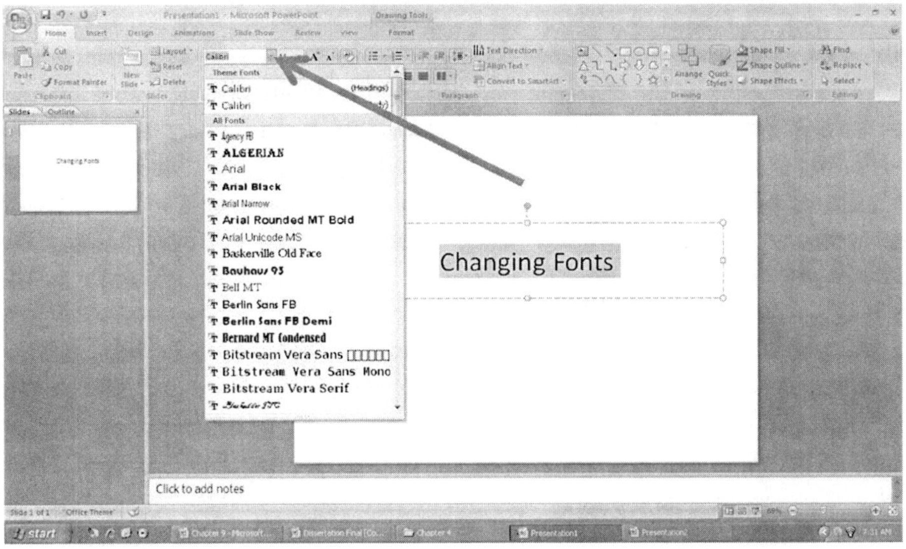

Figure 4. Step 3: Highlight and click the desired font. This will change the font on the slide

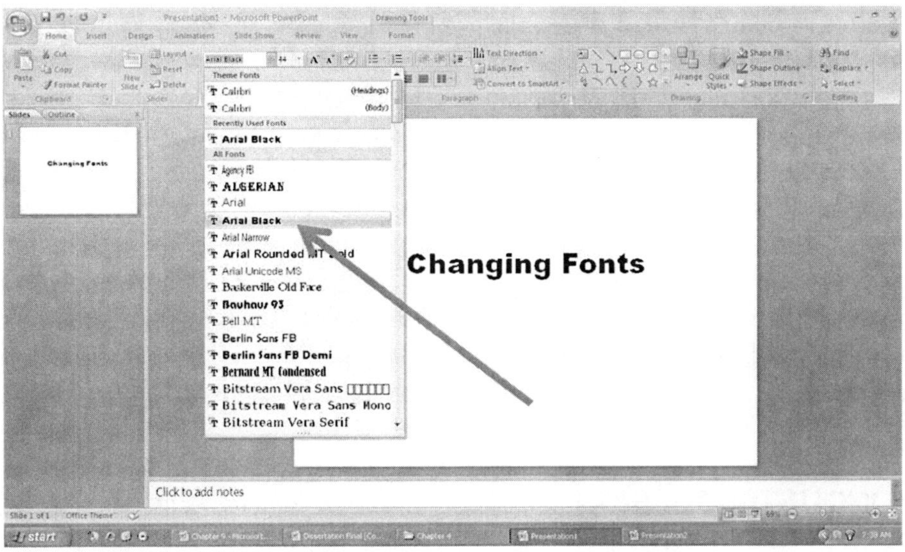

establishes a practice opportunity where students search for articles. When and if students have any difficulty finding appropriate literature, the instructor through email or other synchronous communications can provide feedback and additional information on how better to approach the task. The question the instructor needs to ask themselves is how would you provide feedback and in what form? This type of feedback is also known as formative assessment (as discussed in chapter 8) and is imperative interaction for students to learn and understand the value of the concepts.

Phase 5 Provide a Comprehensive Practice Activity

In this phase the instructor sets conditions for extended practice with attention to transfer of skill to more complex settings or situations. This is important as the student begins to understand the larger application of the skill and sees where the concepts can be utilized. In the example of changing fonts, the instructor could utilize this in conjunction with other skills attained. This could all culminate in the development of a complete PowerPoint presentation where the students introduce themselves in a presentation titled "This is Me."

If we were going to extend the online library literature review that would be included in the researching and writing of a paper. This would then illustrate the need and the application of conducting Boolean literature searches in a library data base. The extended practice not only reinforces individual concepts, but actually combines many concepts in a higher order learning application.

Phase 6 Evaluate Knowledge and Skill Gained by the Student

The final phase involves summative evaluation of the student's progress toward the stated goals. This can be done in a variety of ways. In some cases we can use an exam format as discussed in chapter 8. The instructor can also use a project based assessment with an appropriate rubric to assess student work and mastery of the foundational concepts and skills.

ASYNCHRONOUS DISCUSSION BOARDS AND SYNCHRONOUS VIRTUAL CHAT ROOM

In the foundational course, the use of instructor interaction is vital to assure that foundational knowledge and skills are being learned and not just left to the student's own devices. The use of asynchronous and synchronous communications becomes vital to understanding and assuring that learning is taking place. This becomes a fundamental form of formative evaluation. Instructors need to have frequent checks for learning and student understanding of structure and open up a dialogue about an area or issue as needed (Fuller, 2008, p 159). Instructors need to frequently check that learning is occurring and that students understand. This is an overt move on the part of online instructors conducted in both the discussion boards and through emails. Instructors will frequently open lines of communication with either the entire group for a check of learning or with specific online students that may be exhibiting difficulty with the material as demonstrated through weekly assignments or through weekly interactions. It becomes important for the instructor to structure and facilitate feedback between him/herself and the student (Vrasidas & McIsaac, 1999; Beaubin, 2002). This feedback can be generally facilitated through the asynchronous modes of discussion boards and emails as stated. However, occasionally a student needs to have a synchronous conversation to include both the real contact and the level of dialogue necessary to gain the clarity of understanding the foundational concepts. This synchronous communication can be established through a real time tool such as Skype, Wimba, Adobe Connect or simply a phone call and can be initiated by either the student or the instructor.

While many of the pedagogies are innate to one type of course over another, the pedagogies described in each of the course types provide a myriad of pedagogical opportunity for the instructor to draw upon. The instructor is only limited by his imagination in the ability to meet objectives and student needs. Many of the pedagogies listed and described for use in the foundational course can be used and modified to meet skills based courses, analysis/synthesis courses and used generally across the board in hybrid courses.

Reflections

1. Look at those courses that you have listed as foundational in your online teaching. What pedagogies have you traditionally incorporated?

2. Which of the pedagogies presented and discussed in this chapter could you incorporate?
3. What technological training do you anticipate needing to assist you in the production and development of these to enhance your online course?

REFERENCES

Bandura, A. (1986). *Social Foundations of Thought and Action*. Englewood Cliffs, NJ: Prentice-Hall.

Beaubien, J. (2002). Harnessing the power of complexity in an online learning environment . In Rudestam, K. E., & Schoenholtz-Read, J. (Eds.), *Handbook of Online Learning: Innovations in Higher Education and Corporate Training* (pp. 221–236). Thousand Oaks, CA: Sage Publications.

Bereiter, C., & Engelmann, S. (1966). *Teaching disadvantaged children in the preschool*. Englewood Cliffs, NJ: Prentice-Hall.

Champagne, M. T., Hewitt, D., & Short, T. (2002). Access to opportunity: The Duke-East Carolina partnership for training program. *Journal of Asynchronous Learning Networks*, *6*(1).

Dewey, J. (1926). *Democracy and education: An introduction to the philosophy of education*. New York: Macmillan. (Original manuscript published in 1916).

Feenberg, A. (1999). Distance learning: Promise or threat. *Crosstalk*. Retrieved from http://www-rohan.sdsu.edu/faculty/feenberg/TELE3.HTM

Fuller, R. G. (2008). *Faculty Practices in Asynchronous Online Distance Education: A Study within Health Education Programs*. Saarbrucken, Germany: VDM Verlag.

Kagan, S. (1994). *Cooperative Learning*. San Clemente, CA: Kagan Publishing.

Marzano, R. J., Pickering, D. J., & Pollock, J. E. (2001). *Classroom instruction that works: Research-based strategies for increasing student achievement*. Alexandria, VA: Association for Supervision and Curriculum Development.

Notar, C. E., Wilson, J. D., Restauri, S. L., & Friery, K. A. (2002). Going the distance: Active learning. *Education*, *122*(4), 649–654.

Pallof, R. M., & Pratt, K. (2002). Beyond the looking glass: What faculty and students need to be successful online . In Rufestam, K. E., & Schoenholtz-Read, J. (Eds.), *Handbook of online learning: Innovations in higher education and corporate training* (pp. 171–184). London: Sage Publishing.

U.S. Department of Education. (2009). Office of Planning, Evaluation, and Policy Development. In *Evaluation of Evidence-Based Practices in Online Learning: A Meta-Analysis and Review of Online Learning Studies,* Washington, D.C. Retrieved June 2009, at http://www.ed.gov/about/offices/list/opepd/ppss/reports.html

Vrasidas, C., & McIsaac, M. S. (1999). Factors Influencing Interaction in an Online Course. *American Journal of Distance Education*, *13*(3), 22–36. doi:10.1080/08923649909527033

Chapter 11
Active Teaching Phases:
Skills Based and Analysis/ Synthesis Pedagogies

PEDAGOGIES IN SKILLS BASED COURSES

In designing and teaching skill based courses, courses requiring students to gain a particular mental or physical skill(s) set that is applicable to a specific environment, online learners again, must be engaged learners. The goal with the online skills course is to allow the student to become as naturalized in the skill as possible given the time constraints of the course or training. This requires a focus on assuring that the skill is properly modeled for the student and that ample guided practice is provided and promoted. The instructor needs to give sufficient interactive feedback to allow the student to achieve a high level of competency, as can be measured through a summative assessment tool. The online instructor must utilize the best methods to assure that the learners in the online course are active learners.

In teaching skills online the instructor needs to use similar pedagogies as are incorporated into the traditional face-to-face course. There are several models designed to teach skills which ascend from the inclusion of direct instruction. One method is the DECA system for attaining skills. This method presents a direct instruction focus that provides proper modeling of the skill and sufficient practice and feedback to assist the student toward naturalization of both mental and physical skills. DECA stands for Demonstration, Explain, Criticism, and Assistance.

The first step in the DECA process is to *demonstrate* the skill. This requires that the instructor present the model by showing the procedure and demonstrating the ideal way to conduct the process or perform the task. Modeling in this step provides the student an end target which they can use to match what they are doing with the desired end result. It assists them to self-evaluate their progress toward naturalization of the skill. This requires that the instructor pay attention to detail and provide the textbook way to perform the skill as the student will emulate what he sees the instructor do. If the instructor models the skill with an error, the student not understanding that it is an error will see this as correct, as the instructor is the expert, and perform as the instructor. The

DOI: 10.4018/978-1-61520-865-4.ch011

danger is, the first way a student sees a skill is how the skill process will be imprinted and how they will remember it.

In the online environment, the physical skill can be modeled in several ways. Some may see this as a limitation in the online environment as the student and instructor are separated by time and space; however there are several opportunities that can be as good if not better than the traditional. This does require initial instructor or course developer production time to prepare online demonstrations or publisher created materials may be utilized. These demonstrations can be presented in the course shell as videos and graphic presentations through programs such as PowerPoint or other graphic presentations packages. This can be a stronger demonstration as the instructor can assure through production that the skills are being properly demonstrated utilizing the textbook way with no errors to cause student confusion. The skills can be practiced through the demonstration and culmination of final projects such as with the development of a science lab project or such as the development of CPR skills where the student must practice and demonstrate proficiency in front of a physical preceptor. As discussed in chapter 9, some skills such as healthcare clinical skills may have a physical presence requirement to validate skill attainment.

Cognitive skills can be demonstrated with ease through text or again demonstration of the skill through a narrated graphics presentation (PPT). Instructors can provide a series of instructions on how to conduct the skill that include the steps and procedures with clues for success and a rubric that specifically lays out the criteria for success. The instructor should follow this with an exemplary model of the final product such as a project or paper that demonstrates the culmination of the desired skills. This goes far to model the process and illustrates to students the final skill to be attained.

The second step in the process is to *explain*. Once the model has been presented and the student has a final picture or model in mind, the instructor explains the steps of the skill in detail, actually analyzing the process as if each step itself is a separate skill. The instructor needs to assure that the mental or physical skill process is both accurate and complete during this step. Instructors need to be careful that they don't focus on bad habits that they themselves have developed over the years, but center on proper text book methods with clues for success at each step. In the online education or training program, this is accomplished again through the use of video and narrated graphic presentations.

The third step is *criticism*. This is where the instructor provides an online activity that focuses the student on practicing the newly demonstrated skill. In this mode the instructor needs to be sure that each of the steps are broken down into easily understood components so that the student can practice with a clear understanding of the dynamics of the skill. The instructor can then coordinate activities that have the student demonstrate the skill or a portion of the skill in an online component through email exchange or in a threaded online discussion board. An example skill in this phase might be the development of a focused research question. The activity can have the student chose a subject area and then write research questions. Through the posting of the research questions in a discussion board thread, all in the course can see and learn from each other with proper feedback and suggestions for clarification and greater focus. This is the time for the instructor to spot potential problems and prevent the development of bad habits. This also becomes the "teachable moment" to correct errors and to support proper skill demonstration by the participants.

The final step of the process is *assistance* were the instructor helps the person being trained through encouraging them to ask questions and to grow along Bloom's taxonomy toward the naturalization of the skill. This can be done by perturbing things as Beaubien (2002) states. In the teaching of skills this is done by not only focusing on their questions, but also posing questions that make them think about the skill and applying it in different venues and areas of application. This is also accomplished online by encouraging them to practice and providing different opportunities such as asking them, "How would they apply the skill in this area or another?" If they were developing the skill to write research questions, the instructor could offer different research areas and ask participants how they would phrase questions. This becomes part of active learning were students are engaged in the learning process rather than simple passive recipient of knowledge and skill in an online venue. The level of interaction with the instructor is geared toward guiding the student through the process while facilitating them to be a dynamic learner. As the online instructor observes the online students responses and the development of the skills through practice, he can provide additional DECA as is warranted.

SYNCHRONOUS AND ASYNCHRONOUS COMMUNICATIONS IN SKILLS BASED COURSES

Discussion boards play an integral role in the teaching and interactive review of student progress toward the naturalization of the skills. The goal is to escalate the student up Bloom's psychomotor continuum. In many courses students may only attain a certain precision level of a skill. The use of a combination of synchronous and asynchronous discussion board communications can go far to increasing the level toward naturalization of the skill. The key to student success in the acquisition of skills is the level of interaction and presence that the instructor practices and models for the participants. In the coming chapters, we will look at some examples of skills based courses that will illustrate some possibilities.

Reflections

1. Look at those courses that you have listed as skills based course. Are there courses that you have not taught online that could be taught online? Which skills based courses are you currently teaching online. What pedagogies have you traditionally incorporated?
2. Which of the pedagogies presented and discussed could you incorporate?
3. What technological training would you need to assist you in the development and production of these online activities to enhance online learning?

FACILITATING THE ANALYSIS SYNTHESIS COURSE

In designing and teaching online Analysis/Synthesis courses, which incorporate the ability to analyze a situation and engage in problem solving (Fuller and Kuhne, 2008) three major components need to be considered by the instructor: the presentation of core information, concepts, knowledge and facts and the careful facilitation of analysis and then the synthesis of that information. These are courses where there may not necessarily be a right or wrong view but a series of facts presented that require analysis to break down the concepts for the learner to understand and then synthesis to assist the learner to determine a point of view. The key element is for the instructor to channel students to see all elements and consider all facts to draw their own logical conclusions. This can be accomplished using several pedagogies.

Generally, the Analysis/Synthesis course begins each lesson with the presentation of information on a topic. The information may be presented as a series of facts or descriptions of a current situation. The example used in Chapter 2 was the comparison of the United States health care system versus the Canadian health care model.

Initially, participants in the online course may have a particular opinion on which is the better system as many times issues like this fall along political lines of thinking. The instructor needs to present the unbiased facts regarding both systems during the lesson. These can be presented using a variety of online pedagogies as presented in figure 10.1. The instructor can choose to have the students read text book material that depict the concepts of each health care system and post articles that lay out the systems as they are. He/she can choose to have the students read editorials or opinion pieces on each of the systems through video or view a PowerPoint with instructor voice over that depict key elements of fact and information. The instructor can post a *guided exploration* of web sites that show integral facts, data, statistics and other vital information and then have them write a brief monograph paper for posting on a threaded discussion (asynchronous) that examine and allow the student to begin to draw some conclusions based on the facts. The guided exploration is a posted web site or series of web sites to explore with specific instructions on what to view along with a series of guiding questions that focus the student on the desired information and facts. The instructor can also create or post a publisher's video that depicts fact or an expert's opinion of vital information.

Once the facts have been presented and absorbed by the participants, the next step is for the instructor to facilitate the analysis and synthesis of these ideas. This can be done through a number of pedagogies. The instructor can assign a position paper that requires the student to present the facts and then draw conclusions based on those facts although this can become voluminous in nature for both the student and instructor on a weekly basis. Another option for the instructor to consider is to use a weekly discussion board where students can through a facilitated question or problem statement analyze and synthesize the content information fleshing out all views and sides of the issues. Students can also be facilitated to choose a topic or area of the weekly content, interview someone and then write a monograph paper and/or discuss their issue and what they have found through the guided exploration by leading a discussion board thread. All of these culminate with a clearer understanding of the concepts and a fleshing out of all the facts surrounding an issue or the sides of a topic.

The most difficult element of this is for the instructor not to let his own personal view or bias to be seen by the participants. If he does then the opportunity for the analysis and synthesis skill to develop by the participants becomes lost. The instructor must not display his own view or opinion but plays the role of "devil's advocate" in prodding the system and assuring that students view all sides of the issue. *Synthesis/Analysis* or discussion-based courses teach students to analyze a situation and engage in problem solving. Care needs to be taken not to become authoritative but facilitative in this type of course. Instructors will find that authoritative postings shut down dialogue or that students will simply "parrot" instructor ideas or postings (Fuller and Kuhne, 2008). The "parroting" is most likely due to participants not wanting to be wrong and not wanting to challenge the instructor even if they believe otherwise. The overall danger is stopping the students from thinking and problem solving any further.

Dialogue among participants in the analysis/synthesis course provides regular opportunities for reflection and inquiry and requires the least intervention in the discussion boards of all the course types. Interaction in this manner through subject matter presentation can subsume part of the interaction by causing students to consider different views, approaches and solutions and generally to interact with a course content as well as other participants. There is a need to establish the culture of independent collaborative learning. Instructors respond to key ideas and elements and, through additional questions, guide the learning process. If the discussion is getting one sided or negative the instructor can, through a posted thought, direct the dialogue to view all sides. "That is true but what would 'so and so' say regarding this and why?" One of the general goals with an analysis/synthesis course is to have students view and understand all sides of the issues.

Beaubien (2002) states that the instructor does not need to be intrusive to the online dialogue but his/her presence needs to be known and that he/she is there. Short postings are good for the most part but the teachable moment should be capitalized upon to provide sufficient information and clarification as is necessary. Sometimes the instructor needs to pose questions that will stimulate or lead the discussion in a direction. Instructors need to practice what Vandergrift (2002) describes as restrained presence in an effort to facilitate students' personal responsibility for their own learning and for community building in the online learning environment. Facilitators should preferably coordinate discussions and encourage participation, but at the same time they should avoid being identified with authority (Fisher & Coleman, 2002). Rovia (2002) stated that the threat to community occurs when one or more students or the instructor use an authoritative tone in online discussions, followed by those students who have a more inclusive style of discourse, who feel put off and thus reduce discussion participation.

Discussions in the analysis/synthesis course can be deeper and more reflective, covering a broader range of issues than a traditional face to face discussion. This is generally true as with a traditional face-to-face discussion, some students may be reluctant to participate as they may not trust the relevance of their comments or they don't want to say something that will make them look unintelligent. Face-to-face discussions can also be more superficial as participants may not have had the time to analyze and synthesize key information necessary to make informed comments. The online discussion offered in an asynchronous format allows the instructor to ask thought provoking questions, guiding students to support their ideas in the literature, to generate dialogue and to have students explore all sides of an issue drawing upon greater levels of content material.

Open-ended questions are used in an analysis synthesis type course to set the stage for learning all sides of the issues. These higher-end questions foster students to synthesize a great deal of the content information and then process it to formulate responses and opinions based upon the course content and their own understanding and experiences. The instructor's role is to summarize all postings at the end of the designated time to draw the elements to conclusion acknowledging students' contributions by name and ideas but, with the practiced self-control in their postings to a discussion board, they read all student postings but do not necessarily respond to all. They respond selectively to connect concepts or redirect the group or individuals.

How students are facilitated to interact is an important part of this dynamic. The use of questions and questioning techniques is a staple of the interactive online teacher. If a student is very pro on one side of an issue the instructor should facilitate and gently ask them a series of questions that require them to look at the other side of an issue. In a threaded discussion the instructor can say, "I understand your position and I appreciate your beliefs but what about .....? Asking poignant questions of the original respondents helps them expand beyond their unilateral view of the issue.

USING THE ONLINE DEBATE

One pedagogical technique that can assist in this goal is to institute an online structured debate (Fuller, 2008). Structured differently than the weekly discussion boards, a debate serves to focus student attention in a deliberate, researched collaborative investigation to convince others that their view or assigned view is efficacious. This deliberate thought-out process affords students the ability to take a stance on an issue and to research it toward a logical conclusion. According to the learner centered conception, having learners involved with real situations or simulations of the issue is critical to effectively engaging them and making their experience more meaningful. Learning, as it normally occurs, is a function of the activity, context and culture in which it occurs. This contrasts with traditional classroom learning activities that involve knowledge which is often presented in an abstract form and out of context (Kearsley, 1996).

For example students in an upper-level management course studying the concepts of traditional top-down management philosophies and the contrary organizational learning concepts can each be randomly assigned to different groups with opposing views of management. These views may or may not be in line with their espoused beliefs. The groups meet online through email or the establishment of online group divisions with their own asynchronous discussion boards to allow communication and plan their debate topics. Group synchronous communications can also be established through some LMS platforms that allow real time communications using text based chat rooms or using voice and live feed video. Each group or groups will establish a division of labor using a collaborative learning strategy. They then research and build their cases from the literature and readings and as a team gather convincing information. The instructor can then establish an online debate format to take place over the course of a week or possibly two as needed. The debate format usually takes the form of each side presenting their initial data by a certain time including real world examples from their own experiences as well as those presented in the literature. The sides each have the opportunity to read the other group's initial arguments and then formulate a counter response arguing against the other sides' initial presentation by a later time in the week. Additional points are then posted and final closing arguments are made for their side. The instructor serves as moderator and can if he/she wishes declare a winner, although this is not as important as the facilitation of facts, learning and supported opinions.

SOCRATIC METHODS OF FACILITATION IN DISCUSSION BOARDS

Socratic Teaching is considered by some to be one of the most powerful teaching strategies to influence a student's critical thinking process. This age old strategy focuses on providing students a series of probing and thought provoking questions to guide thinking. The Socratic instructor is less interested in providing answers and is more interested in the student's process for arriving at the answer to those questions. Using Socratic methods in a synchronous and asynchronous discussion board is a vital tool especially in an analysis/synthesis type course; although the technique has merit in the other three courses as well. The instructor must model the type of deep inquiry that continually asks questions and is not willing to accept a superficial response. This is an ongoing process of questioning a student's goals and reasoning, probing the elements of an issue, concept, problem or question that has been posed by the instructor or participants. Each new element presents an opportunity to delve deeper into the critical thinking process incorporating and questioning the logic and content being presented. The instructor can question whether the participant is analyzing the correct information and if there is other relevant data to support their conclusions and responses. This forces the student to consider alternative data and information as well as other interpretations of the facts. This will cause students to question other student's assumptions in a discussion board. The Socratic approach in a discussion board is a powerful tool that can become self-fulfilling as students start to understand and begin to question other student's posts and assumptions. They will begin to bring in alternative facts and information and offer additional points of view. They will each begin to question and ask each other to trace out their responses as well as the implications and consequences of the positions and statements. As this evolves in the discussion board, the role of the instructor becomes to monitor and direct as is needed to maximize the critical thinking and the analysis synthesis process.

Reflections

1. Look at those courses that you have listed as analysis/synthesis in your online teaching. What pedagogies have you traditionally incorporated? Do you used a single model or pedagogy?
2. Which of the pedagogies presented and discussed in this chapter could you incorporate?
3. How can you utilize the Socratic method in facilitating your asynchronous and synchronous discussions?
4. Where in your online curriculum could you include an online debate?

HYBRID COURSES: FINDING THE BALANCE

Hybrid Courses are those that have a combination of the foundational, skills based, and the analysis/synthesis courses and require a mixing or blending of techniques in the preactive and active phases of teaching to facilitate interaction and foster online learning. The advantage for an online instructor is to be aware of the first three types of courses and the methodologies that are effective in facilitating those types of courses and then applying that on the micro application level for the hybrid course.

One of the example classes discussed in chapter 2 was the Leadership course. This is a course that may require a combination of strategies and techniques to achieve the best outcomes for students and program participants. This is a course that presents foundational material in the form of theories of leadership from the literature. This can be presented in the more traditional roles of online lecturing with PPTs and instructor voice over or a streaming video or the reading of a number of text based options that may include the guided exploration of web sites.

This is a course that may include a level of management leadership listening and communication skills. This is a skill that can be facilitated and fostered in the discussion board through the presentation of the DECA method presented in previous pages. A model of a manager effectively listening and then using a reflective response which is similar to counseling techniques designed to elicit and understand a person's thoughts and meanings in a discussion or dialogue can be developed and incorporated. It involves reflecting back what you as the leader believe that you just heard the other person say so that the leader has full disclosure and in-depth understanding. This is then coupled with active listening skills. This can first be presented through a video either instructor or publisher created and then followed up with the notes or a series of directions for how to go about employing this leadership strategy. Then the instructor can facilitate the learning further through a series of exercises that present a scenario and then has the student post their responses to the scenario in text. It can also be conducted as a series of dialogue with the instructor. This can be done asynchronously through discussion board or through a synchronous chat feature. This is where the learner is practicing their ideas and honing their communications skills. This can culminate in a final communication strategy where the student uses the skill in a real life situation and then reports back their findings in a final document or monograph describing a real situation or scenario and the ensuing dialogue that occurred. The monograph or discussion, if the instructor prefers, can discuss the outcomes of employing the technique. This can be a very powerful way to learn as it provides real application and shows the student where and how this will be employed, strengthening the affective domain of learning.

The hybrid course may also have an analysis/synthesis component in which the foundational information discussed is analyzed for efficacy in different situations and circumstances or possibly analysis and synthesis of divergent sides of a particular issue. This can again be fostered in the discussion boards using the techniques of faciliatation and the Socratic approaches discussed previously in this chapter.

Reflections

1. Look at those courses that believe may be hybrid in nature (including one or more of the foundational, skills based, or analysis/synthesis components). Where could you include the different pedagogies described in this and chapter 10?
2. Which online pedagogies that you currently employ are effective and which could you enhance for learner effectiveness?

EMPATHETICAL PEDAGOGIES TO FIT THE 4 COURSE MODEL

In the online teaching and learning environment to effectively meet the needs of all students through the four categories of teaching and learning, the instructor needs to practice not only a level of presence in teaching but also a high level of empathy. Empathy can be defined as the ability of the instructor to put him/herself in the place of the student and understand things from the student's position. This provides the instructor a sense of the student's perspective and provides an insight as to the student's pedagogical needs. Empathy allows an understanding of learner's perspective and effect from the inside, a sensitive awareness of the way learning seems to students. Practicing empathy provides a motivation to learn and influences the learning process in a positive manner. Empathy is fostered by using a variety of techniques that promote positive interaction.

Holmberg (1999) assumed, in his theory of teaching-learning conversation and the empathy approach, if a course consistently represents a communication process that is felt to have the character of a conversation then the students will be more motivated and more successful than if it has an impersonal textbook character. This is accomplished through real conversation (student assignments, comments on the assignments, telephone, email) and by conversational style in printed and recorded subject matter presentation. The conversational approach is meant to help students handle the difficulties of study, including reading difficult texts. When a lecturer presents the intricacies of his subject he/she naturally tries to express problems, arguments and solutions in as understandable a way as possible, thus facilitating the reading of handbooks and articles. Holmberg (1999) believed that his communication theory had great value in relating teaching and learning effectiveness to participant feelings of belonging and cooperation as well as the interactions that come from questions, answers, and arguments in mediated communications. Holmberg (1989,) offered these assumptions for this theory:

1. The core of teaching consists of interaction between the teaching and learning parties. Simulated interaction through subject matter presentation in pre-produced courses can subsume part of the interaction by causing students to consider different views, approaches and solutions and generally to interact with a course.
2. Emotional involvement in the study and feelings of personal relation between the teaching and learning parties is likely to contribute to learning pleasure.
3. Learning pleasure supports student motivation.

4. Participation in decision making is favorable to student motivation.
5. Strong student motivation facilitates learning.
6. A friendly, personal tone and easy access to the subject matter contributes to leaning pleasure, supports student motivation and thus facilitates learning.
7. The effectiveness of teaching is demonstrated by students' learning of what has been taught.

Empathy in the online course becomes an integral part of both instructor and student success. There are several things that an instructor can do to show his empathy for the students and assist them in being successful. Instructors need to develop and conduct their teaching in both the pre-active and active teaching phases in an empathetic, caring manner. To practice empathy in an online course or training there are many pedagogical approaches that can employ to increase the sense of caring in an online course which are described below:

Provide a "Tips for Online Course Success" Document

Instructors should provide a tips page that tells the students both technical ideas for success as well as how to approach the course overall. Posting tips for learning and the skills for self-motivation, adult learning and how best to stay organized will help to maximize the learning opportunity. This can be posted on the shell portal for student reference.

Find Common Ground for Students in Technology and Content

All student technological capabilities are not the same. Some have access to large bandwidths and technology; others do not. The decision about how and when to include large data and media files such as audio, streaming video clips, large PDF files or other data rich files needs to take this into consideration. There are a variety of technological options that instructors can explore to enhance content such as streaming video, audio clips and podcasting. Publishers' course cartridges, web cites and CD ROMs can provide significant information and reduce faculty production time.

Instructor Presence Is Practiced So Students Know the Instructor Is There

Instructors practice presence through selective discussion board postings, frequent email contacts individually and with the group. This becomes a mindset that instructors prepare themselves to actively participant every day. Online teaching requires a higher degree of instructor presence than the traditional learning environment. Students need to know that they are not just sending their material into cyberspace never to be seen nor heard from again. The online instructor needs to interact more with their online students and be more available through email and discussion boards than in a face-to-face class. Instructors should respond to their students through email within 24 hours, seven days a week and established phone conferences with students as necessary. Empathetic instructors provide personalized feedback every week with every assignment. When they do not hear from a student, they make the overt act to communicate. If an instructor is going to be offline for any period of time, they should inform their students so the students do not feel the instructor is ignoring their posts or emails.

Exhibit High and Deliberate Nurturing

Empathetic instructors are always available to their students and need to understand that their students are traveling, juggling education, career and family. The online instructor should be careful in making assumptions about student intentions and responses. If there is a question about the tone of student language and motivation, the instructor needs to contact the student directly for clarification. For example: "From reading this it sounds like you are confused, are you?" These issues are addressed in different ways from the traditional classroom where you can read body language, attitude and facial expressions.

Create a Sense of Trust Early In the Course

Creating an environment of trust allows students to feel that they are important to their instructor. Trust can be promoted by employing by providing real communication with students in the discussion boards, emails and general communication. This sense of trust needs to be established from the beginning of the course and carried out consistently throughout the learning process. Students need to feel that they are able to ask questions and the instructor is both approachable and responsive to student needs.

Use Frequent Formative Evaluation Techniques Checking For Understanding

To apply empathy, instructors can frequently check that learning is occurring and that students understand both content and structure of the class materials, activities and assignments. This is an overt move through discussion boards and emails where instructors frequently open lines of communication with the entire group and specific students. They also monitor communications and postings to assure that learning is occurring. This requires a high level of clarity in the posting of instructions and learner assignments. Students also need to be able to locate information and files with ease through as discussed earlier a consistent approach to the weekly lesson design. Changing structure can lead to learner confusion and detract from the learning.

Increase Interactive Frequency

The empathetic instructor interacts with more regularity and with greater intensity than in the traditional classroom. On a percentage basis, the online instructor will spend more time with their online students than they do their traditional classroom. Students have greater access to the instructor and should be facilitated to take advantage of the increased contact. Generally in a traditional course students have limited access to the instructor outside of the classroom. In the online class students actually have contact with the instructor 24/7. The successful instructor in the online course takes a more active role and provides more one on one teaching and communications.

Reflections

1. Look at those courses that you have taught online. How have your communications, structure and pedagogies established the sense of empathy?
2. Are their areas in your online courses that could benefit from increased clarity?
3. *Which of the above empathetic practices do you traditionally employ and which do you see that would be of benefit for you to add?*

REFERENCES

Bandura, A. (1986). *Social Foundations of Thought and Action*. Englewood Cliffs, NJ: Prentice-Hall.

Beaubien, J. (2002). Harnessing the power of complexity in an online learning environment . In Rudestam, K. E., & Schoenholtz-Read, J. (Eds.), *Handbook of Online Learning: Innovations in Higher Education and Corporate Training* (pp. 221–236). Thousand Oaks, CA: Sage Publications.

Bereiter, C., & Engelmann, S. (1966). *Teaching disadvantaged children in the preschool*. Englewood Cliffs, NJ: Prentice-Hall.

Champagne, M. T., Hewitt, D., & Short, T. (2002). Access to opportunity: The Duke-East Carolina partnership for training program. *Journal of Asynchronous Learning Networks*, *6*(1).

Dewey, J. (1926). *Democracy and education: An introduction to the philosophy of education*. New York: Macmillan. (Original manuscript published in 1916).

Feenberg, A. (1999). Distance learning: Promise or threat. *Crosstalk*. Retrieved from http://www-rohan.sdsu.edu/faculty/feenberg/TELE3.HTM

Fisher, M., & Coleman, B. (2002). Collaborative online learning in virtual discussions. *Journal of Educational Technology Systems*, *30*(1), 3–17.

Fuller, R. G. (2008). *Faculty Practices in Asynchronous Online Distance Education: A Study within Health Education Programs*. Saarbrucken, Germany: VDM Verlag.

Kagan, S. (1994). *Cooperative Learning*. San Clemente, CA: Kagan Publishing.

Marzano, R. J., Pickering, D. J., & Pollock, J. E. (2001). *Classroom instruction that works: Research-based strategies for increasing student achievement*. Alexandria, VA: Association for Supervision and Curriculum Development.

Notar, C. E., Wilson, J. D., Restauri, S. L., & Friery, K. A. (2002). Going the distance: Active learning. *Education*, *122*(4), 649–654.

Pallof, R. M., & Pratt, K. (2002). Beyond the looking glass: What faculty and students need to be successful online . In Rufestam, K. E., & Schoenholtz-Read, J. (Eds.), *Handbook of online learning: Innovations in higher education and corporate training* (pp. 171–184). London: Sage Publishing.

U.S. Department of Education. (2009). Office of Planning, Evaluation, and Policy Development. In *Evaluation of Evidence-Based Practices in Online Learning: A Meta-Analysis and Review of Online Learning Studies,* Washington, D.C. Retrieved June 2009, at http://www.ed.gov/about/offices/list/opepd/ppss/reports.html

Vandergrift, K. E. (2002 July). The anatomy of a distance education course: A case study analysis. *Journal of Asynchronous Learning Networks, 6*(1). Retrieved January 28, 2003, from http://www.sloan-.org/publications/jaln/v6n1_vandergrift.asp

Vrasidas, C., & McIsaac, M. S. (1999). Factors Influencing Interaction in an Online Course. *American Journal of Distance Education*, *13*(3), 22–36. doi:10.1080/08923649909527033

Section 4

Designing Differentiated Course Pedagogies

Chapter 12
Designing Foundational Courses

This chapter and those that follow present example pedagogies from a variety of courses and disciplines. Our goal is to demonstrate the structure and instructional methods used in foundational courses. We want to stimulate your thinking about the design options and potential pedagogies across different programs and courses of study. This chapter is by no means an exhaustive presentation of design features, but serves to illustrate the realm of possibilities that exist within differentiated instruction in the foundational, analysis/synthesis, and skills course types. This chapter will focus on *foundational* courses.

Foundational courses focus on providing basic knowledge and the framework of concepts within a topic or discipline. In traditional university settings, foundational courses tend to be the large-enrollment, lecture-based courses that present factual terms, definitions, and content. In general, there are no prerequisite courses for foundational courses. The foundational learning objectives use low level verbs from Bloom's Taxonomy (1956; 2001) such as identify, explain, describe, list, summarize, and define. Most objectives are in the knowledge domain, but affective domain objectives to build awareness, appreciation, and value of the subject matter are also appropriate. Through the course design and structure, the instructor can help students master the content in both the knowledge and affective domains, plus help students advance their thinking and application in preparation for future courses.

DOI: 10.4018/978-1-61520-865-4.ch012

One of the challenges is designing online foundation courses is balancing the depth and breadth of material covered in the course. More course content is not always better and can actually deter learning, as the students don't learn, but just survive the assignments and assessment. In foundational courses, instructors need to be cognizant of the time required by busy students who engage in online learning. The instructor needs to have a level of understanding and empathy for the workload placed upon students to meet the learning objectives. In the traditional face-to-face classroom, the workload is more easily planned within the time frame for each class session as determined by the clock. In the online environment, this clock does not exist and hence the restraints are different. While the online instructor wants to be sure that the activities and the assignments are not overwhelming to the time commitment that is needed, he/she does need to be sure to provide ample opportunity and resources for the learners to master the objectives. Learning takes time, and time on task enhances the students' learning experience (Department of Education, 2009). A variety of well designed learning activities can increase the time on task and benefit students with different learning styles.

In this chapter, we will look at three sample lessons from courses in Anatomy and Physiology, Introduction to Economics, and Sexual Harassment. While these examples provide foundational content, they do more than march learners through volumes of factual course content. These courses integrate active learning, inquiry-based learning, self-directed learning, and a variety of mediums to engage the students.

Personal Reflection Suggestions

Think about a topic that you know really well. It does not have to be academic–it can be a topic related to business, family, sports, hobbies, or any other subject. Do you consider yourself an expert on this topic? How did you learn this subject? How do you know that you thoroughly understand it? Consider how you would teach this topic to another person.

EXAMPLE ONE: ONLINE ANATOMY AND PHYSIOLOGY COURSE

Generally speaking, an Anatomy and Physiology (A&P) course serves as the *foundation* for a number of biology and health-related programs. Many programs such as nursing, physician training, and allied health programs use an A & P course as foundational knowledge. The information presented and learned in this course serves as not only the basis for other classes but also for practice. A typical A&P course may cover the following topics:

- Basic Terminology
- Basic Structures of the Human Body
- Human Body Chemistry of Life
- Cell Structure
- Cellular Metabolism and Reproduction: Mitosis and Meiosis
- Tissues
- Integumentary (Skin) System
- Skeletal System
- Articular System
- Muscular System
- Nervous System
- Endocrine System
- Blood
- Cardiovascular System
- Lymphatic System
- Reproductive System
- Digestive System
- Respiratory System
- Urinary System
- General Receptor Organs

A typical anatomy and physiology course may have some of the following objectives:

- Define the anatomic terms used to refer to the body in terms of directions and geometric planes.
- Describe the major cavities of the body and the organs they contain.
- Illustrate the anatomical location of anatomical structures and explain their function.
- Identify the major components in each of the body systems and differentiate roles of each in conjunction with the others.
- Identify the anatomical structures in the digestive system and relate them to the aspects of digestion.

Let's look at an example unit or weekly lesson focused on the cardiovascular system. The objectives for such a unit may include:

- Label the anatomical structures of the cardiovascular system.
- List and describe the electrical pathways and their role in heart function.
- Outline and analyze the structures of the heart in scope and design and explain their integration with the respiratory system.
- Explain the role and integral functioning of the cardiovascular structures.
- Appreciate the function of the cardiovascular system in the network of the body.

The online posted lesson may look like the following example weekly module:

Cardiovascular System Online Lesson

I. Weekly Focus
   - *Last week we discussed the* circulatory system including blood and lymph. As you will recall, the heart and blood vessels form the cardiovascular system. *This week we are going to focus on the cardiovascular system, specifically, its anatomy and electrical system pathways and how they integrate to allow the heart to pump and oxygenate blood in conjunction with the respiratory system. There are several activities designed to assist you in learning the cardiovascular anatomy and physiology. So follow along as we go through this interesting and exciting system.*

II. Text Readings
   - In the textbook, please read Chapter 5, "Cardiovascular Systems," and review the questions at the end of the chapter.

III. Instructional Materials
   - There are three components for this lesson on cardiovascular systems: (1) a narrated PowerPoint presentation; (2) an instructional video; and (3) a Web-based tutorial.

A. Microsoft PowerPoint Presentation on the Cardiovascular System
   1. Below is an advanced organizer handout that you should print and have in front of you as you watch and listen to the explanations on the PowerPoint presentation. You can take notes and label the structures as we go through the systems.
   2. Please open and review the following PowerPoint presentation. Be sure that the volume is turned up on your computer as this is a paced POWERPOINT with voice over. In particular, note the graphic illustrations and explanations of the position and function of the cardiovascular structures. The presentation file is a large file and may take a few seconds to load because it incorporates both audio and graphic images.

Cardiovascular System.MICROSOFT POWERPOINTX

B. Cardiovascular Video
   - Please watch the following streaming 6-minute video on the anatomical structures of the heart, the electrical pathways, and their functions to pump blood through the respiratory system for oxygenation. This video provides you with an excellent visual illustration of how all the systems come together to provide oxygenated blood to the body tissues. As you watch the video, create a simple diagram of the cardiovascular system.
   - Click the link (Cardiovascular Video) which will take you to the video:

C. Guided Web View and Tutorial
   - *Please go to the Body Smart Web site at* http://www.getbodysmart.com/. *Here you will find a list of tutorials on different aspects of anatomy and physiology. Complete the* tutorial Circulatory (Cardiovascular System), which focuses on *blood and blood cells, the heart, blood vessels, and circulation. Please click each section and review the material. Each section has several subsections that review and explain the structures and physiology in detail. At the end of the tutorial, take the Visual Quiz. This tutorial will provide you with a greater understanding of the cardiovascular system and help you in this week's discussion board.*
   - When you complete the online quiz, send me an e-mail with your score.

IV. Cardiovascular Quiz
   - Please go to the Cardiovascular Quiz and take the online assessment. This will help you and me to understand your progress toward learning the cardiovascular system. The quiz is designed not only to assist you in memorizing the key elements of the cardiovascular system but also to help you to articulate the practical functions of each of the structures.
   - Cardiovascular Quiz

V. Discussion Board
   - This week's discussion board will help us to understand the functions of the cardiovascular system and how our bodies react to malfunctions in the system.
   - From your knowledge and/or experience, describe an instance when the heart did not work properly.
   - Consider these types of issues: How would the individual react differently to left sided and right sided heart failure? If there was a blockage in the electrical conduction pathway of the heart at the SA node, the AV node, and in the right and left branches, what would be the effect on the heart's ability to pump blood to the body? If oxygen were low in the body tissues, what cardiovascular structures could affect this? If a heart had a septal defect, how would that affect blood flow?
   - Please click the following discussion board link or go directly to the discussion board and find Cardiovascular Discussion.

Rationale of Lesson Design

In this foundational course, the sample lesson focuses on low level objectives from Bloom's Taxonomy (1956). Low level objectives are not less important or inferior to the higher levels of learning indicated in Bloom's Taxonomy. The low levels of learning provide the necessary foundation or framework required for advanced learning and thinking. The purpose of this example A&P cardiovascular system lesson is to provide the basic structures and functions of anatomy and physiology.

This particular course is organized into weekly lessons. Each lesson consistently includes an introduction or weekly focus, readings, instructional material, a quiz, and a discussion forum. The lesson begins with a short overview that helps students recall prior knowledge, introduces the topic for the lesson, and explains why the information is important.

Much of the student learning in this lesson is rote memorization. It is critically important for the course design to incorporate repetition and practice using the core content. Just as basic multiplication becomes second nature to elementary school children, health care professionals have to instinctively know the structure of the human body and how each system functions. The learner must have a deep understanding of the intricacies between all parts of the system. These basic anatomy concepts will be applied in many future lessons and professional practice settings. In designing the course, the instructor needs to introduce content that goes above and beyond simple rote memorization that learners commit to memory for the quiz and then promptly forget. The instruction should provide a view of the cardiovascular system that illustrates transfer and application in a variety of settings and contexts. For example, how does the cardiovascular system work differently in an older adult? What happens to the system when the individual has an eating disorder? What happens to the system during a heart transplant operation or a drug overdose?

Helping the students to understand the logical design and function of each of the human structures will aid in their retention of the A&P concepts. As an instructor and course designer, you want to make the learning as practical as possible. Generally speaking, the students need more diligence than intelligence because there is an overwhelming volume of factual information to absorb in the scope of the typical A&P course. Since anatomy is a visual subject, it is especially helpful to provide learners with video, images, and illustrations. Many videos, anatomy Web sites, and reusable learning objects are freely available for online learning. One instructor created a video about skeletal anatomy of the cranium. He uses three-dimensional or real skulls, shining a flashlight through different areas of the structures to illustrate the frontal sinus cavities or other structures. Visualizing the location and relationship of key structures helps the learners to understand the structure and function of the cranium. For online students, there are also some A&P software programs that provide the learners with the hands-on opportunity to manipulate three dimensional images to understand the structure of human systems. Some instructors provide the text files for flash cards as a portable, low-cost, low-tech study aid.

Anatomy is more meaningful to the learners when the discussions become personal. This can be accomplished by asking questions such as, "Please describe a personal example from you or someone that you know where the heart did not function properly and why." One student shared that her mom had a heart problem and was given a pacemaker. The pacemaker caused an interruption in the electrical system that required intervention, which gave the class a new context for discussing the cardiovascular system. Through interaction, the students benefit from using the terminology in authentic scenarios. The instructor can explain the concepts in realistic terms and make the material practical for students.

In our A&P sample lesson, the online discussion, assignment, and quiz provide formative evaluation feedback to both the instructor and the students. Formative evaluation strategies can help to identify the students' strengths and weakness as they progress toward mastery of the course objectives. By checking students' understanding throughout the course, there are multiple opportunities for the instructor to intervene and guide the students to helpful learning resources. The key element to success in a foundational course such as A&P is to learn the terminology, the anatomical structures, and the purpose and function of each structure.

EXAMPLE TWO: ONLINE ECONOMICS COURSE

Let's look at another example of a foundational class, Introduction to Economics, which some institutions may call Economics 101 or Principles of Economics. This is a course that many universities and colleges provide as a foundation for economics and business majors, but it may also serve as a general education requirement. The basic economic information is applied in later courses and within the profession. Some of the areas of focus may include unemployment, inflation and economic growth, government management of the economy, and resources to produce and distribute commodities. A typical Introduction to Economics course may cover the following topics:

- Principles of Economics
- Economic Terminology
- How Trade Works
- Supply and Demand
- Supply, Demand, and Government Policies
- The Application Elasticity
- Market Trends
- Externalities
- Public Goods and Common Resources
- Costs of Production
- Competitive Markets
- Monopoly and Oligopoly
- Gross National Product
- Unemployment
- Cost of Living Indices
- Growth and Production
- Financial Systems
- Monetary Systems
- The Effects of Inflation

A typical Introduction to Economics course may have some of the following objectives:

- Describe the basic decision-making processes of consumers.
- Interpret the role of supply and demand.
- Define economic terminology.
- Analyze the role of the public and private sectors in the economy.
- Analyze and synthesize the factors that affect unemployment, the development of goods and services, and how the economy as a whole works.
- Identify and appreciate different financial and monetary systems and their interdependency.
- Interpret the factors that affect economic indicators of growth.

Let's look at an example unit or weekly lesson focused on the concept of Supply and Demand. The objectives for such a unit include:

- Define supply and demand, elasticity, price floor and ceilings.
- Identify what happens when demand exceeds supply.
- Identify what happens when supply exceeds demand.
- Explain how economic stability or affluence affect supply and demand.
- Recognize the effects of economic indicators on supply and demand.

Introduction to Economics: Supply and Demand

I. Introduction: Supply and Demand
    - Last week we discussed the basic terms and principles of microeconomics. This week we are going to focus on the concept of supply and demand. We will examine the basic supply and demand curves, and the effects of the free market and government policies. We will review price ceilings and floors and a number of factors that can affect supply and demand. You will complete several activities that explore these concepts and then apply them in your own summation and venues. This should be an interesting week as you discover the many economics conditions that influence prices in your everyday life. As always, feel free to contact me if you have any questions or need clarification. I'm always available to assist you through the learning process.

II. Text Reading
    - Please read Chapter 4, "Supply and Demand," and take notes on the key concepts.

III. Instructional Materials
- There are three components for this lesson on supply and demand: (1) a narrated PowerPoint presentation; (2) a website article; and (3) a choice of reflective exercises.

A. Please review the MICROSOFT POWERPOINT presentation lecturette on supply and demand provided below this paragraph. Be sure that the volume is turned up on your computer as this is a self-running Microsoft PowerPoint with voice over. Of particular importance are the explanations of the supply and demand curves as they are affected by price control. Also watch the examples on the cost of ice cream cones. This is a simple explanation that provides a deep understanding of the concepts.
- SupplyandDemand.pptx

B. Web site Article – Please go to Investopedia's Web site and review the information on supply and demand curves. In particular, review the detailed graphs that show the relationships between supply and demand (quantity and price). http://www.investopedia.com/university/economics/economics3.asp

C. Reflection Exercise: Choose one of the following exercises:
- ***State-by-State Exploration:***
  - Please go to the U.S. Department of Labor Employment Standards Act at the above Web site. Select a state and look at the minimum wage standards. What effect do you believe this is having on the price floors in your own state?
  - http://www.dol.gov/esa/minwage/america.htm.

OR
- **StateMaster.com:**
  - Here you will find information on the economic conditions of all states within the United States. Compare indicators such as education, housing, or employment among the states. How does your state rate compared to others?
  - http://www.statemaster.com/graph/eco_sta_tax_lev_tax_per_cap-tax-levels-taxes-per-capita

IV. Activity
- Supply and Demand Curve Assignment: In this assignment, show the effects of binding and nonbinding price ceilings on the gasoline market. Create and display the effects by creating two supply and demand curves, one for binding and one for nonbinding. Please create these curves in PowerPoint and e-mail them to me by the end of the week.

V. Discussion Board
- *Based upon your exploration of economic conditions and indicators, please* post one example of an instance in which demand exceeded supply, and one instance in which supply exceeded demand. *Support your two instances with personal observations and data. What would have happened if the economics conditions were different? Please respond to at least two of your classmates. I am looking forward to this very interesting and eye-opening dialogue.*

Rationale of Lesson Design

Introduction to Economics provides the basic understanding of concepts and information that prepares students for advanced concepts in other courses or in the profession. The purpose of this example Supply and Demand lesson is to provide both the foundational knowledge of terminology and concepts, and the understanding of how different economic indicators can have an effect on the market structures, including supply and demand. Each of the activities scaffolds and culminates in a thorough understanding of factors that affect supply and demand curves. While basic in nature, these abstract concepts can be difficult for some students to understand. The interactive focus and practice in the lesson lead the students to a deep understanding of the causes and effects of supply and demand. Each activity is designed to help the learners actively engage in the learning through a series of practice, reinforcement, and application exercises.

Structure and organization are extremely important in a foundational course that is built on basic factual information. One of the best practices in course design is to provide a consistent weekly structure. In this course, every lesson has an introduction, readings, instructional material, an activity, a discussion, and a conclusion. This allows the learner to focus on the learning and not on the technology and where to find things. Consistency removes distractions from the course design and keeps the learning focused on the concepts and the activities.

Preparing students with the foundational understanding of concepts and applications involves interaction with the material, the instructor, and possibly other participants. In this example, interaction with the content occurs through the textbook, the online PowerPoint presentation, and the Web article. The initial reading introduces learners to basic concepts, and the follow-up PowerPoint presentation emphasizes key points. This is similar to the focus of a traditional face-to-face lecture where the instructor directs the instruction. It is always a challenge to provide students with enough instructional material to master the objectives without overwhelming them with content. While the Internet is a valuable source for learning material, it can also be a bottomless pit of examples, images, and readings that students perceive as unnecessary "busywork."

The use of the Supply and Curve Demand Assignment allows the instructor to interact with all students to provide detailed feedback regarding their progress and learning. This feedback helps students to check their knowledge of the supply and demand concept. The interaction also helps the student to identify student gaps in learning and guide them toward appropriate resources. As students practice using course concepts, they develop a deeper understanding of the material. The instructor enhances students' satisfaction and learning with a strong teaching presence and providing clarifications and corrections to help the students master the objectives.

The discussion board fosters instructor-student and student-student interaction. The discussion helps students to reflect on additional factors and other applications. The discussion does not necessarily introduce new concepts, just deeper understanding, application, and transfer of foundational knowledge. The instructor's role in this example is to galvanize the discussion by infusing some clarifications and corrections. In addition, the instructor uses probing questions to make all students think about the effects of external influences and how they will affect supply and demand. The instructor needs to carefully monitor the discussions to assure accuracy of information. Some instructors prefer synchronous discussions to ensure controlled, timely correction of misunderstood concepts. The discussion boards often become the area where students culminate and integrate weekly information, assignments, and interactions to achieve the deep learning required in a foundational course.

Personal Reflection Suggestions

In a foundational course, practice activities are used to enhance learning and retention of the key terms, definitions, and concepts. What practice activities are appropriate for the fact-oriented memorization and rote learning common in foundational courses? What types of assessments would you recommend for foundational courses?

ADAPTIVE RELEASE: CONTROLS TO RELEASE CONTENT

Students in a foundational class may need or require more structure to move through and understand the progressive nature of the lessons. This in some cases requires a hierarchy of information presented. To assure that the students access the information in a chronology established by the instructor, a series of rules can be established. This requires the students to access one section before another section is made available. For example, learners must complete Module 1 before the Module 1 Quiz becomes available. In some course management systems this controlled release of course components is called *adaptive release*. This control feature ensures the content structure the instructor intended for the course. Controlled release helps learners to move through the objectives and build from the most basic and fundamental concepts toward a higher understanding. The adaptive release control mimics the type of control and structure that an instructor would present in a traditional face-to-face class where the instructor controls the flow of information and classroom activities. In some online foundational courses, this type of instructor control may be desirable for the maximization of the learning.

Not only does this provide instructor control, it also establishes student accountability toward the weekly lesson or whatever learning sequence is appropriate. It works with the idea that in order for students to see one thing in the lesson, they must do something else first. Another example may be that in order to see the first lesson, they must first access the course syllabus. Until the syllabus is accessed, the first lesson will not be visible. In the Economics 101 lesson, the use of adaptive release could requires students to access the reading material in the text, review and watch the Supply and Demand Microsoft PowerPoint lecturette before the Supply and Demand Curve Assignment is accessed. The Web site exploration would need to be accessed before students are admitted to the discussion board. This provides the learners with a chronological structure similar to how a face-to-face teacher would present and release information in a class.

EXAMPLE THREE: ONLINE SEXUAL HARASSMENT TRAINING

Outside of higher education, foundational courses provide the basic knowledge and framework for learning within many organizations. Most organizations have some type of orientation or initial training that is required of all employees to fulfill either outside-adjudicated regulations or entry-level knowledge and skill deemed important by the institution. One example may be the use of Sexual Harassment Training. This has become a mainstay in many organizations to preempt litigation. By providing this training to their new and existing employees, organizations can limit their risk of exposure to sexual harassment lawsuits.

An efficient delivery mode for many organizations is an online learning platform. It provides them with the flexibility to offer the training in a cost-efficient, on-going basis., and employees have the flexibility to complete the training at their convenience.

Objectives for Sexual Harassment in the Workplace Workshop may include:

1. To define sexual harassment.
2. To identify behaviors associated with sexual harassment.
3. To prevent occurrences of sexual harassment.

Sexual Harassment in the Workplace Workshop

I. Introduction

- Our organization is committed to providing a work environment that is safe, positive, and free from Sexual Harassment. We foster a community where all administration and staff are treated with dignity and respect. We are pleased to provide you this online training program, Sexual Harassment Prevention in the Workplace.

II. Instructional Material

- Sexual Harassment in the Workplace Tutorial
- Please click the link below to access the training program. This is a practical and interactive online training session that will take 35-45 minutes to complete. After completing the course, you will be able to define and identify sexual harassment in the workplace, and act to prevent and stop sexual harassment behavior of fellow employees.
- Read each screen and click the navigation buttons (forward and backward arrows) to maneuver through the presentation as well as listen to the narrators' explanations.
- Sexual Harassment Prevention in the Workplace Training Program

III. Sexual Harassment in the Workplace Competency Assessment

- Now that you have completed the training workshop, please complete the online competency exam. You must earn a score of 75% or higher to receive credit for the workshop. There is no time limit and you may take the quiz multiple times.
- On the first page of the quiz, you will be asked to enter your name, phone number, and department. A copy of your "Certificate of Completion" will be sent directly to the HR department. You should also print and save a copy of the certification of completion for your records.
- Thank you for participating in this vitally important training program.
- Sexual Harassment Assessment

Rationale of Lesson Design

This sexual harassment tutorial is a self-paced program completed at times that are convenient for the employee. There is no interaction between the instructor and the learner or among the learners. Participants interact with the computer-based program only. The learners must complete the narrated PowerPoint tutorial prior to receiving access to the quiz. This ensures that the program and all contents have been reviewed and that participants have heard and seen all of the core information that the organization deems vital. The learners can take the competency quiz multiple times to earn a satisfactory score.

Personal Reflection Suggestion

In the book "Exploring Signature Pedagogies: Approaches to Teaching Disciplinary Habits of Mind," authors share examples of the prominent instructional approaches within their discipline. "Signature" pedagogies are the most common teaching and learning strategies for a subject, and these strategies strive to help learners think and solve problems like the professionals within that discipline. Courses in the arts frequently use peer critiques, composition courses use writing workshops, science courses use modeling, and music courses use one-on-one coaching. What are the common "signature pedagogies" in your discipline?

CONCLUSION

Foundational courses are frequently a learner's first experience with online learning. They tend to be low-level, introductory courses that provide basic terms, definitions, and concepts. The objective content provides a framework for further advanced study. Instructor-student interaction is often limited because the well designed course is organized and highly structured. While it may seem foundational courses are "all about the content," most instructors strive to introduce students to a variety of contexts and applications for the subject matter.

In the traditional classroom the instructor employs a variety of approaches to teaching and learning. Each instructor has to be aware of his or her strengths and style of teaching. The same dynamic holds true for the online modalities. These foundational course examples serve as a tool box of options that can be employed in a wide range of disciplines. Instructors may find a particular pedagogy that is effective; however, the same pedagogy may not work every time or in every learning situation. Instructors who use the same methodology for every lesson run the risk of increasing "learner fatigue." Our hope is that you will consider the pedagogies used in your online foundational courses. A variety of pedagogies offers the learner options and increases their overall motivation, satisfaction, and learning. Identifying the course purpose and outcomes will help you determine the most effective instructional strategies.

REFERENCES

Bloom, B. S., & Krathwohl, D. R. (1956). *Taxonomy of educational objectives: The classification of educational goals, by a committee of college and university examiners. Handbook 1: Cognitive domain.* New York: Longman. Anderson, L. W., & Krathwohl, D. R. (Eds.). (2001). *A taxonomy for learning, teaching and assessing: A revision of Bloom's Taxonomy of educational objectives* (*Complete Ed.*). New York: Longman.

Gurung, R. A., Chick, N. L., & Haynie, A. (2009). *Exploring signature pedagogies: Approaches to teaching disciplinary habits of mind.* Sterling, VA: Stylus Publishing, LLC.

U.S. Department of Education. (2009). *Evaluation of evidence-based practices in online learning: A meta-analysis and review of online learning studies.* Retrieved on July 16, 2009, from http://www.ed.gov/rschstat/eval/tech/evidence-based-practices/finalreport.pdf

Chapter 13
Designing Skills Based Classes

In this chapter we will look at the pedagogical opportunities that exist in online skills-based courses. As previously discussed, skills based classes encompass both cognitive and physical manipulation skills as well as kinesthetic activities. Physical or psychomotor skills are required to perform many practical activities in such areas as health care, physical education, vocation training, and the arts. Cognitive or mental skills are taught in courses that use models, process, procedures, or repetitive tasks such as math, accounting, public speaking communication, and computer science. There are many educators and trainers who are skeptical about teaching skills and incorporating kinesthetic activities into an online environment. In their face-to-face courses, they may use an interactive coaching or apprentice type of teaching that cannot be easily converted to a web-based course. In this chapter we will illustrate through several example lessons and subject areas how teaching skills online and utilizing kinesthetic or hands on activities can be accomplished.

DOI: 10.4018/978-1-61520-865-4.ch013

The skills-based type of course focuses on the attainment of both intellectual and physical skills. Learners not only understand *how* to do something, they also understand *why* they are doing it in this manner. When developing skills-based learning objectives, there are several psychomotor taxonomies (Harrow,1972; Simpson, 1972) with the one created by Dave (1967; 1970) used most frequently. Dave's psychomotor domain consists of the following five-level continuum of skills development: (1) imitation, (2) manipulation, (3) precision, (4) articulation, and (5) naturalization. While naturalization or the automatic performance of a skill may be beyond the scope of any single online or face-to-face course, it is often a professional goal. Nurses take their patients' blood pressure, pianists perform in large concert halls, and computer programmers develop software with the ease that results from mastering objectives or what some experts refer to as "over-learning" their skill. Popular verbs in skills-based courses are perform, operate, use, demonstrate, and construct.

One key consideration when developing skills-based courses is planning strategies that actively engage the learner through reading, writing, discussing, performing, and reflecting on course content. The learner cannot be a passive recipient of information to learn and retain key concepts. Active involvement applies to both the intellectual and psychomotor skills development within the course. In skills-based courses, there are many strategies to engage online students such as video demonstrations chunked into logical steps, performance checklists based on task analysis, experiential tasks for discovery learning, and reflective assessments for the mental review of performances. This chapter will illustrate some of the methodologies that maximize the benefits of online learning. Sample lessons in science and research methods demonstrate the course format, objectives, activities, and assessment methods used in skills-based online learning.

Personal Reflection Suggestion

Consider a physical skill that you would like to teach in an online course (e.g., how to play the piano, drive a car, and lift weights). Even though the skill is primarily physical, there is likely an important cognitive component to teaching the skill. How would you begin the learning process? Should the skill be taught in chunks or as whole process? What is the difference between how a novice and a master perform this skill?

EXAMPLE ONE: ONLINE SCIENCE COURSE

Traditionally, many online instructors are reticent when it comes to presenting physical skills or courses that require physical manipulation of something such as a lab science. Teaching a lab science online for some looses the sense of instructor control and begs the question of whether the student is actually doing the skill or the lab. Are they simply using someone else's work? This frequently asked question about online kinesthetic activities is easily dealt with as in the following example.

Let's look at an online Science Methods Course. The company LabPaqTM provides home science lab experiment kits in a number of science specialties including Anatomy and Physiology, biology, chemistry, physics, geology, microbiology and others. These are not computer simulations of experiments but actual science experiments were students receive a kit at the beginning of a semester and conduct the experiments throughout the semester much the same way that they would in a traditional science lab. The kit includes all the materials that are necessary to conduct the experiments and a laboratory manual with procedures. The cost is comparable to that of a text book.

The topics for the Science Methods Course Lab components include the following in the LabPaqTM kit:

- The Scientific Method
- Measurement: Length, Mass, Volume, Density, & Time
- Experimental Errors and Uncertainty
- Separation of a Mixture of Solids
- Properties of Gases
- Microbes Everywhere
- Spread of Contagion
- Phenotype and Genotype
- Caloric Content of Food
- Introduction to Electrical Circuits
- Pendulum and the Calculation of g
- Crystal Growing and the Rock Cycle
- Radioactive Decay
- Plate Tectonics
- Using Statistics
- MS Excel© and Statistics

Let's look at an example lab lesson that focuses on the Properties of Gases.

The objectives for such a science lab might be that the learners will:

- Examine and report on the physical and chemical properties of gases

- Identify different gases according to their physical and chemical properties.
- Conduct gas experiments using safety precautions
- Report and present experimental data findings given a lab report format.

The online lesson formatting may look something like this:

A. Focus

Last week, we discussed how to use the laboratory equipment, characteristics of the substances in the labs (e.g., toxicity and flammability), and safety precautions to observe in all of your lab work. This week we will look at Gases and their properties. We have several readings, presentations and activities that will help you to better understand the phenomenon of gases and their physical and chemical properties. We will be learning about some of the more common gases in our environment and their interactions and creation. You will be conducting a series of experiments and writing and posting your lab report and creating a lab video presentation of your findings.

B. Text readings

Please read the chapter on Gas Properties in your Science Text book. Please note the example lab results presented along with the focus on the chemical and gas properties.

C. PPT lecture Properties of Gases

Please watch the following 13 minute PPT presentation. It has a voice over lecture so be sure that the volume is up on your computer. Once you open and put it in presentation mode you can follow along. You should also print down a copy and have the handout in front of you as you view the presentation. This may take a minute to download due to the size of the file.

propertiesofgases.pptx

D. Lab Assignment

Conduct Experiment 5 on Gases in your LabPaqTM science kit. Please read all safety precautions first and follow the manual directions completely.

(See Table 1 for example.)

E. Assignment: Lab Report

Complete the lab report format in Word. Once completed, please email your lab report to the instructor.

(See Table 2 for example)

F. Lab Video Report

Using your web cam, please create a video presentation of your lab report and all findings. Please go through each area of your lab report explaining each section in detail. You may refer to information in your lab report as needed for clarity and explanations. Once your video has been created, please load your video on the discussion board for all to view along with your lab report.

G. Discussion Board

Please review everyone else's lab report and please comment on their findings and conclusions. What did you find compelling from this experiment? How did their findings align with your own findings? What did you find surprising from your findings and theirs? Please post your comments under Properties of Gases by clicking the discussion board link.

Figure 1.

Table 1. Lab assignment example

Experiment 5: Properties of Gases **Remember to review the safety sections and wear goggles when working with chemicals.**
Objectives: To investigate some physical and chemical properties of gases, and to use these properties to identify these gases when they are encountered.
Materials: Student Provides: Matches Toothpicks (or wooden splints) Pie tin or similar Drinking straw Marker pen Household white vinegar 3% Hydrogen peroxide (H2O2) Measuring spoons Baking soda (sodium bicarbonate) From LabPaq: Goggles 24-well Plate 2 13x100mm Test tubes From Aux. Supplies Bag: Stopper w/plastic delivery tube Clean and empty pipet Stopper w/copper & gas delivery tube From Aux. Chem. Bag: 6 M Hydrochloric acid (HCl) (To be diluted according to instructions) From Experiment Bag: 3 Wide-neck pipet bulbs Alka Seltzer® Mossy Zn pieces Manganese (Mn) pieces Bromthymol blue Limewater (saturated calcium hydroxide)
Discussion and Review: Several gases are produced frequently in the laboratory and it is important to be able to identify them by their physical and chemical properties. The gases under investigation are hydrogen (H2), oxygen (O2), and carbon dioxide (CO2). These gases will be generated using small-scale techniques and carrying out the following reactions: Hydrogen (H2) Mg + 2HCl → MgCl2 + H2 or Zn + 2HCl → ZnCl2 + H2 Oxygen (O2) 2 H202 MnO2→ 2 H2O + O2 Carbon Dioxide (CO2) NaHC03 + 2 HCl → NaCl + H2O + CO2
PROCEDURES:*Before beginning, dilute the 6 M HCl from the auxiliary bottle as follows: Pour 6 mL of distilled water into the graduated cylinder. Carefully add, drop by drop, 3mL of 6 M HCl directly from the auxiliary bottle. Mix well and pour the total 9 mL of diluted (2 M) HCl into a test tube. Use your 24-well plate as a test tube and pipet holder.* *CAUTION: It may be difficult to insert the rubber stoppers into your test tube. Be very careful, or you might break the tube and cut yourself! Briskly rub the bottom of the stopper between your hands to warm it, squeeze the end with your fingers, then slowly and carefully twist the stopper into the tube. It doesn't need to go far, but should have a tight fit. You can also use a little lubrication if needed. Practice inserting the stoppers before beginning the experiment.*

conitnues on following page

Rationale of the Lesson Design

This science lab example illustrates the possibilities that exist in the online environment. This lesson utilizes a number of activities that lead in the culmination of a kinesthetic or hands on skills manipulation activity conducted in the learners own home. The lesson starts with the traditional text based and instructor online presentation of information that provides the necessary background information on the properties of gases. This all culminates in the learner conducting a well scripted and controlled lab experiment from a pre-developed lab kit. Purchased like a textbook, software, or packets of readings, the kit is part of the course materials. The lab report serves as the summative evaluation of the experiment the same as in the traditional classroom.

The lab video assignment validates that the student actually did the experiment and under-

Table 1. continued

1. Hydrogen: A. Place a small piece of Zn (mossy zinc) metal into the test tube containing the diluted HCl. B. Take the test tube and cap it with the rubber stopper with the short, straight, plastic gas delivery tubing through its center. Place the test tube into one of the wells of the 24-well plate. The test tube must stand up straight, so wrap a little tissue paper around the bottom of the test tube to help wedge it upright into a well opening. Observe the reaction. C. Fill one wide-neck pipet bulb completely with water, invert and quickly place it on top of the test tube's gas delivery tube as shown in the picture at right. D. Place the well plate with test tube assembly in a pie tin as some water will overflow when the water in the pipet bulb is displaced by gas. E. When the water in the collection pipet has been completely displaced with hydrogen remove the collection pipet, keeping it inverted, and quickly place a thumb over the opening to keep any gas from escaping. F. Light a match. While holding the hydrogen filled pipet bulb horizontally with its mouth about 1 cm from the flame, gently squeeze a small portion of the contents of the pipet into the flame andobserve. G. Record your observations. H. With a marker pen mark the wide-neck pipet bulb on the outside into approximately three equal parts. I. Fill the marked pipet bulb with water, invert it, and set it onto the gas generation tube as before. J. When the bulb is filled 2/3 with gas remove it, still keeping it inverted, and set it with the opening facing down into one of the wells of the 24-well plate to be used later. K. Disassemble the test tube, pour the weak acid down the drain, and flush well with water. Dispose of the zinc fragment and paper towels in your trash can. L. Thoroughly rinse the test tube and rubber stopper assembly with water for use in the next section.
2. Oxygen: A. Place a few pieces of Mn (manganese) metal into the second test tube. B. Add enough 3% H_2O_2 (hydrogen peroxide) to fill the test tube to within 1 cm of the top. Place the rubber stopper with plastic gas delivery tube through its center into the test tube, and place the test tube into a well of the 24-well plate. Again, use some tissue to wedge it into a straight position. Observe the reaction and record your observation. How do the two reactions compare? C. Fill another wide-neck pipet bulb completely with water, invert and place it on top of the test tube's gas delivery tube. D. When the water has been completely displaced with oxygen in the collection pipet remove the pipet and place your thumb over the opening to keep gas from escaping. E. Light a wooden toothpick, extinguish it and quickly, while it is still glowing, insert the toothpick into the oxygen-filled pipet. F. Record your observations. G. Give two reasons why we fill the gas generator test tubes almost to the top with chemicals.
3. Hydrogen and Oxygen Mixture: A. Take the collection pipet bulb saved from Part 1, which is partially filled with hydrogen, and place it on the oxygen generation test tube created in Part 2. B. Collect enough oxygen until all the water has been displaced. The bulb should now be filled with 2/3 hydrogen and 1/3 oxygen. C. Remove the bulb and place a thumb over the end to keep the gas mixture from escaping. D. Light a match. While holding the gas filled pipet horizontally with its mouth about 1 cm from the flame, gently squeeze the contents of the pipet into the flame and observe. E. Disassemble the test tube, pour the weak H_2O_2 solution down the drain and flush with water. Dispose of the manganese fragment and used paper towel in the trash. F. Thoroughly rinse the test tube and rubber stopper assembly for future use. G. Write a balanced equation for the reaction between O_2 and H_2.

conitnues on following page

stands the lab procedures and results. This active engagement process provides an increased level of reliability and validity that goes above and beyond what is done in the many traditional labs. Students provide a detailed explanation of their lab report, which leads to a deep understanding of the lab process. The student video confirms that the student actually completed the assignment and achieved the learning objectives. The instructor can see through the video interaction what the student has done and their understanding of the process and results. This may actually be a greater validation of learning than the traditional classroom instruction.

The use of posting the lab report and the video to the discussion board allows all students to see what others have done and to interact and discuss their findings. This also provides a forum for the instructor to discuss with the learners what they did and what conclusions can be drawn.

Table 1. continued

4. Carbon Dioxide: **Part 1:** A. Put .5 to 1.0 mL of limewater into a well of the 24-well plate. B. Place half a teaspoon sodium bicarbonate (baking soda) in the bottom of the generation test tube. Hold the test tube over a pie tin or a sink and add half a pipet full of white vinegar to the sodium bicarbonate. As soon as the sodium bicarbonate and the vinegar are combined, they will react vigorously and some may overflow. That is all right. As soon as the overflow has stopped, insert the stopper with copper and plastic (c&p) gas dleivery tube into the test tube. C. Place the open end of the c&p gas delivery tube into the limewater previously placed in the well. D. What is happening to the limewater? **Part 2:** A. Put .5 to 1 mL of bromthymol blue into another well of the 24-well plate. B. Thoroughly rinse the gas generation test tube under running water in the sink and set up another test with sodium bicarbonate and vinegar as in Part 1 above. C. When the stopper assembly is in the test tube place the open end of the c&p gas delivery tube into the bromthymol blue. Observe and record the reaction. D. Remove the stopper and c&p gas delivery tube from the generation tube. E. Light a toothpick or match and insert the flame into the upper part of the gas generation test tube. F. Record your observation. **Part 3:** A. Pour the chemicals from the above experiments into a sink and flush with water. Then thoroughly rinse the test tubes, stopper, and c&p gas delivery tube for reuse. B. Put .5 to 1 mL of limewater into another well of the 24-well plate. C. Crumble the small piece of Alka Seltzer® tablet into the generation test tube. D. Add 1 pipet full of water to the Alka Seltzer® and then immediately insert the stopper with c&p gas delivery tubing into the generation tube. E. Place the open end of the c&p gas delivery tube into the limewater in the well. F. Observe and record the reaction. What does it mean? G. Thoroughly rinse the gas generation test tube under running water in the sink. **Part 4:** A. Place .5 to 1 mL limewater into a small test tube. B. Insert a straw and blow gently into it for a few seconds. C. What do you observe? Explain. D. Pour the limewater into a sink and flush with water. **5. Other:** Make a table of the gases studied. Tabulate their colors, the effect on lighted or glowing splints, and other properties one might use to identify them.
Cleanup: Flush remaining liquid chemicals down the sink and throw solid metals in the trash. Rinse and dry all equipment and store it for future experiments. (Reprinted with permission from LabPaqTM)

This interaction provides a learning activity that facilitates the students to evaluate and synthesize the experimental findings beyond the traditional affording a deeper understanding and learning of the properties of gases.

Figure 2.

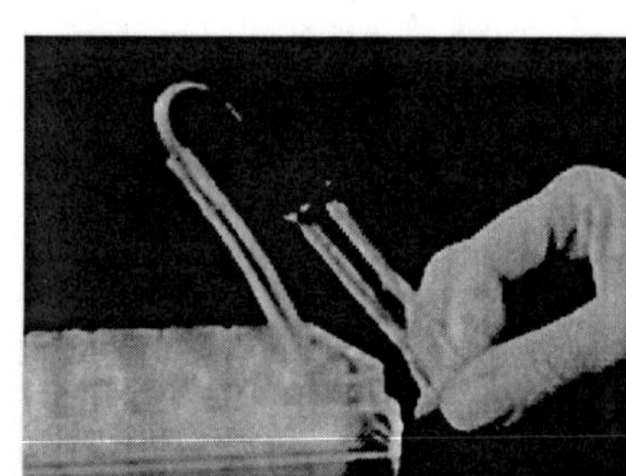

Personal Reflection Suggestion

Think of the traditional or face to face skills based courses that you teach. What physical skills are part of that course? How could you transfer the teaching of those skills in the online environment? How could you assess the skill development along psychomotor Domain described byDave (1967)?

Table 2. Lap report example

Lab Report Form Name__________________ Date______________ Experiment Title: *Purpose/Problem* State the reasons why you are doing the experiment. State the problem that is being investigated. This section can be stated as a question with an explanation. *Background Information* Explain what you already know about the problem and any suppositions about the experiment. Use the information learned from lectures, text readings or other information sources. This grounds your experiecment in what you already know about the underlying principles and information. What do you expect to find in conducting the experiment? This section should also have a hypothesis statement that should use the "If..., then..." statement. The 'If' is what you know, the 'then' statement is conjecture on the outcome. The experiment is designed to test the hypothesis and whether it is found to be true or not. *Materials/Supplies* Provide a listing of all equipment, supplies and chemicals (with amounts of each) used to conduct the experiment. *Procedure:* Writing in the past tense this section describes the exact procedures used to conduct the experiment. Accuracy must be maintained throughout this section describing what you did including steps, time frames and procedures applied as this effects the results and the findings of the experiment and allows the reader an accurate depiction of what was done. *Data Collected and Observations* Data and observations are reported in this section without conclusions. This is the raw data that was observed and is reported without commentary. This should be reported in tables, drawings, graphs or text descriptions of what was observed and any numerical findings during the experiment. *Conclusion* The conclusions explain and describe the observations and links the data findings directly back to the problem and the hypothesis statement. This section is written as text format that should explain the findings and what conclusions that the experimenter logically draws from the findings as it relates to the hypothesis and the questions. The conclusion should state whether the data found supports or rejects the hypothesis stated. This section should also make suggestions for additional experimentation and possible predictions based upon the findings in this experiment.

EXAMPLE TWO: ONLINE RESEARCH COURSE

Let's take a look at a graduate level research class. While there is foundational knowledge provided, the majority of a research course is focused on the cognitive skills of design, implementation and conducting of research. This research example is an online graduate course that focuses on the ideals of quantitative and qualitative design structures as well as the skills associated with applied statistics within research. The overall objective of the course is for the learner to leave with the skills necessary to develop and conduct research. Each of the lessons focus on building the essential skills necessary to achieve this goal.

The course description may look something like the following:

Applied Research and Statistics; 3 credits

Basic statistics and research methods used in the social sciences are covered in this course. Creating research questions, hypotheses, and literature review skills are presented. The identification of appropriate statistical tests to research design and interpretation of findings will be evaluated through the review of current research. Evaluation of current research and its application to practice will be emphasized.

A set of typical Course Objectives might be:

After completion of this course the student will be able to:

- Define and identify reliability, validity (internal, external, construct), sensitivity, and specificity and demonstrate how these are assessed when evaluating research.
- Develop the following research designs

including their relative strengths and weaknesses:
  - stratified
  - randomized controlled
  - longitudinal
  - cross-sectional
  - case-control
  - cohort
  - retrospective
  - prospective
  - meta-analysis
- Describe blinding and double blinding and illustrate proper use.
- Develop a null hypothesis and alternative hypothesis.
- Differentiate and apply descriptive and inferential statistics.
- Perform and demonstrate proper use of normal distribution and 3 measures of central tendency.
- Compare and contrast parametric and non-parametric statistics.
- Define and Apply the following statistical terms:
  - variables
  - statistical significance
  - probability
  - P value
  - population
  - subjects
  - sample (random, convenience)
- one and two-tailed tests
  - correlation
  - association
- Describe statistical power and its relationship to sample size.
- Describe the importance of controlling for confounding variables.
- List and describe three measures of variability (range, standard deviation, standard error).
- Apply the use of t-tests and ANOVA in research.
- Define, describe, and list some examples of bias, Type I Errors, and Type II Errors.
- Contrast tests of difference with tests of relationship.
- Define and describe the function of the following statistical tools:
  - regression analysis
- confidence intervals
- Define and describe relative risk reduction, absolute risk reduction and Number Needed to Treat
- Explore statistical software use to perform statistical measures.
- Identify and use appropriate citation methods and formats.
- Review original research journal articles from the literature evaluating its study design, results, and relevance to practice.

The semester long assignments in this course are also designed to engage learners in the skill development necessary to conduct research and achieve the above objectives.

This focus establishes the expectations that the instructor has and the level of interaction required in a discussion thread. The focus for these discussions is the generation and development of weekly skills. This is a process that requires all students to participate and interact with the material as well as with each other and the instructor. In an analysis/synthesis type of course an instructor may not want to respond to all posts as it can change the dynamic of the discussion. In a skills based class such as this research example, the instructor will want to post and respond frequently to assure that skill development is being attained by all participants. This takes careful facilitation and greater presence by the instructor to assure skill growth and improvement. As the instructor sees skills developing, he needs to provide positive feedback and constructive criticism to guide the student to proper skill proficiency. This becomes an integral part of the formative assessment discussed

Table 3. Syllabus 1

Assignments	
Weekly Assignment Postings	2.5 points/wk (30 total)
Quizzes	5 points each (10 total)
Article Critiques	8 points
Statistic Group Work	8 points
Proposal Outline	6 points
Annotated Bibliography	8 points
Synchronous Chat room Participation	5 points
Final Project	25 points
Total:	**100 points**

Weekly Lessons: Students will complete the weekly assigned readings and lectures. These will be posted in the Topics of Study area. A summary of assignments and deadlines appears in the Organizer area of this Syllabus. The Discussion Board area contains questions that must be answered. The answers may be brief but must be substantive. **Original responses should be posted as early in the week as possible to allow adequate time for discussion.** In addition, all students must respond to at least three posting from a classmate although more postings are encouraged. That response must also be substantive. Application of the weekly content and the addition of other articles and readings will assist you in the forming your substantive responses.
Participation: You must respond to at least three of your classmate's postings on the Discussion Board each week; this should be relevant and at least 100 words, and will count towards the overall grade. "Relevant" means expanding on a discussion topic, analyzing that topic, weaving in personal or workplace experiences etc. Use of appropriate references from the weekly readings and text along with your own references may prove helpful. Grades for discussion board activities will be posted weekly and accounts for one third of the semester grade. 1.5 points will be awarded for the original posting and an additional 1.0 points be awarded for response to a classmate's postings. Deadline for responding to each other's postings is 2359 hours (11:59PM) the Wednesday following the beginning of the week. Discussion Boards will be closed after that time or when the instructor announces.

in previous chapters. This is also not so different to how traditional education and training function.

Each of the above assignments is designed to build and develop research skills. This all culminates in a final research proposal that allows all of the skills to come together in one project. This engages the student and promotes active learning of research. The Chat Room function is a synchronous form of communication that can provide clarity for the student and feedback for the instructor to understand where the students are and what they may need to further develop the research skills. This is provided as an option for learners and has proven to be beneficial by students who have participated. This can be accomplished through a number of synchronous communication tools. Innate to most learning management systems is a virtual chat function that allows real time interaction. Connections can be through text communication or a combination of

Table 4. Syllabus 2

Quizzes: Two online quizzes will be completed by the assigned due dates.
Article Critique: One journal article will be written in a narrative format using the criteria found in the Article Critique Worksheet as a guide. These must be submitted in the appropriate area (e.g. Article Critique) by the designated due date. Finding articles in your area of interest for your project and that can form part of your literature review is a smart approach to these assignments.
Proposal Outline: The outline is to assist you in organizing and identifying the elements essential for the actual proposal.
Annotated Bibliography: This forces you to cite and note the essential findings from the literature review and preparation you complete for the proposal. It should be inclusive of the material you research independently for the proposal creation.
Final Project: You will develop an idea to include your research question, hypothesis (if applicable), literature review, research methodology, and approach to data analysis. This is a project you will build upon each week as you explore the many facets of research process. Your final project will be the creation of a research proposal. Keep in mind that the capstone project can form the basis of the work for this class. Review the capstone guidelines for more direction.
Chat Room: There will be three chat rooms (synchronous communications) throughout the term. Each student is required to attend at least one. Students are encouraged to participate in more.

text writing and voice communication with web cam visualization. The use of a product such as Adobe Connect or Skype allows learners and instructor voice communications and a combination of text interaction with posting of documents and instructional materials. Other options include the use of traditional telephone with conference bridge communication which is traditionally audio only however can be enhanced with synchronous web communications.

The topics of study in a course like this may be:

- Identifying a Topic
- Searching, organizing and Analyzing the Literature
- Developing and Refining Research questions
- Statistics: Normal Distribution
  - Measures of Central Tendency
  - Standard Deviation
  - Research methods continued
  - Validity and Reliability of Measurement
  - Correlation
  - Regression
  - Probability
  - t-Tests
  - ANOVA
  - Chi Squared
- Qualitative Analysis
- Qualitative Methods
- Quantitative Methods
- Human Rights Issues & IRB's
- Using statistical software
- Evidence base management

Lets take a look at an initial lesson that could be "Identifying a Topic." This section may include the identifying of a topic, establishing research questions, hypothesis development and purpose of the study statement. The objectives for this lesson might be that the student will be able to:

- Identify a viable researchable topic.
- Create functional focused research questions.
- Establish a research hypothesis.
- Develop a purpose of the study statement.

Opening Announcement Posted on the Announcement Page

Week One - Welcome and Identifying a Topic

Hello to all: Welcome to Applied Research and Statistics. We will help you navigate the process so don't hesitate to ask questions. I think that you will all enjoy this course. Each week we are working on activities that will assist you in building research skills and understanding the research process ultimately culminating in a final research project proposal. We will not have time this term to actually conduct the research but to plan out and develop the process. This course will be the foundation for your final capstone project to assist you in graduating from the program.

Research and statistics has its' own language in the terms and definitions. We will be reviewing these as the term progresses but please review your previous research course work to gain deeper understandings. During this term, you will be doing individual work as well as group projects to assist in the learning process. To make a group project work you will need a high level of involvement and communication among your group to be effective. You can use several different methods to do this - through Blackboard, email, phone conferences or any online method - Yahoo, Skype, Google, live meetings, etc.

Please take advantage of all that this course has to offer and explore all avenues of the research process. As stated above you can begin to explore areas of interest that could serve as a capstone.

Each week we will have a series of readings, activities and discussion work to assist us all in a greater research skill development and the scary statistics part. We will have three live conference chats (via phone conference bridge) that will allow us all some great opportunities to interact in real time. (You must make one of the three, but are encouraged to participate with all.)

Please begin the first week by doing several things. Please review the Course syllabus located under the Syllabus button on the left, then go to the <u>Topics of Study and begin with Week one Identifying a Research Topic</u>. This first week we are going to begin by identifying areas of interest and starting the research process.

Please know that I am always available to assist you. The easiest way is to email me. If the question can't be answered online, we can set up a time to talk via phone conference. Research is a great process and one that you will enjoy. You will all find that after a couple of weeks that the lights will go on and you will get it. That's when it becomes fun.

Have a great week. See you in the discussion boards and emails.

A. Topics of Study Week One Focus

Identifying a Topic

What is research? Better yet what is not research?

In general use, you will see "research" referred to whenever there is the need to impress. Research says .... whatever, so we should accept that finding and act upon it. Eat eggs? don't eat eggs? You will find that the quality of research is one reason why you need to study how research should be done and the elements that go into the methods or the how to do part. Being a knowledgeable consumer means you understand what to look for and how to evaluate if a study is well done and one you want to use in your area of study. This course will ask you to create a research question and explore the many facets that match that research question, create a hypothesis, conduct a literature review and write the analysis. What method or study design is most appropriate to conduct your study? Do you have the resources to do it? Do you need to modify? How will you obtain a sample and conduct meaningful data analysis?

At the same time we will be exploring statistics. What are the many types of statistical tools in use? Which go where? When? How? We look forward to guiding your journey. We will have a phone chat next week to discuss some research basics.

B. Bio intro

Tell us about yourself, who you are, where you are in the program, where you work, what is your background, why are you taking this course of study, what some of your areas of research may be, hobbies, likes, dislikes, and any other personal or other information you would like to tell us. Please answer what research is.... What do you think Research is? What does research accomplish in your mind?

When you write your personal e-mail introduction, write it in the third person as if you were introducing someone else. Please have some fun with this. Click Email to go to the email section of this learning platform and please email your response and ideas to everyone in the class. This will allow each of us the opportunity to learn about and interact with each other.

C. Text Readings

Please read: Please read the chapters in the text book on:

Essentials in Research and What do I Research and the Research Process. These chapters will focus on the scientific process and how to establish the framework for research. Please focus on the research questions, hypothesis and purpose portions in the examples provided.

D. Please read the attached notes on Formulating Research Questions.
FORMULATINGRESEARCHQUESTIONS.docx

E. PPT Presentation on Identifying a Topic.
Please click on the PPT lecturette below. The lecture is less than 30 minutes and has voice over explaining, Variables in Experimental Studies, Research Hypotheses, Purposes, and Research Question Development and also discusses Operational Definitions of Variables.
Identifying a Topic.PPTX

F. Article Review
Please find two research articles through the electronic library on any topic area you desire. Make sure that they are research based primary research (original research). Once you have obtained two good articles, please begin to review the research. Look at the research questions, the hypothesis, and the purpose statement. Please in a review of the articles, please list these and critique them. Are they good or could they benefit from some clarity. How would you reword them to make them better? Please send your reviews of these sections as a Word Document to me in an email. Additionally, please send an electronic copy of the articles in either PDF or HTML format as you received them from the electronic library. They will be returned to you with comments. This will allow us to dialogue about the research process.

G. Discussion Board
This week's discussion board will help us focus on developing the skills of identifying a researchable topic, writing research questions, establishing a hypothesis and a purpose of study statement.

1) You have all read the chapters for the week. Please list and discuss as many topics that you think need and should be researched in your field and why you believe they are important. These do not need to be specific here, but just a laundry list of topic ideas.
2) Utilizing the list that you generated in #1 or the list that others have generated in this discussion board, and develop the beginnings of a research project by: listing three to four research questions, a hypothesis statement, a statement of purpose. Through this week's interaction with each other and the instructor, we will help each other to focus our questions and hone the hypothesis and the purpose statement. This is a skill that takes some practice along with some feedback from others. By sharing these ideas in this discussion board and brainstorming ideas and possible research directions this will assist in the process to "funnel" questions down to researchable topics, a very viable research skill.

Please click the discussion board link or go directly to the discussion board and post your information and ideas under Identifying a Topic.

Rationale of the Lesson Design

Instructor presence plays a significant role in the skill development in this lesson. Students are learning to identify viable research topics, write questions, develop hypotheses and establish research purpose statements, all important initial research skills. These skills do not stand in isolation but are the cornerstone for the rest of the research process. The skills they learn and develop in this lesson will carry through the rest of the course and be used to establish viable research methodologies. If the students do not develop these skills in this lesson, the development of additional research skills will be difficult.

This lesson and the activities are progressive in scope and do require significant instructor feedback to assure that the skills are being developed and understood by all students. Many of the activities require not only interaction with the content such as the narrated PPT presentation but instructor review to formatively assess student progress toward the stated objectives. The article review assignment in this lesson serves to provide an example of how the skill is to look and allows the instructor to review and interact with the learner through email providing feedback on research questions, the purpose statements and the hypothesis.

While in other types of courses, an instructor may not want to answer and address each discussion board post, most skill based classes require the instructor to respond to all posts assuring that each student is attaining the skills. The discussion board further facilitates the development of the skills by allowing all students to see each other's postings and allows the instructor to provide the feedback and help students hone their skills. This requires the instructor to respond to all learners and interact more on a one on one basis to assure the skills are being developed properly. Without this feedback the student may not attain the desired skill level. The interaction through email contact and discussion board feedback aids greatly in student clarity and skill articulation. The use of the synchronous communication as discussed in the opening focus, allows the instructor to provide clarity and additional instruction with real time discussion and dialogue to assist learners with clarity and the appropriate skill enhancement.

As this was the first week of the course, the instructor chose to include an opening introductory activity. Each student was required to provide a brief biography to help everyone get to know a little about each other. This can in some cases help students to interact and provide the instructor general background information and a better understanding of the student, who they are and what they may need. An interesting twist with this introduction activity is the use of the third person. This can sometimes make it easier for students to provide information about themselves and can be something unique and different. This information can allow students to interact and make connections with each other which can be helpful in cooperative activities or online group work as the next lesson illustrates.

Personal Reflection Suggestion

In the courses that you have identified as skill based, what types of online pedagogies have you used? Are there others that you could employ? How have you traditionally facilitated online discussions in these classes? Are their changes that you would make to the way that you structure and interact with students in discussions and through emails?

EXAMPLE THREE: ONLINE RESEARCH STATISTICS LESSON

This next example lesson is part of the above research class and illustrates how online cooperative learning or group work can be incorporated into skills training and education. The use of group work provides the learner the opportunity to be an active engaged learner in online skill development and application. Conducting and applying statistics is an area that many students fear or avoid. Statistics however is not hard. Calculating statistics is generally not difficult as it is solving for an equation with basic math skills or using a software program such as Excel or SPSS to complete the computations. The difficulty that many students have is the ability to apply the correct statistic in the right setting and then interpret the relevance of the final numbers.

One of the traditional methods of integrating statistics is to provide activities where information is presented regarding descriptive and inferential statistics with learners applying the appropriate method to example cases. These are generally effective, however to provide a more active learning environment students can be engaged in a cooperative learning exercise. The following lesson is in part extended over the course of three weeks and allows interaction between students in groups and with the entire class.

Objectives for this section may include:

- Differentiate between applications for descriptive and inferential statistics
- Perform and demonstrate proper use a normal distribution and 3 measures of central tendency.
- Apply parametric and non-parametric statistics.
- Apply the following statistical terms:
    - variables
    - statistical significance
    - probability
    - P value
    - population
    - subjects
    - sample (random, convenience)
    - one and two-tailed tests
        - j. correlation
        - k. association
- Describe statistical power and its relationship to sample size.
- Describe the importance of controlling for confounding variables.
- List and describe three measures of variability (range, standard deviation, standard error).
- Apply the use of t-tests and ANOVA in research.
- Evaluate Type I Errors, and Type II Errors.
- Contrast tests of difference with tests of relationship.
- Define and describe the function of the following statistical tools:
    - regression analysis

A. *What do we do with Data? Weekly Focus*

For the next three weeks, we are focusing on some of the key areas of statistics: Normal Distribution, Measures of Central Tendency and Standard Deviation all the way through parametric and non-parametric tools. As you will see, the class is divided into groups to work on these projects. Each of you needs to read all of the material presented with the examples to understand and apply the basic assumptions and use of these statistics. The small groups will provide additional material for you to review as well as illustrate the applications of statistics. We will use the Week 6, 7 and 8 discussion board area for this 3 week block. You are expected to read all postings and provide substantive comments as appropriate. In addition to the discussion board points for weeks 6, 7 and 8, there will be a separate grade awarded each group member for the work that is accomplished and presented as you lead the discussions on each area.

The groups are as follow:

Students 1, 2 and 3 - Chi Square, Correlation

Students 4, 5 and 6 - Regression, non-parametric

Students 7, 8 and 9 - T Test, ANOVA, post hoc

Students 10, 11 and 12 - Central tendency measures, including

standard deviation and probability
Each member of the group is requested to email the instructor a grade for each group member and a justification for that assessment at the end of week 8. This will assure that all members provide equally to the project.
Please begin by reading the Word file on descriptive versus inferential information. You are looking to identify when each measurement is appropriate and how interpretations can change based on which measurement is used.
Many files are attached addressing different statistical measures. Using the readings and links you should develop a reasonable understanding of the use of these statistics. The links and readings will support weeks 6, 7 and 8.
We also have a guest lecturer this week, Dr. Smith who is a statistician and professor of research at the university. He will be assisting us to better understand statistics. He will also join us on the next live chat.
There is a lot of material posted here- work your way through it over the course of the next three weeks. Each of these activities should provide you some clarity in understanding and applying statistics in research. The groups should assist in concentrating on the data analysis techniques.

B. *Descriptive vs Inferential Statistics*
Please begin by reviewing these documents.
Descriptive_vs_Inferential_Statistics.doc (42 Kb)
dmmstatslecture b.zip

C. *Text Readings - for weeks 6, 7 and 8*
Please read Chapter 6 on Survey Research. For week 7 read chapters 7, 8 and week 8 read Chapters 9 and 10 There are several articles for reference to read and use in the "Course Documents" section. These are here as supplemental readings and can be used to better understand statistical use and application. Please use them individually to understand and in your groups as needed.

D. *Discussion Board*
The next 3 weeks, we will explore statistics a little differently. Everyone has a group and topics to delve into and post. Identify the definition, use and give one or two examples of how the information gained from your statistical measure can be used in "real life". Your presentations each week can be posted as text, PPT, video or audio discussion board threads of the concepts and ideas in line with the weekly tasks as listed below.
Group page areas have been established for each of the four statistic presentation teams in the communication area. This will provide you access to your own group discussion board that only your group can see. Here you can post documents and interact to plan and develop your statistical presentations. You also have access to email, announcements, and messaging systems. It is up to your group to decide how and when to meet as well as the division of labor.
Tasks- week 6 working as a group define your assigned area and explain the concept and its use. This is a group project so everyone must participate-do choose a weekly person to post and organize the material you create. All in your group however need to interact and dialogue as the rest of the class migrates to your posted thread and material.

Task- Week 7 Show examples of how your measure has been used in previous research. In these existing studies, was it the appropriate statistic? Why or why not? Attach the study your group is using as your example as a PDF or HTML file for all to see and review and then lead your discussion.

Task- Week 8 Develop a narrative statement about how your assigned measure might be used in a study that your group designs. (You can use the ideas you are developing for your final proposals as is appropriate). Again each member of the group must provide input to the entire class.

Group members:

Students 1, 2 and 3 - Chi Square, Correlation

Students 4, 5 and 6 - Regression, non-parametrics

Students 7, 8 and 9 - T Test, ANOVA, post hoc

Students 10, 11 and 12 - Central tendency measures, including standard deviation and probability

E. *Topics Correlation and regression*

This week we discuss the statistical use of correlation and regression - what it is and can do for you in your research. On of the nice features of the technology age is that you can use software to manipulate your data. The key is understanding how to collect and code your information and then how to use the software program you choose.

Go to this site: http://math.about.com/gi/dynamic/offsite.htm?zi=1/XJ/Ya&sdn=math&cdn=education&tm=21&gps=75_12_1012_536&f=10&tt=14&bt=0&bts=0&zu=http%3A//www.statsoftinc.com/textbook/stathome.html

Begin to work through the types of statistics we have discussed. This will take some time but it is a pretty clear site that makes sense out of stats.

The concepts of reliability and validity need some discussion. From the instrument viewpoint, how do you know you are evaluating the correct elements? Will you obtain the same results each time you use this instrument or tool?

F. *Probability*

Please read through the short Word file on Probability and then continue with the other chapter readings.

Probability_and_Statistics.doc (47.5 Kb)

Additional material on Probability - Web Sites

Explore the information on the following web sites. They may also shed some light on the probability concepts.

http://www.probabilitytheory.info/index.htm

http://www.math.csusb.edu/faculty/stanton/m262/probstat.html

G. *Web Sites*

Please take some time and study the following URLs. They all offer great insights to t testing and their uses.

http://www.statsoft.com/textbook/stbasic.html

and click on the two sections that deal with t tests.

http://www.socialresearchmethods.net/kb/stat_t.php

http://faculty.vassar.edu/lowry/ch11pt1.html

H. *ANOVA Example*

Please read through this ANOVA example. This may help put this into perspective and its use in research.

LetstakeanexampleofanANOVA.doc (44.5 Kb)

I. *Guest Lecturer/Presenter*

Dr. Smith will be our guest presenter this week. He has provided audio file lectures that have been zipped for size. They should open without difficulty. If you have difficulty please contact me for assistance.

While you are reviewing the audio files and Dr. Smith's presentations, please keep the handouts, which are posted as PDF files in front of you, either in printed hardcopy or on screen. Dr. Smith will refer to these files in his presentations and discussions.

Descriptive and inferential statistics

Descriptive Statistics.pdf (186.455 Kb)

descriptive statistics 1 smith3.zip (Package File)

Inferential Statistics.pdf (238.002 Kb)

inferential statistics smith.zip (Package File)

Rationale for the Lesson

Applying statistics in research is a foundational proficiency that becomes part of the skill set of developing research projects. In the previous example, *Identifying a Topic* there were several skills being developed that required the instructor to interact with every student's posting to provide feedback and clarification toward the naturalization of the skill. In the present statistics example however, it is more prudent for the instructor not to respond to every posting. The instructor needs to monitor the cooperative learning group presentations for clarity and correctness of information and should post when there is an issue or instruction is necessary. If the instructor posts too much in this forum or thread, then the students may not dialogue and interact for fear of instructor interruption. However the students need to know that the instructor is present and there as a safety net so that they are sure that the information and skills they are learning are correct. This becomes a fine line that the instructor must formatively assess and read to understand when to post and when to monitor to maximize student learning.

Cooperative learning like the example presented here has some innate learning opportunities as students are active rather than passive learners. They get to use a larger number of their senses toward learning as they are preparing, presenting and coordinating the activities of their individual group efforts. The group learns from each other and the learning can be magnified by their input to the group presentation and interaction with other students in the entire class.

Their however can be a downside to the group work. Occasionally, some students may not put forth maximum efforts within the group structure, sitting back allowing others to take on a larger share of the labor. This can cause some animosity among students as they step up to take on a larger role in fear of not receiving a good grade on the project and can be further exacerbated as they watch those who did not do their fair share receive credit for work not done. The way to combat this, causing an equal distribution of work and learning for all students in the group, is to provide a mechanism for the students to evaluate each other on their contributions to the project. As in the above example, students email the instructor a grade for each of the participants in the group. This remains confidential and allows the instructor to modify grades accordingly given learner assessments of each other.

We know that not all students learn the same and that by providing a number of learning activities and options we as instructors are more likely to increase the overall learning of the online class. This statistics lesson example does just that. There are several learning skills and materials presented over the course of the three weeks in a variety of manners from lectures and discussions, to reviews, articles and text material and a variety of learning web sites that students can use to learn. This differentiation of instruction does not mean that all students must read every word of every article or text displayed, but serves to provide the students a number of learning options. These choices help the students to be self-directed in a portion of their learning. What is required from time to time in a lesson such as this three week section is for the instructor to monitor student progress not only in the discussion boards and the group sections, but to also check for understanding frequently. With this volume of work and lessons organized in this self-directed manner many students will flourish while others may fall behind. The instructor needs to monitor progress throughout to assure all are engaged in the learning process. This can be monitored by watching the level of engagement of each of the students. Communications can be accomplished through email and through a synchronous chat if deemed necessary by either the student or instructor.

In a traditional class, instructors will occasionally bring in a guest speaker to provide a specific level of expertise and to supply a perspective different from their own. This can be a valuable learning opportunity for students. The same holds true in the online course. A guest lecturer such as the one described in the above example with Dr. Smith, allows students to see yet another level of expertise and a different learning point of view. The variety again differentiates the learning.

Personal Reflection Suggestion

How have you or could you utilize cooperative learning or group work in your online courses? Is there someone's expertise that you could use as a guest lecturer in one of your online courses? How would you use them in your online class? How do you differentiate the materials that you present in the online environment to meet all student learning needs? Are there things that you could do to enhance this?

THE HYBRID COURSE APPROACH

As with any of the course types, there will be a cross-over of pedagogies or a hybrid approach to designing and teaching in the four course types. Given the cognitive skill development as discussed in the research examples above there is both foundational information presented that serve to remind students of previous knowledge that will be applied in the skill development as well as an analysis/synthesis component to the skill. In the application of statistics, the cooperative learning task with groups presenting and leading discussions, allows students to analyze the statistical application and then apply them in new circumstances (synthesize). The group lead discussions help all students to both analyze and synthesize the new statistical skill.

SUMMARY

Traditionally, instructors, teachers and trainers, may have shied away from teaching skills and kinesthetic activities in an online course. As the examples in this chapter illustrate, a carefully designed course can help students to achieve both physical and intellectual outcomes. Course lessons should be designed to lead learners from a logical progression such as knowledge-based concepts, to observation, to guided practice, to independent practice, to reflection, and, ultimately, to transfer and retention.

Hands-on activities are certainly opportunities that exist for online learning, and as the technology continues to grow more tools will become available. Technology is no longer used just for the delivery of online courses. Easy-to-use video and digital image cameras are readily available to many learners who want to document their performance in a course. In addition, there are web-based tools that offer audio and video conferencing with inexpensive microphones and web cameras. These examples create a rich tool box of ideas and media that can be employed to guide and assess learners as they develop skills.

Personal Reflection Suggestion

Are there courses that you teach in the traditional that you could now see being taught online? What pedagogies could you employ? How do you monitor student progress of online skill development? What can you add to make your evaluations more efficient in both formative and summative assessment?

REFERENCES

Dave, R. (1967). *Psychomotor domain.* Berlin: International Conference of Educational Testing.

Dave, R. (1970). Psychomotor levels . In Armstrong, R. J. (Ed.), *Developing and writing behavioral objectives*. Tucson, AZ: Educational Innovators Press.

Harrow, A. (1972). *A taxonomy of the psychomotor domain. A guide for developing behavioral objectives*. New York: McKay.

Chapter 14
Designing Analysis/ Synthesis Courses

In this chapter we will explore examples that illustrate the pedagogical opportunities that exist in online analysis/synthesis courses. Whether they are graduate or undergraduate courses, analysis/synthesis classes tend to be the more advanced courses in a program of study. They often have perquisite courses providing foundational subject matter. As previously discussed analysis/synthesis courses are used to teach students to analyze content and engage in reasoning, critical thinking, and problem solving. This type of course requires unique pedagogies and instructor interaction as well as teaching and social presence to maximize the learning opportunity. The interactions are generally more in depth and may require a different instructor skill set as facilitation in the analysis/synthesis course may have a different focus than that of the foundational or skills based online course.

As noted in earlier chapters, the goal of the foundational course is to master basic material and how and where it will apply, assisting the student to understand beyond rote memorization. Furthermore, foundational courses often help students to appreciate and value the material being learned. In the skills based courses, the interaction leads students closer to the naturalization or automatic application of the skills, whether cognitive or physical in nature. This is facilitated in a number of ways that help students learn concrete acts, tasks, or processes. The focus of the course design and interaction in an analysis/synthesis type training or education course is to have the learner analyze information or a particular body of knowledge. This information is then integrated into the students' own understanding and mental models. Analysis/synthesis courses use the higher order thinking skills referenced in Bloom's Taxonomy (1956) such as assess, critique, defend, manage, or develop. Writing and collaborative exercises often serve the purpose of helping students to explore, organize, and clarify their thinking. In an advanced course, learners may share an argument or opinion that requires evidence to support and defend. To analyze a concept is to break it down into parts, while synthesizing is to take those parts and build or apply them in a different area.

DOI: 10.4018/978-1-61520-865-4.ch014

In order to facilitate student learning in an analysis/synthesis course, instructors need to integrate higher level thinking activities into their courses. These learning activities may include discussions with probing questions, authentic case studies, problem based and decision making exercises, debates, or other activities skillfully written for reasoning and critical thinking. Technology tools such as wikis or blogs may be used as students collaborate to create their own knowledge. Through these activities, students review all sides of issues and concepts to develop their own judgment in an unbiased manner. Halpern explains that "critical thinking skills can be taught and learned, and when students learn these skills and apply them appropriately, they become better thinkers" (p.70). If learners appear to be too one sided in their thinking, it becomes the instructor's role to guide them to evaluate all aspects and dynamics of an idea. Many learners come to a learning situation with a plethora of life experiences to draw upon which Knowles (1999, 1984) states is a rich resource for learning; however, this can also restrain students in their ability to analyze and synthesize new material. Hopefully, the course will help the students to grow beyond their preexisting comprehension and assumptions. In an analysis/synthesis course, the thinking process is often more important than the final product or conclusion.

Let's take a look at three examples of analysis/synthesis courses and activities. These courses require a strong foundation of understanding the basic concepts of the discipline. The analysis/synthesis courses tend to address complex, multifaceted issues that rarely have one correct answer or approach. The courses may have "Issues" in their title, but these are not the only courses that fit this category.

Personal Reflection Suggestion

How can an instructor or course developer teach learners to think? How can you model critical thinking in your discipline? Advanced training does not necessarily teach participants how to think. Yet, thinking and analysis are highly valued skills in the workplace and classroom. As demands for problem solving, reasoning, decision making, and other cognitive process become more frequent and complex, how can we prepare our students?

EXAMPLE ONE: ISSUES IN HEALTHCARE DELIVERY

The first example is from a course that may be titled, "Issues in Healthcare Delivery." The perquisite knowledge for this analysis/synthesis course is from an introductory course on the U.S. healthcare system. The description for the course may look something like the following:

Course Description

This course is an examination of the international healthcare delivery systems and will spotlight the major trends, issues, and problems challenging policy makers and healthcare professionals. Topics includes the structure, finance, and management of healthcare services and the role of healthcare professionals.

Healthcare is a complex, dynamic subject with many influences and challenges. The course objectives may include some of following:

Upon completion of the course, participants will be able to:

- Compare and contrast the complexity and diversity of international healthcare systems.
- Assess healthcare issues as they relate to their own professional discipline or area of competence.
- Analyze a country's healthcare system based on that country's level of development and socio-political system.
- Rationalize and advocate legislative and policy initiatives which will serve to affect the healthcare delivery system.

The topics for a course may include:

- Public and private financing in healthcare
- Management and international healthcare
- Quality assessment and improvement
- Outcome measurements and use
- Managed care
- International healthcare
- Healthcare reform
- Labor management issues

Let's look at an online example lesson from the course "Issues in Healthcare Delivery." Prior to the start of the week, the instructor may post the following announcement:

Announcement: International Healthcare Delivery Systems

Welcome to Week Three. This week we are going to kick it up a bit. We will continue to look at some additional international healthcare systems. Last week's discussion boards were very interesting and gave us all an introductory view of some of the other systems differences, strengths and comparisons to the U.S. system. As everyone read, we all have different opinions on the efficacy of the JCAHO standards. Some felt it good, some bad, some not sure how to get all systems in this country to comply beyond scheduled site visits.

As I stated in my postings, you have hit on some of the central issues. I'm not sure there is a perfect system out there or one that could be developed. I think there are flaws and loopholes in any system. Standards are good as they set norms that can and should be attained. That is not to say that there are not differences of opinions about what those standards should be and which ones are important and which are frivolous. Each institution has standards that they feel are very costly and maybe unnecessary for improved care, but they follow them anyway. Many felt that there was a need to centralize the standards through some type of government department or cabinet post.

I think you are all thinking about multifaceted issues and that is the point to our discussions, to view healthcare from all angles and to gain new insights and perspectives. We all have opinions. The key is to see different perspectives and learn from them. In this lesson, you will see some things that you absolutely agree with and you will see things that you don't. The goal is to understand the different ideas and then to formulate your own ideas based on more complete information. You will also explore some different political views, because there truly is no way to separate healthcare issues from political ideology. They go hand in hand. When possible, please refer to our readings and present evidence to support your postings.

The module for this lesson may by organized with an overview or weekly focus, lecture notes or instructional material, readings, an activity or assessment, and an online discussion.

I. Weekly Focus
  - This week we are going to begin exploring healthcare systems used by countries outside of the U.S. We will examine the delivery of healthcare services, insurance issues, and the overall differences/similarities in these various healthcare systems. This lesson includes several readings and activities. In our discussion, we will focus on the differences between the U.S. healthcare system and that of Canada. This is a hotly debated issue that should yield some interesting perspectives.
  - We will begin conceptualizing the Semester Paper/Presentation and you will select the country that you want to research.

II. Instructional Materials
  A. Microsoft PowerPoint Presentation on International Healthcare Issues.

- Please click on the PPT lecture below. The lecture is less than 30 minutes and has voice over explaining some of the elements that fuel the healthcare debate and what to look for as we explore the different healthcare system variables.

◦ International Healthcare Issues. PPTX

B. Text Reading

- Please read Chapter #2 through #12 in our text "Issues in Healthcare." These are short chapters that provide some different perspectives on other international healthcare systems.
- Chapter #11 addresses the Healthcare provided in Canada. This is a system pointed to by many experts as the way the U.S. should redesign our system. This issue has caused great debate within the halls of the U.S. Congress and has been a central political issue in the minds of many for years. As you will realize, this topic has established polarizing views as to what is right and wrong for this country. What are we doing correctly and what needs changing?

C. Article Reading

- Please read the following articles by Enthoven and Kronick on Universal Health Insurance. They have an interesting perspective on the issues in implementing Canada's payer mix in the United States and provide some alternative ideas. Please also read the articles on the U.S. healthcare system. There are several experts that provide different perspectives on the systems.
- Universal Health Insurance.pdf
- US Healthcare.pdf
- Healthcare in America.pdf
- The Status of our system.pdf
- Overview of the U.S. Healthcare System.pdf

D. Web Site Activity

- Please go to the following Web site about the Canadian Health System: http://www.hc-sc.gc.ca/english/care/romanow/index.html . Consider whether Canada's system has long-term sustainability. Review the Report: Commission on the Future of Healthcare in Canada. This is a PDF file on the Commission report by Roy Romanow from November 2002. Please read "A Message to Canadians" and read Chapters #1, #2 and #3. This information is very practical and will help you to understand how Canadian citizens receive their health care services.

III. Assessment

◦ Semester Paper/Presentation

◦ This week we are going to begin looking at International Healthcare Systems Paper/Presentation, which is due on Week 10. Check your syllabus for a detailed outside of the paper and presentation, plus the rubric listing the grading criteria. The purpose of the paper is to conduct a literature review on the health care system of one sountry and share that information with the rest of the class. The synthesis paper is 8 to10 pages, and must include a minimum of 15 references. Your presentations will need to be comprehensive and go beyond that material presented in class or through the course readings. However, I do not want your paper to exceed 10 pages.

- ***A good place to start your search is the World Healthcare Organization's Web site (***www.who.int/en/), ***which provides information on international healthcare issues. Withn the navigation button "Counties," there is a significant list of countries and several links to each.***
- Start thinking and searching for the country you want to explore for this paper/presentation. Your task this week is to select the country for your syntesis report and presentation. When you have decided, please post the country you plan to analyze in the discussion forum "Topic of Healthcare System Paper/Presentation." We want to cover as many countries as possible so everyone should pick a different country.

IV. Discussion Board

- Providing the highest quality of healthcare in a timely manner and at an affordable price is an ongoing dilemma in healthcare. This week, we'll compare the healthcare systems of the U.S. and Canada.
- Go to the discussion board forum "Canadian Healthcare System" and contribute your thoughts on the following: (1) In your estimation, what are the pros and cons of the Canadian system? What are the pros and cons of the U.S. system? (2) What could the U.S. policy makers learn and use from the Canadian system? What could the Canadians policy makers learn from the U.S. system? Please quote our weekly readings or Web sites to support your thoughts and ideas.
- Please post your initial response to these questions by Thursday. Respond to questions from other students regarding your initial post and follow up with at least two other student posts by Sunday. Remember that course discussion is a large part of course grade. The expectations and grading rubric for participation in online discussions are stated in the syllabus.

V. Conclusion

- This week we began our exploration of international healthcare systems. Undoubtedly, the challenges of managing an effective healthcare system are overwhelming. As we compared the Canadian system to the U.S. system, you identified some positive aspects of each system and some aspects that should be changed. In the coming week, we will continue to investigate both private and public healthcare delivery systems throughout Europe.
- Have a great week. See you in the e-mails and discussion board. As always if you have any questions, please feel free to contact me electronically or if you wish you may contact me by phone at the numbers on the syllabus. Remember that I am available to you.

Rationale of Course Design

The design of an analysis/synthesis course lesson, like the above example, often provides a great deal of information about the topics and concepts being studied. Students who take this healthcare course have perquisite knowledge on the U.S. healthcare system which provides a strong basis for comparison and an opportunity to develop higher order thinking. Armed with well established concepts, the learner enters the analysis phase with the necessary understanding of the basic tenants to examine all aspects from a variety of vantage points. This is accomplished in the above example lesson through the presentation of text based reading materials, various analysis and opinion articles, an instructor created lecture, options to explore information of their choice through a guided web exploration, and a threaded online discussion. The discussion board serves to foster the analysis of material and to better formulate their own meaning and application of the concepts.

INSTRUCTOR INTERACTION IN AN ANALYSIS/SYNTHESIS DISCUSSION BOARD

The purpose of the discussion board in an analysis/synthesis course is to have the students interact with the content using writing and reflection to apply and analyze the concepts. One valuable aspect of asynchronous online discussions is the time students have to think and develop their responses. Synchronous discussions can be effective if students have a clear purpose, activity, and agenda to prepare for the interaction. In a learning community, students will be comfortable questioning one another, responding to one another, and respectfully challenging one another. If a student is viewing one side of an issue and becoming myopic to the elements of the issues and concepts, then it becomes the instructor's role to facilitate the learner to explore and be open to all sides.

It is not the goal for the instructor to lecture or provide new information during the discussions, but to serve as a guide toward this higher-level thinking and learning. This process is often accomplished by the instructor practicing restraint in their discussion board postings. While they should read and formatively assess postings during the discourse, they in general should limit their own posts, allowing the students to generate the discussion and dialogue. Instructors find that authoritative postings shut down dialogue or that students simply parrot instructor ideas or postings (Fuller & Kuhne, 2008). The parroting or repetitive statements may be from students who have not sufficiently analyzed the course content or who are concerned that challenging the ideas of others may result in a lower grade. Early instructor intervention may also deter discussion as students wait for faculty to provide "answers", fix problems, or point to evidence. The instructor's role, as Beaubien (2002) states, is to generate student thinking and additional dialogue if the discussions have stalled. The instructor also provides clarification and corrections to student posts as necessary to assure proper dissemination of information.

Example Discussion Board Post and Interaction with Instructor

The following student and instructor postings deal with the above discussion question comparing U.S. and Canadian healthcare systems:

Subject: Canadian Healthcare System
Author: Kathy
Posted date: Monday, February 3, 6:00 PM EST

From the readings on Canada and everyone else's posts, I have learned a lot about the Canadian Healthcare system. To me, the most important part of their system is that everyone has healthcare insurance.

Reading through several articles the Canadian Healthcare Act gives a baseline as to what is expected from healthcare services so that the provinces and territories get the money they are supposed to receive which is called the "full federal cash contribution". There are several other benefits of this act as well. It makes sure that ALL residents have access to insured services on a prepaid basis so there is no charge when service is provided.

The role of the federal government is very clear, for example:

1. They make sure that the principles are set for the insured health services in the C.H.A.
2. They provide direct services for such groups as: Veterans, Military and Inmates of Federal prisons.
3. Their functions are: health protection, promotion and disease prevention.

Each province or territory has the responsibility of delivery and administration of healthcare services. With federal funding assistance these provinces and territories plan, finance, and evaluate the hospital care and physician services.

The Canadian Health System offers "comprehensive, universal, first-dollar coverage" to all Canadian citizens, but I'm not clear on what this truly means. This system prides itself on looking at the patient as a "sick person" rather than a "consumer". Because of very strict cost capping measures, this health system can offer all its citizens coverage and is founded on "equity, fairness and solidarity" (Commission on the Future of Healthcare in Canada, 2002). Because the Canadians look at healthcare from the "supply" side, they limit the number of doctors, hospitals, and clinics. A new product must be scrutinized by cost-analysis before being offered to citizens due to tight money controls.

The key differences between the U.S and Canada in the healthcare arena are their views. The U.S. is the capitalist not issuing cost capping. Canada on the other hand is the socialist providing healthcare for all citizens. The U.S.'s entrepreneurial views treat patients like "consumers" and allow for "demand" side tactics where cost sharing is employed due to the out of control prices for service. In the U.S. you get what you pay for (the more money you have, the more services you get). Although the government does provide assistance to the less fortunate, there are still inequities between the rich and poor. Because Canada offers the right for every citizen to be entitled to healthcare, they have to take a conservative approach and budget their money appropriately. The U.S. government has little say in who is insured and what kind of care they receive.

The U.S. could learn a few things from the Canadian Healthcare system, the first being treat patients as "sick people" rather than "consumers". Because the U.S. treats its patients like "consumers" and the "you get what you pay for" approach is the sign of times for the sick. As much as it would go against the capitalistic way, cost capping may be appropriate in order to gain some control over prices. Sometimes efficiency is not the way of the American people, too much time gets spent on what the interior design of a doctor's office is rather than how much the patient is paying for it. Just like American cars, doctors have all the power in the world but limited efficiency. The Japanese cars are very comparable in power with a lot more efficiency.

Subject: Canadian Healthcare System
Author: Instructor Response
Posted date: Monday, February 3, 9:00 PM EST

Kathy, Interesting post. "First Dollar Coverage" indicates that health insurance covers from the first dollar meaning no co-pay in many cases. This generally indicates that the healthcare costs are covered and the responsibility to pay lays with the government not the individual person. This is the big difference in how Canada and the U.S. approach healthcare.

Read Michael's article because he elaborates on this "first dollar approach" to healthcare..

You have brought up some very interesting ideas from the readings about the strengths of the Canadian System. What do you see as the negative issues or areas where the Canadian or U.S. system is lacking? As a citizen, where would you rather live and why?

In the above example, the instructor practices restraint in the discussion board with limited posting. A final thought at the end of the discussion board serves as a culminating post bringing all the thoughts together in a summary of ideas. This adds closure to the dialogue, emphasizes key points, and allows students and the instructor to move to new subject areas. An example closure post for the above lesson may look something like this:

Subject: Canadian Healthcare System Final Thoughts
Author: Instructor
Posted date: Monday, February 8, 8:00 AM EST

This has been a very interesting discussion board. I think that you have all hit on the key issues that separate the Canadian system from the U.S. system. Each has some very strong points and each has their shortcomings. While the Canadian system provides comprehensive care for all, they lack the innovations that come through an open market approach. Their care while comprehensive has not lead to the level of research that has found new medicine. In our free market, the U.S. has and continues to advance medicine further and faster than Canada or any other country. The issues in the U.S. are sky-rocketing healthcare coverage, coverage issues with HMOs and PPOs, and coverage for all Americans. There are advantages and disadvantages in a free market system such as ours. It does open up our system to abuse. If you look at the increased patient flow to Emergency Department (ED) in this country, you would think that we are becoming a sicker nation at least on an emergency basis. But the truth is that the patient acuity levels (rating of how sick people are) is getting lower. We are seeing an increase patient flow of those patients who should be seen at their family doctor as opposed to the ED. ED care is far more expensive than a physician office. We also are seeing an increase of malpractice insurance spawned by an increase the number of lawsuits and some exorbitant payouts. We also have a very high population of indigent care. In my history of healthcare experience, most people who present to an ED without insurance coverage are treated with the same care as those who can fully pay. There are exceptions, but most are treated.

Many of you stated that we have the best healthcare system in the world and that you would not want to be treated anywhere else. Which is also supported by the number of foreign patients that are treated in the U.S. as described in the articles by Enthoven and Kronick. How do we improve our system to control healthcare costs and assure coverage for all Americans who need treatment? Some can be learned from Canada, and much can be learned by understanding the flaws in our own system. Education plays a considerable role as Mario stated in several posts. Education of our people and education of our politicians who are fairly polarized by the solutions is necessary as concluded by several of you this week. There are those politicians and government officials who see all the issues as you all have discussed here. Most of you concluded that the Canadian system in its entirety would not work here. But the questions arise as to what parts would. We need to keep the innovations that afford us to advance medicine and plug the holes in our own system.

In the coming week, we are going to explore European health care.

As has been stated, the analysis/synthesis course goal is to have students examine all the areas and then develop their own view of the issues. This helps them build their own framework of thinking. It becomes important throughout the presentation and discussion for the instructor to facilitate students to understand all sides of an issue and to be careful that he does not insert his own views and opinions as this may again steer learner perceptions and not allow them to take advantage of the critical thinking and problem solving skill development innate to this type of course. While most instructors have certainly developed strong opinions, these must remain transparent to the participants. Learners, especially adult learners, come to learning situations with a wealth of life experience that may cloud their ability to see other views. It is the instructor's role to foster and encourage the student to consider and learn all views and relevant information.

Personal Reflection Suggestion

Think about the analysis/synthesis courses that you teach in either the traditional setting or in the online arena. What assignments and pedagogies do you use in these courses? Do the assignments reflect the higher levels of thinking reflected in your course objectives? If you use online discussions, do the questions or case studies incorporate an analysis of course concepts? Reflect on your level of interaction with the students.

EXAMPLE TWO: MANAGEMENT LEADERSHIP COURSE EXAMPLE

The next example uses an online debate that will assist to accomplish a similar outcome using a different pedagogy. Let's look at a business leadership or management course. This is a course that can be found in most business programs and can take on the elements of an analysis/synthesis course.

Course Description

This course builds on the principles covered in previous courses. The topics include theories and models that serve as a basis for professional management and leadership practice during periods of rapid change. It focuses on the early recognition, methods of coping, and prevention of disruptive situations within an organization. Students will explore a variety of management and leadership concepts to develop a framework for implementation within their own systems.

Course Objectives

Management and leadership is a broad topic that could include objectives dealing with communication, motivation, teamwork, and a wide range of additional business-related topics. Following are some examples of course objectives.

Upon completion of the course, participants will be able to:

- Determine organizational structures and the impact of structural and technological change on organization members.
- Analyze learning organization concepts in their own professional setting.
- Develop decision making processes that apply learning organization concepts during times of rapid change.
- Integrate leadership and motivation principles into the management of personnel.
- Compare and contrast organizational designs and the implications for managers and systems.
- Examine the implications of different leadership and management philosophies on organizations.
- Analyze steady state issues for stability and security.
- Evaluate the components of leadership and management to apply managerial skills and abilities.

Throughout this course many of the following topic areas may be covered including:

- Leadership Theories
- Five Practices of Exemplary Leadership
- Managers and Managing
- History of Management
- Planning Theory

- Decision Making and Administrative Issues
- Basic Organizational Designs
- Communication Issues
- Managerial Communications
- Organizational Asset Management
- Motivational Leadership
- Building Teamwork
- Individual Behavior and Motivation
- Power and Conflict
- Cultural Diversity
- Organizational Learning
- Learning Organizations
- Managing Change
- Teams and Groups

This practical course could include several semester long assignment activities that would help participants to integrate the knowledge into their own setting and framework of ideas. An Action Plan would allow learners to analyze and implement change within a familiar organization. Students could also research a topic such as crisis management and develop a paper on the topic. As students think through their Action Plan, it is valuable to have peer feedback to support or challenge their thinking.

In a analysis/synthesis course, one of the activities could be an online debate to explore and evaluate different management and leadership opportunities within organizations. Let's look at an example lesson. The initial debate planning process will take several weeks. Students should be allotted enough time to explore and prepare their arguments and materials. The following is a message that may appear early on in the course, several weeks prior to the actual debate process.

Team Debates Planning

Over the course of the next several weeks you and your team members will prepare for an online debate. The purpose of the debate is to analyze your position on an assigned topic and defend your position using evidence from our readings and additional references. Ultimately, your goal is to persuade those holding differing opinions to conform to your opinion. This debate will be between teams who will be randomly assigned either the topic of (1) Traditional Top Down Management or (2) Organizational Learning. Each team will have their own group page on the learning management system platform to communicate and plan their debate. This will allow each group to divide tasks, research areas, and report back to the group. Each group will be responsible for researching their assigned area, developing a strategy to argue their side of the debate, and presenting information. There will be four phases to the actual debate.

- **Phase One:** Each side will develop initial arguments supporting their position/argument. This should include 400 to 500 words on background information and the scope of the issue. Phase One may be presented as a Microsoft Word, PowerPoint, or any other format that the team feels will be persuasive. On Monday of Week 8, post your team's document in the appropriate Discussion forum ---- either "Team Debate: Top Down Management" or "Team Debate: Organizational Learning".
- **Phase Two:** After each team has read the other's initial position/argument, your team will post a rebuttal of the other team's initial posting on the discussion board by Wednesday of Week 8. This 250 – 300 word posting should be completed as a team post (communicate on your group page). Preparation before the week of the debate should focus on strategies to refute what you believe the other team may state in their opening arguments. Do not wait till the week of the debate to plan this. You should be prepared ahead of the debate week although it is anticipated that you may need to seek additional information depending upon the other team's argu-

ment. Post the rebuttal as a new thread within your team's debate forum.

- **Phase Three:** After reading the opponent's rebuttal, your team will develop their final Closing Remarks of 150 to 200 words. Planning should focus on how your team will bring all the arguments together to draw a conclusion that supports your side. Planning and strategy to support your arguments and counter your opponent's position should be developed and considered throughout the process. Post your team's Closing Remarks by Saturday. Once again, post this as a separate thread within your term's debate forum.
- **Phase Four:** After you and your team have completed the closing remarks, go to the forum "Final Forum: My Position" and post your individual stance or opinion on each of the debate topics. Where do you stand?

Rationale for Course Design

For this collaborative project, students need to be provided several weeks of planning time with their group. This allows them to gather information and to investigate all elements of their side. This provides the opportunity to interact with other students, to dialogue and discuss all aspects of their topic area. The planning phase prior to the week of the debate serve as a great interactive learning tool as students review and discuss options for their arguments, rebuttals, and final remarks. They also discuss strategies that assist them to explore all positive and negative aspects of their argument and their opponents premise as well.

In most learning management systems, the instructor can design a series of group pages to divide the class into teams. This allows them a communication platform with some collaborative tools such as asynchronous discussion forums, synchronous chat rooms, and perhaps wikis for document posting. The instructor can monitor group progress and discussions, which is an advantage over individual private e-mails sent between learners, Once again, the instructor should practice restraint in posting information unless she/he sees the group going in the wrong direction.

One of the key elements to making this debate a successful activity is to establish clear directions and expectations upfront. The debate activity needs to be seen as an important part of the course and a vital component of the learning and assessment process. As with any interactive activity, instructor presence throughout the process helps to assure that it runs smoothly during the planning process and during the actual week of debate. If the instructor sees that the phases are not moving forward smoothly, then he/she needs to intervene to get teams and individuals back on track. What gets graded is often what gets accomplished in an online course, so there may be benefit in dividing the assessment by phases of the activity. The value of this learning is high end as students are analyzing and synthesizing a great deal of information. A debate forces students to see and argue all aspects of the issue, in this example the differences and strengths of the traditional Top Down Management philosophy versus that of the Organizational approach. In previous activities, throughout the term, an instructor may notice that one or more students are lining up behind one of these two directions becoming very single minded. If this is the case, the instructor should assign the student to argue the other side in the debate process. This forces the student to learn all of the vital information and synthesize it into their own framework of thinking.

The online debate builds learning communities that allow students to work collaboratively to achieve important, mutually established goals. Participants learn from each other by working together with a common purpose on a common task (Buckingham, 2003). In an education setting, students come to the learning task with varying backgrounds, which they share through collaborative learning (Driscoll, 2000). A community can be defined as a group of people who are socially interdependent, who participate together in discussion and decision making, and who share certain practices that both define the community and are nurtured by it (Bellah, Madsen, Sullivan, Swindler, and Tipton, 1985). McMillan and Chavis (1986) state that a community offers a feeling that members have a belonging, a feeling that members matter to one another and to the group. The development of a sense of community in a semester long course does not arbitrarily occur. It must be planned for and be facilitated by the instructor. Bielaczyc and Collins (1999) described community as one that embodies a culture of learning in which everyone is involved in a collective effort of understanding. While appearing seamless to the participants, this involvement becomes a deliberate purpose planned for by the instructor.

Analysis/synthesis course tend to be smaller, advanced courses. In a larger enrollment course, the instructor can establish multiple debates that are conducted simultaneously. This assists with the organization of the debate structure and allows for greater interaction and a stronger sense of community among learners. Students are divided into their respective debate teams and groups and can then come back after the debate to the larger community. While they are debating their opponents, several other debates are occurring. This becomes a rich resource for all students after the debate week has concluded. At this time the instructor can make all the debate platforms visible for all students to review. Here they will find some redundant information as each debate was arguing the same issues, but they are able to see and learn from the other group's research, strategies and information blending. This then broadens the reach of the debate and the learning community.

EXAMPLE THREE: ISSUES IN EDUCATION

The above two course examples are structured around the premise that there may be two or more opposing vantage points on an issue that can be multifaceted in nature. Sometimes an analysis/synthesis course does not present diametrically opposed viewpoints, but requires the examination of information to establish meaning and to be used in decision making and application. Learners in our next example are presented with information and concepts, and then data to analyze and synthesize to determine a conclusion.

A typical "Issues in Education" course may cover a number of subject areas and explore a number of perspectives that can change over time. The topics can fluctuate given the culture, the political environment, and the economy of the country. For example, when there is a change in political focus within government, there is invariably a change in the education system.

Some of the topics addressed in an "Issues in Education" course may include the following:

- Classroom Management
- Student Achievement and Outcomes
- No Child Left Behind
- State Mandatory Testing
- The Nation at Risk Report
- Public School Teacher Salaries
- Standards for Teachers
- Teaching Adults versus Children
- State and Federal Control
- Unionization of Education
- Online Learning
- Cyber Charter Schools
- Ethics in Adult Education
- Ethics in Education
- School Vouchers
- Instructional Technology

Let's take a look at an example lesson that focuses on the No Child Left Behind (NCLB) legislation and the effects on individual school districts. Objectives for a lesson may be:

The student will be able to:

- Outline the fundamental principles of the No Child Left Behind legislation.
- Analyze how states are postured to meet Annual Yearly Progress (AYP).
- Critique the provisions within NCLB considering the impact each provision has on K-12 education.
- Compare and Contrast school systems to determine the correlation of finance to student outcomes.
- Develop an Annual Yearly Progress report based on the federal standards for 2014.

I. Weekly Focus
   - Over the past few weeks we have been working with the issues surrounding adult education. This week we are going to shift our focus to public school education and the No Child Left Behind (NCLB) legislation enacted under the Bush (43) administration. This federal law that is presently driving our public school education system. Each state must have a plan in place to meet the federal standards on an annual basis. We are going to explore this legislation and the historical events that drove this policy. We have several activities this week and an analysis project that will help you to better understand NCLB and the effects at the local school district level.
   - Please follow along with this week's lessons and activities. Many of us have children in grades K through 12, and it will be interesting to share our perspectives.

II. Instructional Materials
   A. Lecture Notes: Please review the text lecture materials on the NCLB legislation and the mandates for states to enact. This document outlines the history of the legislation and the events that lead to its implementation. It also presents the standards and what each state must do to report their progress toward those standards. It discusses the finances that come into play with regard to federal and state contributions. This is a Word file. Pay particular attention to the information on the standards at each of the years.
      - NCLB.docx
   B. Text Reading
      - Please read Chapter #5 in our Issues text on No Child Left Behind. Pay particular attention to the progressive nature of the standards from its conception through 2014. Please reflect on whether you believe that these standards can be met by all school systems across the country.
   C. Article Reading
      - Please read the following Nation at Risk summation article.
      - Nation at Risk Summation.pdf
   D. Report Reading
      - Please read the American High School Today Report
      - American High School Today.pdf

III. Collaborative Wiki
   - Now that you have read through the Nation at Risk and the American High School Today, reflect on what these reports have in common and what role they may have played in the current legislation. What similarities do you see between these reports issued in 1958 and 1983 and the driving factors that lead to NCLB? Please post your ideas on the class wiki in the appropriate section for either similarities or differences.

- Add your statements of similarities or differences to the appropriate list in our class wiki.

IV. Data Mining Activity

- Please complete the following assignment. Respond to each question in a Word document and submit it through the assignment drop box by midnight on Sunday. We will use this school district data as the basis for our Discussion Board during the week.
- We will each collect data regarding three school district test scores and financial information. You will be reporting the information that you uncover and then comparing/contrasting that information to better understand the relationship between finances and test scores.
    1. Access http://www.schoolmatters.com. Select a District and then a state from the State drop down list. Select and review data from one of the school districts.
    2. Using the latest data, find three school districts—one that has a median household income of $90,000 or higher, one that has a median household income between $55,000 and $75,000, and one that has a median household income below $45,000. Clue: start by selecting school districts in an area in which you are familiar and believe may fit this criteria.
- Access the median household income by clicking the Community Demographics link. Scroll down to the District Household Income Distribution and figure the median income range for each of the three districts.
    3. Click on the District Financial Information for each district. In a table, report the percent of revenue that comes from Local, State, and Federal sources for each district. Write a one paragraph summary explaining the data in the table and a second paragraph that discusses the conclusions you can draw from the data in the table.
    4. In the District Financial Information section find the District Spending & Revenue ($ per Student) at the top of the page. Report the Operating Expenditures per student and the Instructional Expenditures per student for each district. Calculate the percent of the Operating Expenditures per student that is comprised of the Instructional Expenditures per student. Write one paragraph explaining the data in the table and a second paragraph that discusses the conclusions you can draw from the data in the table.
    5. Go to http://wdcrobcolp01.ed.gov/Programs/EROD/org_list.cfm?category_ID=SEA
- This is the US Department of Education's Education Resource Directory of State Education Agency (State Department of Education) websites. Select a state, and locate the state test and AYP results for the most recent year recorded. Go to the School Districts that you have been reviewing and locate the District Level Math and Reading test results. Review and report the findings for the math, reading, and writing scores for your three school districts in a chart.

Determine whether or not these districts are making adequate yearly progress and if there are any deficiencies noted.

  - In 250 to 300 words, report your findings and draw conclusions from this data. What can you conclude about these districts based upon the data that you have reviewed? Try to project whether or not these schools are in danger of not meeting AYP by 2014.
  - Please complete this in a Word document and email your results to me. This will be graded according to the criteria in your course syllabus.

V. Discussion Board

  - Based on the readings this week and your data mining analysis activity, what can you conclude about the NCLB legislation? Is it going to improve education? Do districts that have higher incomes and more local funding do better than districts that have lower? What overall assumptions can you make regarding NCLB and finances? Please support your posts with information from the articles, presentation, and specific examples from your data mining assignment.

Rationale of Course Design

This lesson from "Issues in Education" does not have a dichotomy of issues, as do the previous two example lessons. This lesson has a single premise to be analyzed, the value of NCLB. Basic information is presented through text, articles, and an instructor created text based lecture. While the Internet provides easy access to government reports, online journals, e-books, and other digital information, some Internet information is not credible. As student review Web sites, they develop critical thinking skills that help them become better consumers of media, which is a valuable life skill and often a desired educational outcome.

The massive amounts of material on the Web do not make a better course; therefore, the instructor is very clear about the purpose of each Web site. The data mining activity forces the students to delve deeper into the data analysis by first showing them how to gather data and then providing a basis for using and comparing the data. While there may be no right or wrong conclusion to their findings, it serves to assist them in understanding the dynamics and effects of the NCLB legislation. The readings and activities culminate in the discussion board where the students can compare their findings to the findings of other participants.

Once again, the instructor discussion board interaction should be limited to give students a chance to ask and answer important questions. Students should have the opportunity to develop their problem solving skills and to inductively develop their thinking. The "guide-on-the-side" instructor can help foster learner thinking with guiding questions, clarification, or examples. At the end of the week or the designated time period for closing the discussion, the instructor should post final thoughts that serve to emphasize key points. It is important to remind students what they learned through the discussion process.

HYBRID COURSES

Blending foundational or skills based courses with analysis/synthesis courses is extremely common. The foundational and analysis/synthesis courses are each at opposite ends of a continuum and courses may be structured to help students advance along the continuum. The foundational courses tend to be a larger enrollment introductory courses, and the analysis/synthesis courses are smaller, more advanced courses. The foundational level courses are the prerequisite courses with more objective concepts, and analysis/synthesis courses focus on the thinking of complex issues. Introductory courses may structure some end of term activities that strive for higher level thinking. A basic physics course includes the topics velocity, energy, and acceleration. After mastering basic concepts, students have to apply these principles in a more advanced activity that analyzes what went wrong in an amusement park roaster coaster accident. They are given diagrams and data to summarize the accident, and develop a presentation summarizing what went wrong. Through the activity, learners move to higher levels of thinking and relate concepts to real-world examples.

The hybrid analysis/synthesis and skills-based courses are common because there are many healthcare and vocational activities that require an individual to diagnose a problem and perform a task. Many health and safety issues require quick, high level thinking and action. In an online hybrid course to certify athletic trainers, participants need to learn to (1) collect vital information from clients regarding their health and goals; (2) develop a training program; and (3) teach clients appropriate exercises by modeling the form and process. The certification training includes analysis of client data, synthesis to develop an exercise plan, and physical skills to methodically teach the exercises. The skills and the analysis skills are equally information for successful training outcomes.

CONCLUSION

In this chapter, you have seen three examples of analysis/synthesis courses from three different disciplines – Issues in Healthcare Delivery, Management Leadership, and Issues in Education. Each example provides a different opportunity and perspective for students to engage in the learning process. In analysis/synthesis courses, students build on prerequisite knowledge gained through foundational and skills based courses. The courses are likely to prepare students for professional practice or more advanced study. Learners tend to be interested and motivated because these course are electives or within their program of study. In many cases, the courses are not focused on developing a product or single outcome, they are likely to focus on a high level thinking process. In many areas such as ethics, healthcare, education, law, and business, there are no clear answers to the complex, multifaceted issues. Activities in analysis/synthesis courses often engage learners through authentic case studies, simulations, roles plays, debates, guest speakers, and presentations.

The instructor-student and student-student collaborative interaction is a critical aspect of most analysis/synthesis courses. Students want interaction and detailed feedback. Instructor feedback is especially important as the instructor takes on the role of facilitator, mentor, and coach. As students mature, they also gain respect for the learners in their courses who bring knowledge and valuable life experience to the class discussions. This respect contributes to the camaraderie and dedication of a learning community. Analysis/synthesis courses address some controversial issues and respect for co-learners is critical. Discussions may provoke divergent thinking that can lead to disagreement among students, but learners can grow from understanding the assumptions, priorities, and viewpoints of others. The analysis of information, the instructor feedback, the peer interaction, and the divergent views contribute to the students' enhanced knowledge base and new mental models.

Personal Reflection Suggestion

Look over some of your most recent posts to student discussion boards. How do you interact with students in your courses? Do you post too much or too little? Does your interaction and postings cause students to seek out different thinking and analysis opportunities? Do you use your postings to cause students to look at all sides of an issue? Do your questions foster high level critical thinking?

REFERENCES

Beaubien, J. (2002). Harnessing the power of complexity in an online learning environment . In Rudestam, K. E., & Schoenholtz-Read, J. (Eds.), *Handbook of Online Learning: Innovations in Higher Education and Corporate Training* (pp. 221–236). Thousand Oaks, CA: Sage Publications.

Bellah, R. N., Madsen, R., Sullivan, W. M., Swindler, A., & Tipton, S. M. (1985). *Habits of the heart: Individualism and commitment in American life*. New York: Harper.

Bielaczyc, K., & Collins, A. (1999). Learning communities in classrooms: A reconceptualization of educational practices . In Reigeluth, C. (Ed.), *Instructional-design theories and models: A new paradigm of instructional theory* (pp. 269–292). Englewood Cliffs, NJ: Lawrence Erlbaum.

Bloom, B. S., & Krathwohl, D. R. (1956). *Taxonomy of educational objectives: The classification of educational goals, by a committee of college and university examiners. Handbook 1: Cognitive domain*. New York: Longmans.

Buckingham, S. (2003). Perspectives on the experience of the learning community through online discussions. *Journal of Distance Education, 18*(2), 74–79.

Driscoll, M. P. (2000). *Psychology of learning for instruction* (2nd ed.). Boston, MA: Allyn and Bacon.

Fuller, R. G., & Kuhne, G. W. (2008, January). Fostering Meaningful Interaction in Health Education Online Courses: Matching Pedagogy To Course Types. *International Journal of Information and Communication Technology Education, 4*(1).

Halpern, D. E. (1999). Teaching for critical thinking: Helping college students develop the skills and dispositions of a critical thinker. *New Directions for Teaching and Learning, 80*, 69–74. doi:10.1002/tl.8005

McMillan, W., & Chavis, D. M. (1986). Sense of community: A definition and theory. *Journal of Community Psychology, 14*, 6–23. doi:10.1002/1520-6629(198601)14:1<6::AID-JCOP2290140103>3.0.CO;2-I

Palloff, R., & Pratt, K. (1999). *Building learning communities in cyberspace: Effective strategies for the online classroom*. San Francisco: Jossey Bass.

About the Authors

Richard Fuller is Associate Professor of Education currently serving as graduate faculty at Robert Morris University in the Department of Secondary Education and Graduate Studies. He has served as the Dean of Education for a career college and as Program Director and Assistant Professor for graduate Leadership studies at Drexel University. In addition to his university work, Dr. Fuller serves as a consultant having worked on projects for the Department of Transportation, the Department of Health, higher education institutions, corporate and government entities for education and leadership. Dr. Fuller was elected to the Phi Kappa Phi National Honor Society and is the recipient of the James Naddeo Academic Award in 2002. He speaks nationally and internationally each year on education, distance education, workforce leadership, recruitment and retention, personal motivation and brain compatible learning.

Gary W. Kuhne is an Associate Professor of Education at The Pennsylvania State University serving on the graduate faculty in the Adult Education Program. He is currently the Professor-In- Charge of the Adult Education Program, as well as the Lead Faculty for the World Campus M.Ed. in Adult Education. In addition to his work with the university, Dr. Kuhne is a consultant to business and industry, government agencies, various higher education institutions, and various religious organizations and churches. Dr. Kuhne is also the President of the Institute for the Study of Ministry Dynamics and the Pastor/Teacher of North Coast Christian Fellowship. His primary research interests include Continuing Professional Education, needs assessment and program evaluation, leadership and staff development in the public, private, and nonprofit sectors, and distance education, asynchronous learning and applications to higher education and staff development. The author of numerous books and articles, Dr. Kuhne is listed in Who's Who in American Education, was elected to the Phi Kappa Phi National Honor Society, was the winner (along with Joe Donaldson) of the 1995 Award For Excellence in Research and Publication from the National University Continuing Education Association (NUCEA), and was the winner of the 2000 Outstanding Distance Education Teaching Award, Pennsylvania State University and the 2002 Stellar Program Award, Pennsylvania State University

Barbara A. Frey received her D.Ed. from Pennsylvania State University and her M.Ed. from the University of Pittsburgh. She is a Senior Instructional Designer in the Center for Instructional Development and Distance Education at the University of Pittsburgh where she provides support and training to faculty on a variety of teaching and learning projects. In addition, she teaches as an Adjunct Assistant Professor in the Learning and Performance Systems Department of Pennsylvania State University World Campus. Her research interests include online learning, instructional design and technology, and human resource development.

Index

M

N

O

P

R

S

Breinigsville, PA USA
01 September 2010
R3922900001BB/R39229PG244007BVX1BB/1/P

9 781615 208654